THE WALDENSES.

THE PROTESTANT CHURCH AT BOBBI, VAL PELICE.

Philadelphia
Presbyterian Board of Publication
821 Chestnut St.
J. LYONS SC.

AVENGE, O Lord, thy slaughtered saints, whose bones
Lie scattered on the Alpine mountains cold;
E'en them, who kept thy truth so pure of old,
When all our fathers worshipped stocks and stones,
Forget not: in thy book record their groans,
Who were thy sheep, and in their ancient fold
Slain by the bloody Piedmontese, that roll'd
Mother with infant down the rocks. Their moans
The vales redoubled to the hills, and they
To heaven. Their martyred blood and ashes sow
O'er all the Italian fields, where still doth sway
The triple tyrant; that from these may grow
An hundred-fold, who, having learnt thy way,
Early may fly the Babylonian woe!"

MILTON.

THE WALDENSES:

SKETCHES

OF

The Evangelical Christians

OF THE

VALLEYS OF PIEDMONT

COMPILED FOR THE BOARD OF PUBLICATION
CHIEFLY FROM "THE ISRAEL OF
THE ALPS"

Philadelphia:
PRESBYTERIAN BOARD OF PUBLICATION
AND SABBATH-SCHOOL WORK,
No. 1334 CHESTNUT STREET.

SLOTE & MOONEY, Stereotypers.

PREFACE.

THE Waldensian Church is the "BURNING BUSH" of Christendom. The history of that people presents to us little else than a series of ferocious persecutions, endured with the most heroic constancy. Planted in the valleys of Piedmont, almost within the shadow of the Papal throne, their scriptural faith and order have been a perpetual and most significant protest against the corruptions of that colossal Hierarchy. Everything pertaining to them has contributed to give point and pungency to this testimony. In age, they antedate the usurpations of the Roman See. Their uncontradicted traditions run back nearly to the Christian era, and warrant the presumption that their church was founded either by the apostles or their immediate successors. They have authentic documents, dating many hundred years before the Reformation, from which it appears, that they never acknowledged the supremacy of the Popes—that they rejected from the beginning the monstrous dogmas and superstitious mummeries which Rome has baptized with the sacred name of Christianity—that they have steadfastly adhered to the BIBLE as the only rule of faith and practice—and that their doctrine and polity have, from the first, been precisely what they are now. Such a Church must needs have been persecuted. It was a standing memento of the great apostacy — a living testimony against its abominations, which Rome could not be expected to tolerate. Again and again, therefore, did her priests and her princes decree its extirpation, and send forth their armies to carry havoc and carnage through all its mountain fastnesses.

The records of these infamous crusades constitute some of the blackest chapters even in the history of that power, which an inspired pen has delineated as being "drunk with the blood of the saints." The narrative, therefore, is necessarily a sad one. But it has its alleviations. No other annals supply instances of more generous and sublime heroism, than are to be found here. It is something for the Christian to be able to point to a church, which has, from century to century, exemplified the power of the Gospel, as well to sustain individuals and communities in scenes of the deepest suffering, as to guard them against the common dangers and temptations of life. And the devout observer of Divine Providence, may find here new cause to admire and adore the sovereignty and the faithfulness of Him who is "wonderful in council and excellent in working." It is not, therefore, surprising that enlightened Protestants of every name and country, have always taken the liveliest interest in the history of this most remarkable people.

Let us, too, then say with Moses in Horeb, "I will now turn aside and see this great sight, why the bush is not burnt."

Illustrations.

Contents.

Appendix.

MAP OF THE WALDENSIAN TERRITORY.

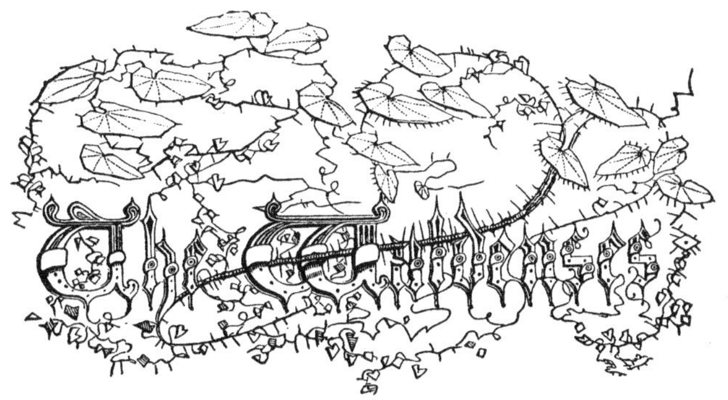

Chapter First.

DESCRIPTION OF THE COUNTRY.

In the northern part of Italy is the beautiful plain of the Po. Beyond this region, and separating it from ancient Gaul and Germany, is the great natural barrier of the Alps. These mountains extend in the general form of a crescent, from the western side of the gulf of Genoa, to the eastern side of the gulf of Venice. They are known, in different parts of their course, by different names, as the Maritime Alps, the Cottian Alps, the Rhetian Alps, the Noric

Alps. The Cottian Alps, in the times of the Romans, formed one of the most common routes in passing from northern Italy into Gaul. This route was also sometimes taken in going from Italy into Spain. The country at the foot of the Cottian Alps, on the Italian side, is called Piedmont, while on the side of Gaul it has received the names of Dauphiny and Savoy. High up in the mountain valleys of Piedmont, on the Italian side of the Cottian Alps, has lived from time immemorial the remarkable people whose history we are about to sketch.

The Waldenses are at once mountaineers and dalesmen. The valleys in which they live are remote from the plain, closely hemmed in by mountains, and in many places accessible only by narrow and precipitous ravines. Much of their time is spent upon the declivities of mountains topped with perpetual snow. Hardy and adventurous, exposed from childhood to a life of toil and danger, they have all that simplicity of character, and that sturdy independence, which seem in all climes to be the natural inheritance of the mountaineer. It is, however, from their character as dalesmen, or men of the valleys, that they have received their name. This name, derived primarily from the Latin *vallis*, a valley, is variously spelled. The French form of the word, which is *val*, gives rise to a plural *vaux*, and thence to the adjective *Vaudois*. The Italian form of the word gives the adjective Vallenses, strengthened into Valdenses, and thence corrupted in English into Waldenses. The first of these names, Vaudois, is that which they call themselves, and by which they are almost universally known on the continent of Europe. The last, Waldenses, is that by which they are generally called in England and the United States.

Politically, the Waldenses are hereditary subjects of

the house of Savoy. The princes of this house, originally dukes, have gradually risen in dignity to the rank of kings. Their kingdom now includes Savoy, Piedmont, the territories of Nice and Genoa, and the island of Sardinia. From this last of its possessions is derived its name, the Kingdom of Sardinia. The Waldensian territory lies wholly within the duchy of Piedmont, and its southern border is about thirty miles from Turin, which is the capital both of Piedmont, and of the whole kingdom.

The Waldenses were formerly much more numerous than now, and their territory covered a much larger area. Persecution, through a long succession of centuries, has gradually reduced them to their present number of about twenty-three thousand, and at the same time hemmed them in within their present narrow limits, extending not more than eighteen miles in length by fourteen in width, and containing an area of less than three hundred square miles.

This territory, as before stated, is within the province of Piedmont, lying in a southwesterly direction from Turin, and about thirty miles distant. It is somewhat triangular in shape, the base of the triangle being the high dividing ridge of the Alps, which separates Piedmont from Dauphiny in France. From this high ridge, the mountains on the Italian side gradually slope down towards the valley of the Po, and several streams rising near the top of the ridge run an easterly course, converge as they descend, and finally unite and empty into the Po. It is the union of these streams that forms the apex of the triangle. These streams are the Po itself at the south, the Pelice in the centre, and the Clusone at the north. They lie between bold mountain spurs that shoot off from the high dividing ridge which has been named. Between each two of these mountain spurs is a valley, forming the natural bed of a river. Each valley and river become in turn the receptacle of numerous small lateral streams and valleys, and so the whole territory is a continued series of lofty mountains and deep valleys.

The river Pelice drains the valley of Luserne, and has several important tributaries. At the entrance into the valley is the parish of St. Jean, with a village of the same name. Beyond St. Jean, and near the junction of the Pelice and the Angrogna, stands La Torre, the Waldensian capital. It has been the scene of many calamities, and is, of course, very celebrated in Waldensian history. The next village of importance in passing up this valley is Villar, and beyond that still, high up among the mountains, is Bobbi. The valley of Luserne, in its lower portions, at St. Jean and La Torre, is of considerable width, and contains a good deal of alluvial, or bottom lands, on the banks of the Pelice. Farther up, however, this alluvial slip becomes gradually less, and cultivation is carried on chiefly by terraces on the mountain sides. At Bobbi, the scene changes from the beautiful into the sublime, and even into the awful. The level alluvial land just about Bobbi expands into the shape of a basin, but higher up it contracts into a narrow strip of a quarter of a mile in width, and finally disappears altogether. Thence up to the mountain ridge which forms the French boundary, there is nothing but deep, and even apparently unfathomable ravines, in which lie the channels of the head stream of the Pelice and its highest confluents, overhung by stupendous masses of rocks. There is not in all the Alps any scenery which is more grand and imposing. Nor are these ravines without inhabitants. Little hamlets are to be found at various points, in all directions, wherever it is possible to find a spot on the sides of the mountains, in the shape of a basin or terrace, or little hollow, that is susceptible of cultiva tion.

The valley of Rora incloses the little stream called Lusernette, which falls into the Pelice below the town of Luserne. The village of Rora, though inconsiderable in size, has been rendered famous in history by the gallant exploits of its people. The scenery of this district, like its history, is full of romantic interest. Few portions of the valley contain so much that is bold, picturesque and beautiful in external nature, or so much that is truly marvellous in its heroic reminiscences. It is equally remarkable for the strong attachment of its inhabitants to their native soil. Bleak and barren as the soil is, particularly in the more elevated and rocky portions, yet few of its people have sought a home elsewhere.

On the north side of the Pelice, is another and large tributary, called the Angrogna, which drains a valley of the same name. This stream takes its rise in a wild mountain region, among high Alps, in the very centre of the Waldensian territory. From its secluded position, rendering it almost inaccessible to a hostile force, the Angrogna has been in all ages the "Holy Valley" of the Waldenses. Though geographically and physically secondary in its character, and only a branch or tributary of the Luserne, yet in its moral and historical bearings, the valley of Angrogna ranks as first in importance. To this retired region have the people often withdrawn, as to an asylum that could not be invaded, when most sorely pressed by their foes. Within this region was the spot, the "Shiloh" of the valleys, where in former ages the Waldensian Synod often met, and where, above all, was their "school of the prophets." In the Pra del Tor, very high up towards the head waters of the Angrogna, secure from interruption, their young men, from the earliest ages of which we have any account of them, were accustomed to assemble from the different valleys, to pursue under the direction of competent pastors such studies as would fit them to preach the gospel. It was perhaps a rude institution, as compared with the well appointed theological Seminaries of this day. But it sent forth many noble bands of missionaries, to preach the pure gospel of Christ, long before the period of the Reformation, and when the rest of the Christian world was enveloped in thick darkness. Whilst, in the monasteries and the theological schools of the rest of christendom, the Bible was a forbidden or an unknown book, the simple minded young dalesmen of the Pra del Tor prepared themselves for the work of the ministry mainly by committing thoroughly to memory the entire gospels and the epistles.

Leaving the region of the Pelice, and going northward, we come to the river Clusone. This river rises in the extreme northwestern part of the Waldensian territory, and runs in a southeasterly course till it unites, first with the Pelice, and a little further on with the Po. The union of these three streams forms the apex of the triangle of which the Cottian Alps are the base. The region drained by the Clusone has three different names. In the highest part of its course, is the valley of Pragela, lower down is the valley of Perouse, and farther still the valley of the Clusone. The first and the last of these valleys have ceased to belong to the Waldenses. That part of the valley of Perouse, which lies east of the Clusone, and which is by far the most extensive and fertile, has also been taken from them. The only part, therefore, of the region drained by the Clusone, that now remains to the Waldenses, is a narrow strip on the western bank, in the middle part of its course, including the three parishes of Parustin, St. Germain, and Pramol.

On the eastern side of the Clusone, are three important Roman Catholic towns, whose names occur but too often in Waldensian history. These are Pignerol, Perouse, and Fenestrelle. The first named of these has been for many ages the stronghold of those who have persecuted most bitterly the people of the valleys. Hundreds of unfortunate victims have here pined away in prison, or have been burnt at the stake, and within its walls have been concocted most of those schemes of mischief which have involved the adjoining valleys in slaughter.

Napoleon, the imperial road-maker, constructed a noble highway through this valley across the Alps. This road begins at Pignerol, passes Perouse and Fenestrelle, and thence from the upper end of the valley of Pragela, it crosses Mont Genévre into France, descending through the valley of the Durance by Briançon and Embrun. It is the precise route supposed to have been taken by Julius Cæsar on his way to Gaul, and by Hannibal on his invasion of Italy, as it was also by Irenæus and the other early Christian missionaries, who first carried the gospel into Gaul.

Opposite Perouse, the Clusone receives an important tributary, the Germanesca, which drains the valley of St. Martin. Near the mouth of the Germanesca, and in the small triangular space between it and the Clusone, is the parish of Pomaret, containing a village of the same name. At the distance of a mile or two above Pomaret, the Germanesca passes through a narrow defile, which is there barely wide enough to allow the river to rush through. Stupendous rocks are piled up on each side of the stream, and form a scene of surpassing grandeur. This is the natural gateway of the valley of St. Martin. This wonderful defile seems to have been cleft by the hand of God to form an outlet for the waters of the river. As a space, barely wide enough for a road, has been hewn out of the solid rock, nothing could be easier than to block it up, and effectually prevent the entrance of a hostile force—a measure which the Waldenses have often actually adopted.

The scenery in the valley of St. Martin frequently changes from the most wild and rugged aspect to the most attractive beauty. Throughout its entire length there is very little bottom land. Wherever there is a spot that is susceptible of cultivation, whether it consists of several acres, or is a mere nook, there the hand of man is at work to turn it to account.

The first parish above Pomaret is that of Ville Séche, so called from its chief village, which occupies an acclivity on the left bank of the Germanesca. It was in this parish that Leger was born, the well known historian of the Waldenses.

Higher up the valley the scenery becomes still more wild and savage. The bottom grows more and more narrow, and the sides consist of alternate projections of masses of naked rocks and deep intervening wooded ravines. In the ravines which have a northern exposure, and which are far up towards the summits of the mountains, masses of snow are seen in midsummer. Everything indicates a region belonging to the High Alps. In this Alpine region, however, is found a parish, Maneille, including a village of the same name and several hamlets, and containing several hundred inhabitants.

Pursuing still a northwest course, and ascending yet higher the deep and gloomy valley, through which a mountain torrent comes pitching down, we arrive at the parish of Macel. The valley, long before one reaches this point, becomes exceedingly picturesque. In several places, rocks surmounted with larches and pines, rise perpendicularly, in awful grandeur, from almost the very edge of the water, so that it would seem impossible to make a road between them and the river. In the upper part of this parish, just beneath the Col-du-Pis, is the hamlet of Balsille, on the left bank of the torrent, and opposite to the famous, cone-shaped mass of rocks, called Balsi. This spot is known as the Thermopylæ of the valleys. Here a few hundred dalesmen defended themselves a long time successfully against twenty thousand French and Savoyard troops, and finally retreated to the mountain in the rear, with scarcely the loss of a man.

The two parishes last described are not on the Germanesca, but on a small branch that comes in from the north-west. The Germanesca itself, in the upper part of its course, comes from the south-east. Ascending this stream, one is struck with the increased wildness and barrenness of the country. The side of the mountain which bounds the river on the right bank has a considerable growth of timber in his ravines. But that on the left bank is composed, for the most part, of naked rocks. There is scarcely any bottom land throughout its entire course. What there is, is covered, in many places, with masses of rocks which have detached themselves from the mountain sides. In some cases, the river is almost blocked up with them.

At first sight, a stranger would suppose that no human being would ever think of taking up his abode in a region, abounding indeed in sublime and imposing scenery, but withal so utterly wild and dreary. Yet even here are two populous parishes. The first is Rodoret, the second and highest is Prali. This last is decidedly the wildest and most barren of all the parishes of the Waldenses. The pines that grow on the sides of the mountains are few, scattered, and dwarfish. On the south the valley is completely shut in by the lofty range of mount Julien, whose elevated peaks and sides are covered with snow even in July. Not unfrequently the whole parish is covered with snow during eight and nine months of the year. Avalanches are frequent, and often very destructive. Among the heights south of Prali, are twelve little lakes or ponds, formed by the melting of the snows on mount Julien. They are nearly on the route from Prali over to Bobi, in the valley of Luserne.

LA TOUR VAL PELICE.—(THE WALDENSIAN CAPITAL.)

Chapter Second.

ANTIQUITY OF THE WALDENSES.

THE Waldenses are in all essential particulars Presbyterian in order, and Calvinistic in doctrine. But they are not, technically speaking, Protestants, nor are they to be counted among the Reformed churches. Though Italians, and living upon the very confines of the papacy, they have never had any connection with the church of Rome, and have had therefore none of its corruptions from which to reform. Their poverty and their inaccessible situation were their protection from encroachment, during the earlier centuries, whilst the papal power was gradually acquiring its colossal dimensions. When the reformed churches of Germany, France, and England threw off the yoke of the papacy, and began to restore Christianity within their borders to its original simplicity and purity, the Waldensian Christians received the tidings with gladness, and had numerous conferences with the Reformers, to their mutual benefit; but they claimed, at that time, as for centuries previous they had claimed, before their temporal sovereigns, that the faith, the worship, and the ecclesiastical organization prevalent among them then, had been handed down among them by uninterrupted tradition from the very earliest ages of Christianity.

Of the conversion of the Waldenses to Christianity, history gives us no authentic account. Romish historians as far back as the year A. D. 1250, represented them as the oldest sect of heretics, though unable to tell when or how their heresy began. Their own account of the matter uniformly has been, that their religion has descended with them from father to son by uninterrupted succession from the time of the apostles. There certainly is no improbability in the conjecture that the gospel was preached to them by some of those early missionaries who carried Christianity into Gaul. The common passage from Rome to Gaul at that time lay directly through the Cottian Alps, and Gaul we know received the gospel early in the second century at the latest, probably before the close of the first century. If the apostle Paul ever made that "journey into Spain," (Rom. xv. 28,) which he speaks of in his epistle to the Romans, and in which he proposed to go by way of Rome, his natural route would have been in the same direction, and it is not impossible that his voice was actually heard among those retired valleys. The most common opinion among Protestant writers is, that the conversion of the Waldenses was begun by some of the very early Christian missionaries, perhaps by some of the apostles themselves, on their way to Gaul, and that it was completed and the churches more fully organized by a large influx of Christians from Rome, after the first general persecution under Nero. The Christians of Rome, scattered by this terrible event, would naturally flee from the plain country to the mountains, carrying with them the gospel and its institutions.

Such is the opinion of Henry Arnaud, one of the most intelligent of the Waldensian pastors. "Neither has their church ever been reformed," says Arnaud,* "whence arises its title of *evangelic*. The Waldenses are in fact descended

* Glorious Recovery by the Waldenses of their Valleys. Preface, page 14.

from those refugees from Italy, who, after St. Paul had there preached the gospel, abandoned their beautiful country, and fled, like the woman mentioned in the Apocalypse, to these wild mountains, where they have, to this day, handed down the gospel from father to son, in the same purity and simplicity as it was preached by St. Paul." This is not following fables, for there is nothing in the relation either improbable or absurd. When the Christians at Rome were bound to stakes, covered with pitch, and burnt in the evenings to illuminate the city, is it wonderful, if the glare of such fires should induce those yet at liberty, to betake themselves for shelter, to the almost inaccessible valleys of the Alps, and to the clefts of the rocks, trusting to that God in whose hands are the deep places of the earth, and considering that the strength of hills is his ?

The words of Arnaud were written near the close of the seventeenth century ; but we have others of a much earlier date. The Waldenses complain, that it has been the cruel policy of their persecutors to destroy all the historical memorials of their antiquity. About the year 1559, the Roman Catholics, with a view to exterminate the protestants of the valleys, cruelly butchered them, and in order to obliterate every memorial of them, diligently searched for their records, which they committed to the flames. Though on this account the testimonies of their antiquity are not so ample as could be wished, yet we possess a variety of their own declarations on this point previous to the period just mentioned, which have been preserved in the wonderful providence of God. In the Noble Lesson, dated 1100,* are contained the following assertions:

* This treatise, dated 1100, Leger tells us was found quite entire in a book of parchment, written in manuscript in an old Gothic character In Leger's time two exemplars were preserved, one at

"Now, after the Apostles, were certain teachers,
Who taught the way of Jesus Christ our Saviour.
And these are found even at the present day.
If any man love those who are good, he must needs love God and Jesus Christ.
Such an one will neither curse, swear, nor lie.
Now, such an one is called a *Waldensian*, and worthy to be punished.
For, I dare say, and it is very true,
That all the Popes, which have been from Silvester to this present,
And all the Cardinals, Bishops, Abbots, and the like,
Have no power to absolve or pardon."

In 1530, the Waldenses thus addressed Ecolampadius and other reformers: "That you may at once understand the matter, we are a sort of teachers of a certain necessitous and small people, who already, for more than four hundred years—nay as those of our country frequently

Cambridge, and one at Geneva. Only the latter is now to be found. Mr. Jackson saw it in 1825. The Lesson is in verse, in their own ancient tongue, that it may be more agreeable to the reader, and that the youth may more easily imprint it upon their memory. The original begins thus:—

O frayre entende una nobla Leyçon.
Sovent deven velhar e istar en oreson.
C. nos veen aquest mont esser pres del chavon
Mot curios deorian esser de bonas obras far
C. nos veen mont de la fin apropriar, &c.

O Brethren give ear to a Noble Lesson.
We ought always to watch and pray,
For we see this world to be near a conclusion,
We ought to strive to do good works,
For we see the end of this world to approach,
A thousand and one hundred years are fully accomplished.

relate—*from the time of the apostles*, have sojourned among the most cruel thorns, yet, as all the pious have easily judged, not without the great favour of Christ; and having been stung and tormented by the same thorns, have been delivered by promised favour."

Robert Olevitan, whom Leger* the historian describes as "one of the most excellent pastors of the valleys," in a preface to his French version of the Bible, dated from the Alps, Feb. 12, 1335, dedicates it to God, and not to the rich and pompous, but to the poor church: "No," adds he, "it is to thee alone I present this precious treasure, in the name of a certain poor people, thy friends and brethren in Jesus Christ, who, ever since they were blessed and enriched with it *by the apostles and ambassadors of Christ, have still possessed and enjoyed the same.*"

In presenting their Confession of Faith to Francis I. of France, 1544, the Waldenses protested that their belief is "entirely such as they have received from hand to hand

* John Leger, one of the Waldensian pastors, in the seventeenth century, carefully collected a number of ancient documents of the Waldensian doctrine. In the persecution, 1655, the plunderers of the Waldenses deprived him of every leaf of M.S. in order to bury in oblivion all knowledge of their former existence, or long continued principles. With incredible diligence he commenced a new search in the Valleys on the French side of the Alps, where the destruction had not been so severe, and found authentic copies of the same treatises. A number of these he has published in his valuable history of the Waldenses. The Originals he delivered to Sir Samuel Morland, who presented them in 1658 to the library of the University of Cambridge. Twenty-one volumes were there deposited, but the first seven are now missing, though Allix quoted from one of these seven in 1690. Copies of some of these are preserved in Geneva. The remaining fourteen volumes, from H to W, are still to be seen at Cambridge.

from their ancestors, according as their predecessors, in all times and in all ages, had taught them it."

These declarations were given by the Waldenses, while in full possession of their documents; but after the most of these were destroyed in 1559, they still refer to the fact of their antiquity. Accordingly, in 1580, they of the valleys complained to their prince, that a mission of Jesuits and troops possessed themselves of their temples at the hour of public worship, preventing the ministers on the Sabbath from performing their duty, and that the Jesuits had along with them a judge, or lord, and sometimes the lords of the valleys, who were furnished with his Highness' letter. They then add; "It is a thing true and notorious, most serene Duke, that his said subjects and their ancestors have been taught for *a great many hundreds of years*, in the true Christian religion, by their ministers, whom they call honourably Barbas, and that they have sometimes taught them in secret and nightly assemblies, in imitation of the primitive church, to avoid the persecution of the ecclesiastics: but afterwards, observing that they took from that quarter a pretext to calumniate them, the matter was reckoned of such consequence, that they have wished to preach publicly, the holy doctrine in which they have been instructed *from all antiquity, and from hand to hand by their fathers.*"

In one of the manuscripts, dated 1587, and deposited in the library of the University of Cambridge, the question is put:—"At what time have the religion and state (stata) been preached in the valleys?" The answer is:—"About five hundred years, as can be collected from many histories; but according to the belief of the inhabitants of the valleys, it has been *from time immemorial, and from father to son, since the time of the apostles.*"

During the dreadful persecutions of 1655, the churches of Piedmont, in a Confession of Faith, publicly declare their agreement, "in sound doctrine, with all the reformed churches of France, Great Britain, the Low Countries, Germany, Switzerland, Bohemia, Poland, Hungary, and other places, being ready to subscribe to that eternal truth of God with our own blood, *even as our ancestors, since the days of the apostles.*"

Let it be observed, then, that the Waldenses maintain, and have done so from the date of their earliest existing histories, that their ancestors inhabited the country which they now occupy, and held the faith which they hold, since the days of the apostles. They are of opinion, that the gospel was preached to their forefathers in those valleys by Christian missionaries from Rome, or other cities in Italy where it had gained extensive ground, or that it was introduced by those who fled from the plain country; perhaps some of them from Rome itself, or the neighbourhood thereof, during the persecutions under the Roman emperors. It is probable, that the truth was introduced by both these means. In a petition, presented by the Waldenses to Philibert Emanuel, duke of Savoy and prince of Piedmont, in the year 1559, they use the following language: "We likewise beseech your Royal Highness to consider, that this religion which we profess is not only ours, nor hath it been invented by men of late years, as is falsely reported, but it was the religion of our fathers, grandfathers, and great grandfathers, and other yet more ancient predecessors of ours, and of the blessed martyrs, confessors, prophets, and apostles; and if any can prove the contrary, we are ready to subscribe, and yield thereunto."

Leger, their great historian, states, that all the petitions and addresses of these people to their sovereigns, from the earliest times, contained a sentence to the same effect, namely, that they had been in the enjoyment of liberty of conscience, "da ogni tempo, da tempo immemoriale," from all time, from time immemorial. "And is it not extraordinary," asks Leger, "that it has never once happened, that any of the dukes of Savoy, or their ministers, should have offered the least contradiction to the pretensions of their Waldensian subjects? Again and again it has been asserted by them, 'We are descendants of those, who from father to son have preserved entire the apostolical faith in the valleys which we now occupy.' Their pretensions have been passed over in silence. They have been suffered to repeat their demands from reign to reign, and to carry them to the feet of their sovereigns:—'Permit us to enjoy that free exercise of our religion which we have enjoyed from time out of mind, and before the dukes of Savoy became princes of Piedmont.' I have still the copy of a remonstrance, in which I myself inserted these very words, and which the President Truchi, the ablest man in the state, has endeavoured to answer on every other point but this. He has, however, never dared to touch upon our antiquity. And formerly, in the year 1559," continues Leger, "when Emanuel Philibert was told, that his Waldensian petitioners professed the faith which had been handed down to them from their forefathers from the time of the martyrs and apostles, would that great prince and his court have endured to be told this by these poor people, if there had been one particle of truth to be discovered to the contrary, by the ministers of his royal highness, or by his ecclesiastics, or if any of them could have maintained the opposite, and shown, that they did not descend from father to son from the times of the martyrs, and confessors, and holy apostles?"

To the above-cited testimonies of the Waldenses themselves in regard to their origin, it may not be amiss to add what they modestly say on this point, when addressing the Reformers, in the sixteenth century:—"Our ancestors," say they, "have often recounted to us, that we have existed from the time of the apostles. In all matters, nevertheless, we agree with you; and, thinking as you think, from the very days of the apostles themselves, we have ever been concordant respecting the faith. In this particular only, we may be said to differ from you; that, through our fault, and the slowness of our genius, we do not understand the sacred writers with such strict correctness as yourselves."

Let us now see what their enemies have said on this point. And here there is an abundance of testimony, from which, however, we can extract only a single instance. Reinerius uses the following language respecting these people, whom he denominates Leonists. "Concerning the sects of ancient heretics, let it be observed, that they have been more than seventy in number; all of which, save those of the Manicheans, the Arians, the Runcarians, and the Leonists, which have infected Germany, have, through God's favour, been extirpated. Among all these sects, which either still exist, or which have formerly existed, there is not one more pernicious to the Church [of Rome] than that of the Leonists; and this for three reasons. First, because it has been of longer continuance; for some say, that it has lasted from the time of Sylvester; others, from the time of the apostles. Second, because it is more general; for there is scarcely a country, in which it does not exist. Third, because, that whilst all other sects, through their monstrous blasphemies against God, strike horror into the hearers, this of the Leonists has a great appearance of piety, inasmuch as they live justly before men, and believe, not only, all the articles of the creed, but every sound doctrine respecting the Deity; only they speak evil of the Roman Church and clergy, to which the multitude of the laity are quite ready to give credence."

That Reinerius speaks of the Waldenses under the name of Leonists, is quite clear, from what he says in other places. In addition to this, Pilichdorf, a writer of the same century, expressly says, that the persons who claim to have existed from the time of Pope Sylvester, were the Waldenses. And Claude Scyssel, Archbishop of Turin, in the latter end of the fifteenth century, and in the beginning of the sixteenth, and who, from his vicinity to them, as well as from the fact that they were geographically comprehended in his diocese, must have had good opportunities of knowing their origin and history, tells us, that the Waldenses of Piedmont took their origin from a person named Leo, who, in the time of the emperor Constantine, execrating the avarice of Pope Sylvester, and the immoderate endowment of the Roman Church, seceded from that communion, and drew after him all those who entertained right sentiments concerning the Christian religion.

These statements prove, not that the Waldenses originated as this writer suggests, but that they were incontestably the people meant by the Roman Catholic writers, when treating of the ancient Leonists.

On the subject of the antiquity of the Waldenses, M. Renouard, author of an elaborate work on the Provençal language and literature, and who discusses this question not as an ecclesiastical historian, but simply as a philologist, says that "the dialect of the Waldenses is an idiom intermediate between the decomposition of the language of the Romans and the establishment of a new grammatical system; a circumstance which attests the high antiquity of this dialect in the country which this people inhabit."

In speaking of the Noble Lesson, the oldest work which the Waldenses have, and which was, as is conceded on all hands, written in the twelfth century, and consequently more ancient than the greater part of the songs and other writings of the Troubadours, this author says:—"The language seems to me to be of an epoch already far separated from its original formation; inasmuch as we may remark the suppression of some final consonants; a peculiarity which announces, that the words of the long-spoken dialect had already lost some portion of their primitive terminations.

The philological fact, here stated, proves the high antiquity of the Waldenses; for they must have retired to those valleys at a remote period indeed, if they left the plains of Italy before the establishment of the new grammatical system, of which M. Renouard speaks. "Hence," remarks Mr. Faber, "the primevally Latin Waldenses must have retired from the lowlands of Italy to the valleys of Piedmont, in the very days of primitive Christianity, and before the breaking up of the Roman empire by the persevering incursions of the Teutonic nations. But it is scarcely probable, that men would leave their homes in the fair, and warm, and fertile country of Italy, for the wildness of desolate mountains, and for the squalidity of neglected valleys—valleys, which would require all the severe labour of assiduous cultivation, and mountains, which no labour could make productive—unless some very paramount and overbearing cause had constrained them to undertake such an emigration. Now a cause, precisely of this description, we have in the persecutions, which, during the second, third, and fourth centuries, occurred under the emperors Marcus Aurelius, Maximin, Decius, Valerian, and Diocletian."

Chapter Third.

CONDITION BEFORE THE REFORMATION.

The character of the early Waldensian church is set forth with singular truth and beauty in their ancient insignia, a copy of which is here given. That church was indeed a "*light shining in darkness*," and blessed be God its candlestick has not yet been removed from its place. The Waldenses of Piedmont are, in our view, primitive Christians, who have been preserved in these valleys from the alterations successively introduced by the church of Rome into the evangelical worship. It is not they who separated from Romanism, but Romanism which separated from them, in modifying the primitive worship. Hence the impossibility of assigning a precise late to their origin. The church of Rome, which, in its commencement, also formed part of the primitive church, did not modify itself all at once; but, as it became powerful, it assumed, together with the sceptre of rule, the display, the pride, and the spirit of domination which ordinarily accompany power; whilst, amid the Waldensian valleys, this primitive church, existing in comparative obscurity, remained in its isolation, free, and without tendency to abandon the pure simplicity of its infancy. The independence of the diocese of Milan, and that asserted by the episcopal see of Turin, in its resistance, in the ninth century, to the worship of images, contributed to maintain them in this position.*

* The following account of the opinions of Claudius, bishop of Turin, 817—839, is derived from Allix's "Remarks on the Ecclesiastical History of the Ancient Churches of Piedmont:"—

"We need only read his commentary upon the Epistle to the Galatians, to assure us, that he everywhere asserts the equality of all the apostles with St. Peter, though the occasions seemed naturally to engage him to establish the primacy of St Peter, and that of his pretended successors. This we find in ten several passages of that commentary; he only declares the primacy of St. Peter to consist in the honour he had of founding the church both amongst the Jews and Gentiles, p. 810. And indeed everywhere throughout his writings he maintains, that Jesus Christ is the only Head of the Church.

"He overthrows the doctrine of merits in such a manner, as overthows all the nice distinctions of the papists on that subject.

"He pronounces anathemas against traditions in matters of religion: so far was he from giving occasion to others to suspect that he made them a part of the object of his faith, as the church of Rome at present doth.

"He maintains, that faith alone saves us, which is the point that so extremely provoked the church of Rome against Luther, who asserted the same thing.

"He holds the church to be subject to error, opposite to what at this day the Romanists pretend in so unreasonable a manner.

The Waldensian valleys could not always preserve that obscure independence which constituted their security. Romanism, gradually invested with a new worship unknown to the apostles, daily rendered more and more conspicuous the contrast between its pompous innovations and the antique simplicity of the Waldenses.

To reduce them within the despotic unity of Rome, there were sent against them the agents of a ministry equally unknown in the apostolic period: these were the inquisitors (1308). In consequence of the resistance which they encountered in these remote mountains, the valley of Luserne was ultimately (1453) put under interdict. But this measure only established more manifestly the line of demarcation which was forming between the two churches; for although the Waldenses were not separated schismatically from the Romish church, the external forms of which

"He denies that prayers after death may be of any use to those that have demanded them.

"He very smartly lashes the superstition and idolatry which then began to be renewed, being supported by the authority of the Roman see.

"These things we find in his commentary upon the Epistle to the Galatians: but the other writings of this great man, manuscript and printed, show us yet more of his mind. Indeed, we find him giving very public marks of his zeal for the purity of religion in several points. First, he proposeth the doctrine of the church, in reference to the eucharist, in a manner altogether conformable to the judgment of antiquity, following therein the most illustrious doctors of the Christian church, and showing that he was, as to that matter, at the farthest distance from the opinions which Paschasius Radbertus advanced eighteen or nineteen years after that Claudius had writ his commentary upon St. Matthew."

It was worth our while to take notice of these opinions of Claudius, because the papists have owned that the valleys of Piedmont preserved the opinions of Claudius in the ninth and tenth century.

still included them, they had their own clergy, their own worship, and their own parishes.

Their pastors were named *barbas*, the Waldensian term for *uncle*. It was in the almost inaccessible solitude of the Pra-del-Tor, that their school was situated. There those who were preparing to be *barbas* learned by heart the gospels of St. Matthew and St. John, the catholic epistles, and a portion of those of St. Paul. They were instructed, further, in Latin, Romane (old French), and Italian. After this they passed several years in retirement, and they were then consecrated ministers by the administration of the sacrament and the imposition of hands.

They were supported by the voluntary contributions of the people, distributed among them annually in a general synod. A third of these contributions was given to the ministers, a third to the poor, and a third was reserved for the missionaries of the church.

These missionaries always journeyed in pairs, a young man and an old man, the latter being designated *regidor*, the former *coadjuteur*. They traversed all Italy, where they had fixed stations at different points, and in almost all the towns adherents: at Venice, for example, no fewer than 6000, and at Genoa as many. Each pastor being, in his turn, a missionary, the younger men thus became initiated in the delicate duties of evangelization, each being under the experienced conduct of an elder, whom discipline established as his superior, and whom he obeyed in all things, alike from duty and from deference. The old man, on his part, thus prepared himself for his repose, by forming for the church successors worthy of it and of himself. His own task finished, he could die in peace, with the consolatory assurance of having transmitted the sacred deposit of the gospel to prudent and zealous hands.

Besides this, the barbas were instructed in some trade or profession by which they might provide, in whole or in part, for their own living. Some were hawkers, some artizans, the greater number surgeons or physicians; and all were versed in the cultivation of the soil and the nurture of flocks.

At the annual synod, held in the valleys, the past conduct of the pastors was closely investigated, and their mutations of residence regulated. These mutations took place every third year among the younger pastors; the old barbas were not removed. A director-general of the church was appointed at each synod, with the designation of President or Moderator; the latter title ultimately prevailed, and subsists to this day.

There was nothing more remarkable about the early Waldenses, than their missionary spirit. It was by sending out missionaries, two by two on foot, to visit their brethren dispersed in various lands, that they kept alive the little piety which existed in the world at that day. These missionaries knew where to find their brethren; they went to their houses, held little meetings, administered the ordinances, ordained deacons, and sustained the faith and hopes of the tempted and persecuted ones. It is said that these missionaries could go, at one period, from Cologne to Florence, and stay every night at the houses of brethren. It is on account of the great number of missionaries which these little and poor churches in the valleys sustained, that we read of there being sometimes one hundred and forty or fifty ministers at the meetings of their synods. But few of these were needed at home; the most were engaged in the foreign work.

It is also remarkable that almost all the men whom God raised up from time to time, in France, and other countries, for more than six hundred years before the Reformation, seem to have had more or less to do with the Waldenses; such as Peter Waldo, Peter Bruys, Henry of Lausanne, and Lollard.

Not only did preachers go out from the valleys to proclaim the glorious gospel, but humble pious pedlars, or itinerating merchants, of whom there were many in the middle ages, scattered the truth by carrying some leaves of the Word of Life, or some manuscript tracts, beneath their merchandize, which they engaged those whom they found to be favourably disposed, to receive and read.

The following beautiful verses, descriptive of this traffic of the Waldensian pedlers, were published in a valuable religious Journal, a few years ago.*

THE VAUDOIS MISSIONARY.

I.

"O, lady fair, these silks of mine
  Are beautiful and rare—
The richest web of the Indian loom
  Which beauty's self might wear.
And these pearls are pure and mild to behold,
  And with radiant light they vie;
I have brought them with me a weary way:
  Will my gentle lady buy?"

II.

And the lady smiled on the worn old man,
  Through the dark and clustering curls
Which vailed her brow as she bent to view
  His silk and glittering pearls:

* The London *Christian Observer.*

And she placed their price in the old man's hand,
  And lightly turned away:
But she paused at the wanderer's earnest call—
  "My gentle lady, stay!"

III.

"O, lady fair, I have yet a gem
  Which a purer lustre flings
Than the diamond flash of the jewelled crown
  On the lofty brow of kings;
A wonderful pearl of exceeding price,
  Whose virtue shall not decay;
Whose light shall be as a spell to thee,
  And a blessing on thy way!"

IV.

The lady glanced at the mirroring steel,
  Where her youthful form was seen,
Where her eyes shone clear and her dark locks waved
  Their clasping pearls between;
"Bring forth thy pearl of exceeding worth,
  Thou traveller gray and old;
And name the price of thy precious gem,
  And my pages shall count thy gold."

V.

The cloud went off from the pilgrim's brow,
  As a small and meagre book
Unchased with gold or diamond gem,
  From his folding robe he took:
"Here, lady fair, is the pearl of price—
  May it prove as such to thee!
Nay, keep thy gold—I ask it not—
  For the Word of God is free."

VI.

The hoary traveller went his way—
  But the gift he left behind
Hath had its pure and perfect work
  On that high-born maiden's mind;

And she hath turned from her pride of sin
  To the lowliness of truth,
And given her human heart to God
  In its beautiful hour of youth.

VII.

And she hath left the old gray walls
  Where an evil faith hath power,
The courtly nights of her father's train,
  And the maidens of her bower;
And she hath gone to the Vaudois vale,
  By lordly feet untrod,
Where the poor and needy of earth are rich
  In the perfect love of God!

The first combined measures taken by the secular authority for the destruction of the Vaudois, do not appear to date before 1209. At that epoch, the emperor Otho IV. having, after the death of his rival, Philip of Suabia, been recognised by the Diet of Frankfort, repaired to Rome, for the purpose of being consecrated by pope Innocent III. who had always favoured him against Philip. On his way he passed through Piedmont. The then reigning count of Savoy, Maurice, had taken part against him in his disputes with Philip, and the latter had given him, as a reward, the towns of Quiers, Testona, and Modona. Otho, now triumphant, resolved to punish the partisan of his competitor, by enfeebling him in his own states; and he accordingly conferred on the archbishop of Turin, who was a prince of the empire, authority to destroy the Waldenses by force of arms. Thus, the long train of persecution which this people had to undergo was not opened by the house of Savoy, but by its enemies; and when, later, the house of Savoy itself entered on the path of cruelty and depopulation, it was not of its own motion, but ever under foreign influences, the most vindictive of which was that of the court of Rome.

Thus was the primitive church preserved in the Alps up to the epoch of the Reformation. The Waldenses are the chain by which the reformed churches are connected with the first disciples of our Saviour. In vain has popery, renegade from evangelical truths, sought, a thousand times, to break that chain; it has resisted every shock; empires have crumbled away, dynasties have fallen, but this chain of scriptural testimony has not been broken, for its strength came, not from men, but from God.

Chapter Fourth.

PERSECUTION BY YOLANDE AND CATANEO.

It was a foreigner, the sister of Louis XI., who first commenced the systematic persecution of the Waldenses. This was Yolande, who, having married Amadeus IX., one of the best and most charitable dukes of Savoy that ever honoured his dynasty, became, in 1472, as his widow, the regent of his dominions. Her name, from Yolande, was converted into Violante, either from some alteration of orthography in the public documents, or in allusion to her violent and vindictive character.

On the 23d of January, 1476, without putting forth any other complaint against the Waldenses, or alleging any other ground for her rigour than their creed, she ordered the seigneurs of Pignerol and Cavours to bring them, at whatever cost, within the bosom of the Romish church: the Waldenses, in their turn, demanded that the Romish church itself should be brought back to the gospel. The duchess convoked her great vassals to deliberate on the means of reducing to silence these daring protestants—if we may employ the term a century before the Reformation. But she had not the opportunity of carrying her projects into effect, being herself made prisoner by order of the duke of Burgundy, who, being at war with Louis XI., desired to prevent her giving aid to that monarch. The Waldenses, however, had pertinaciously refused to abjure their alleged

POMARET.—(VALLEY OF ST. MARTIN.)

heresy, and Charles, Yolande's second son, accordingly directed an inquiry to be made into this contumacy (1485). This inquiry for the first time officially manifested the profound difference which time had established between the Waldenses, still faithful to the primitive faith, and the Romish church, more and more degenerate. The result was laid before the holy see in 1486.

In the following year, Innocent VIII. fulminated against the Waldenses a bull of extermination, by which he enjoined all the temporal powers to arm for their destruction. It invited all catholics to take up the cross against them, "absolving from all ecclesiastical pains and penalties, general and particular, those who should take up the cross; releasing them from any oaths they might have taken; legitimatizing their title to any property they might have illegally acquired; and promising remission of all their sins to such as should kill any heretic. It annulled all contracts made in favour of the Waldenses; ordered their domestics to abandon them, forbade all persons to give them any aid whatever, and empowered all persons to take possession of their property."

Forthwith several thousands of volunteers—vagabond adventurers, ambitious fanatics, reckless pillagers, merciless assassins—assembled from all parts of Italy to execute the behests of the pseudo-successor of St. Peter. This horde of brigands, suitable support of a profligate pontiff, marched against the valleys, in the train of another army of 18,000 regular troops, contributed in common by the king of France and the sovereign of Piedmont.

Yet no crime was alleged against the unhappy Waldenses, even by the pope himself. His exterminating bull itself admitted that their chief means of seduction was their marked manifestation of sanctity. The destruction of this feeble folk seemed inevitable at the hands of so overwhelming a force of foes; but God undertook their defence, breathing a spirit of confusion into the ranks of their enemies, of steady courage into their own.

The papal legate who was charged with the execution of these sanguinary orders, was an archdeacon of Cremona, named Albert Cataneo, or de Cataneis. He took up his abode first at Pignerol, in the convent of San Larenzo, whence he despatched preaching monks to essay the conversion of the Waldenses, ere he assailed them with arms. These missionaries obtaining no success, he himself advanced into the valleys. The inhabitants sent to him as delegates, John Campo and John Desiderio, who thus addressed him:—"Do not condemn us without hearing us, for we are Christians and faithful subjects; and our barbas are prepared to prove, in public or in private, that our doctrines are conformable with the word of God. True, we have not followed the transgressors of the evangelical law, who have so long departed from the tradition of the apostles; we have rejected their corrupt precepts, and refused to recognise any other authority than that of the Bible; but we find our happiness in a pure and simple life, wherein alone the Christian faith takes root and flourishes. We despise the love of riches and the thirst of dominion, wherewith our persecutors are devoured. Our hope in God is, however, greater than our desire to please men: beware how you draw down upon yourselves his anger by persecuting us; for remember, that if God so wills it, all the forces you have assembled against us will nothing avail."

This noble confidence was not deceived. At the will of God this army of invaders vanished from the Waldensian mountains as rain in the sands of the desert.

The inhabitants concentrated themselves on the most

inaccessible points; the enemy, on the contrary, spread themselves over the plains. From strategetic incapacity, or from an ostentatious desire to make a great display of military force, Cataneo resolved to make an attack simultaneously on all the leading points, to that from the village of Biolet, in the marquisate of Saluzzo, to that of Sezanne, in Dauphiny, his shallow lines occupied the whole country. It was his idea to stifle with one blow the hydra of heresy: with one blow his own power was shattered, his lines broken, and his battalions assailed, in their precipitate flight, by those whom they had come to crush.

The only weapons employed were pikes, swords, and arrows. The Waldenses constructed shields and cuirasses of skins, covered with the thick bark of the chestnut-tree, and these arrested the enemy's arrows, which, shot from below, penetrated without piercing these defences; while the Waldenses, vigorous and skilful, full of confidence in God, and better posted, discharged their weapons from above with triumphant advantage. There was one post, however, which, despite the energy of the defence, seemed about to be forced by the enemy—the central point of this great line of operations, on the heights of San Giovanni, near the Angrogna mountains, at a place called Roccamanante.

The crusaders having by degrees ascended the mountain, had reached this natural bulwark, behind which the Waldenses had placed their families. These, seeing them draw back, fell on their knees, and exclaimed with fervour, "O Lord God, help them! O Lord God, save us!" The enemy, who from a distance beheld their suppliant attitude, sent forth a contemptuous shout of laughter, and hastened their march. "You shall be saved with a vengeance," cried one of their chiefs, named, from his dark complexion,

Il Nero di Mondovi; and as he spoke he raised his visor, in scorn of the poor folk, whom he thought he could insult with impunity; but at the very instant an arrow, shot by a young man of Angrogna, called Peter Revelli, pierced the forehead of this modern Goliath between the eyes, and laid him dead on the spot. His men, struck with panic and fear, drew back in disorder; the Waldenses, taking advantage of their terror, sallied forth, and, rushing upon them, drove them down to the plain, where they dispersed in flight.

A fresh endeavour was made next day to obtain possession of the redoubtable post. The enemy, adopting a different route, proceeded along the valley of Angrogna, on their way to the Pra-del-Tor, whence, ascending by La Vachera, they would have rendered themselves masters of the whole country. But one of those thick fogs which, at times, suddenly arise in the Alps, came upon them, just as they were involved in the most dangerous and most difficult defiles. Ignorant of the locality, advancing in doubt, uncertain which way to turn, and unable to advance in a body over these rocks, bordered with precipices, they were checked by the first attack of the Waldenses, and speedily defeated. The first who were repulsed fell back on those who were behind them, these on the next, and in a few minutes utter disorder prevailed: retreat soon became flight, flight catastrophe, the fugitives falling over the humid rocks into the fatal abysses below. Few of the assailants escaped; and this decisive rout, due to the will of God rather than to the arms of the Waldenses, completed the deliverance of this valley, which was not again visited by Cataneo's troops.

On the mountain of Roderi, in the valley of Pragela, the Waldenses, favoured by the nature of the locality, put to flight the crusaders, by rolling down upon them avalanches of rocks; after this they descended, attacked them, man to man, and prolonged the fight till the evening. The legate then drew off to Dauphiny. There a battalion of his forces, 700 strong, entering the village of Pommiere, in the Val-Louise, which they designed to plunder, were suddenly attacked by the Waldenses; and all those who escaped the fury of the first assault perished within a few days in the gorges of the mountains. The standard-bearer alone, after remaining concealed in a ravine for two days, came forth to avoid death by starvation and cold, and yielded himself up to the Waldenses, who afforded him sustenance and asylum, with that generous forgiveness of injuries which Christ has inculcated on his faithful. The prisoner's strength restored, he was permitted to depart; and it was he who made known the total defeat of his companions.

After these futile and inglorious expeditions, the duke of Savoy withdrew his troops, dismissed the legate, under pretext that his mission was completed, and sent a bishop to the Waldenses to induce them to make overtures for a peace, which, they were assured, would be granted them. The interview of this envoy with the evangelical Christians of the Alps took place in the hamlet of Prasuyt, on the borders of the parishes of Angrogna and San Giovanni. It was there agreed that the Waldenses should send a representative from each of their churches to wait upon the prince, who was to repair, for that purpose, to Pignerol. At this meeting it was that the prince required to see some of their children, in order to ascertain whether it was really true that they were born with black throats, hairy teeth, and goat's feet, as the Romanists asserted. "Is it possible," he exclaimed, when he saw several of these children,—" is it possible that these are the children of heretics! What charming creatures! They are the finest children I ever beheld!" The prejudice thus dissipated may appear ridiculous, but it was calculated to be of potent effect in an ignorant age. Superstition, which obscures the moral and religious sense, throws also its veil over all the other parts of the human intellect; as, on the other hand, the light of the gospel, in illuminating the soul which has received it, elevates, aggrandizes, and purifies all the intellectual powers.

Chapter Fifth.

HISTORY OF THE VAL-LOUISE.

In the general description of the country of the Waldenses, which is given in the first chapter, we have confined ourselves to the present limits of that people. They extended, however, at one time, far beyond those limits, into similar mountain valleys on the other side of the Alps, into Savoy on the north, into Provence and Dauphiny in France on the west, into the valley of the Po, and into the plain country between their present territory and Turin. In regard to some of these Waldensian settlements, it is difficult to say whether they were the original population, or whether they were early emigrants from the Piedmontese valleys. They were, however, all homogeneous in character, and they all looked to the Piedmontese valleys as a sort of mother country, the recognized centre and starting point of their race and their religion. Some of the earliest records of the history of this people of God relate to those valleys from which they have been since expelled, and where few, if any, of their name or faith are now to be found.

Among the French valleys, formerly occupied by a Waldensian population, the first to be named is the Val-Louise. This is a deep, cold gorge, which descends from Mont Pelvoux to the basin of the Durance. The earliest ascertained persecution of the people of this valley was between 1238 and 1243. A century later, in 1335, we find, in the accounts-current of the bailli of Embrun, this singular article; *Item, for persecuting the Waldensian, eight sols and thirty deniers, gold;* as though the persecution of these Christians of the Alps had then become a regular department of the public service!

Chabert, one of the Waldensian brethren of the valley of Luserne, more than five hundred years before, had bought, from the dauphin John II., a large house in Val-Louise, which he had presented to the brethren of that district for the purpose of their religious assemblies. This edifice the archbishop of Embrun destroyed, in 1348, excommunicating beforehand any persons who should attempt to rebuild it, and burning, at the same time, twelve Waldenses who had been found in the house by the archbishop's satellites. These unfortunate captives, being taken to Embrun, and collected in the square facing the cathedral, amid a crowd of people, and more immediately surrounded by fanatic monks, were enveloped in a yellow robe, on which were painted flames, symbolizing those of the hell to which they were declared doomed; their heads were shaved, and they were publicly anathematized; then, with bare feet, and ropes round their necks, they were fastened to the stake and strangled; fire was then applied; their bodies returned to dust, their souls ascended to their God.

A young inquisitor, Francesco Borelli, obtained from pope Gregory XI. pressing letters to the king of France, the duke of Savoy, and the governor of Dauphiny, enjoining them to unite their forces for the purpose of extirpating from the Alps this inveterate heresy. The inquisitor undertook the charge of the temporal arms that were confided to him; and his persecutions left not a single village unassailed. Like the fabulous robe of the centaur, which destroyed whatever it touched, it seized whole families, whole populations, so that the prisons were soon inadequate to receive the multitude of prisoners. New dungeons were constructed for them, of mere bare walls, designed only to secure and inflict suffering on the captives.

Borelli began with summoning before him all the inhabitants of these valleys: they did not appear, and he condemned them for not appearing. Thencefoward, exposed to be surprised by his satellites, they suffered the double anguish of their own perils and the anguish of their families. One was seized on the highway, another in his field, another by his fireside; for fifteen years did this work of extermination proceed.

At length, on 22d May, 1393, all the churches of Embrun were decked as for a grand solemnity, and the cathedral especially, where the mass of the local clergy, covered with their theatrical decorations, were grouped in the choir, while, near them, a double line of soldiers served at once to keep back the people in the nave, and to guard a troop of prisoners, soldiers of Christ, condemned, for their vindication of his word, to be burned alive. Presently the list of these martyrs was read out to the people. There were eighty from the valleys of Frayssinières and Argentiere, and one hundred and fifty from the Val-Louise—a large proportion of the population of that valley; and after each name was pronounced the fatal formula that condemned the living bodies of these two hundred and thirty victims to the stake! The solitude of the desert now reigned in these depopulated mountains; and as the wolves abandon the exhausted charnel-house, the inquisitors withdrew from these impoverished valleys.

For a while France had enough to do in saving herself

from utter destruction at the hands of the English, owing her final safety only to the enthusiasm of a young girl, Joan of Arc. Meantime, the Waldensian churches gradually raised up their heads once more, as violets from amid the rocks, the breath of persecution propagating their evangelical faith, as the wind bears afar the fragrance of the flower. But the haughty and brutal animosity of the papacy grew also; and towards the close of the fifteenth century, Innocent VIII. proclaimed against the Waldenses that war of extermination, the conduct of which, as we have seen in a former chapter, he committed to Albert Cataneo.

It was in the month of June, 1488, that this worthy legate of the pope, having fruitlessly essayed to subjugate the valleys of Piedmont, passed into France by Mont Genevre, where he caused to be strangled eighteen of these poor folk whom he had made prisoners. Thence he made an onslaught upon Briançon, a town which had been indicated to him as a nest of heresy; and from this marched upon Frayssinières, whose few and poorly armed inhabitants retired to a rock overlooking the church, where they were surrounded by the troops, and made prisoners.

Cataneo's ferocious fanatics thence entered the deep gorge of Val-Louise. The Waldenses, feeling that they could not resist a force twenty times greater than their own, abandoned their poor habitations, placed their old people and children in their rustic carts, with their domestic utensils and such provisions as they could collect, and, driving their herds before them, and singing canticles, retired to the rugged slopes of Mont Pelvoux. This part of the Alps rises more than six thousand feet above the level of the valley. A third of the way up there is an immense cavern, called Aigue-Froide or Ailfrede, from the cold springs, nourished by the snows, which are found there. A sort of platform, accessible only over fearful precipices, extends at the mouth of the cavern, the majestic vault of which, after subsiding into a narrow passage, expands once more into an immense hall, of irregular form. Such was the asylum which the Waldenses had selected. They placed at the extremity of the grotto, the women, children, and old men; the cattle and sheep occupied the lateral cavities of the rock, and the able-bodied men posted themselves towards the mouth of the cavern, which, after having first barricaded with large rocks the path that led to the grotto, they had walled up with similar materials. Cataneo states, in his Memoirs, that they had with them provisions for more than two years. All their precautions thus taken, they deemed they had nothing to fear; but in reality they had to fear this very confidence in mere human precautions.

Cataneo had with him a daring and experienced leader, named La Palud. This captain, seeing the impossibility of forcing the entrenchments of the grotto on the side by which the Waldenses had reached it, led his own men back into the valley; then, with all the ropes he could collect, he ascended Mont Pelvoux, and, making his way to the precipice overhanging the entrance to the cavern, descended, by means of the ropes, to the platform. Nothing could have been more easy than for the Waldenses either to cut the ropes, or to slay each soldier before he reached the ground, and then hurl him into the abyss; but a panic terror seized the unhappy besieged. Some who rushed out from the cavern precipitated themselves down the rocks. Those who essayed resistance were slaughtered by La Palud, who then, not venturing to involve his men in the depths of the cavern, piled up all the wood he could collect at the entrance, and set fire to it. Those who attempted to issue forth were either destroyed by the flames, or by the sword of the enemy, while those who remained within were stifled by the smoke. When the cavern was afterwards examined, there were found in it four hundred infants suffocated in their cradles, or in the arms of their dead mothers. Altogether there perished in this cavern more than three thousand Waldenses—including the entire population of Val-Louise. Cataneo distributed the property of these unfortunates among the vagabonds who accompanied him, and never again did the Waldensian church raise its head in these blood-stained valleys.

Chapter Sixth.

HISTORY OF BARCELONNETTE, QUEYRAS, AND FRAYSSINIERES.

THE valley of Barcelonnette in Savoy is a hollow closed in on all sides by almost inaccessible mountains. The period of the first advent hither of the Waldenses is unknown; but we find that when Farel came to preach here in 1519, at Josiers, the population rejoiced to hear, by the voice of the reformer, the doctrines of *their forefathers* proclaimed aloud in all their evangelical purity.

In 1366, a rigorous order enjoined all the Waldenses of Barcelonette either to embrace Romanism, or to quit the territory of Savoy within a month, under penalty of death and confiscation of their property. Most of them resolved to retire to the valley of Frayssinières, which belonged to France; but it was now deep winter; the roads were covered with snow and ice; the women, children, and old men could advance but slowly, so that wearied and cold, they were fain to lie down for the night on the snow, and numbers were frozen into the sleep of death. The survivors reached with difficulty the paternal asylum that had been opened to them. When, however, the governor of Barcelonnette proposed to distribute the property of the proscribed amongst the catholic population of the valley, these noble men refused to accept the gift, and the exiles were thereupon permitted to return and resume their possessions, the authorities perceiving that otherwise the land would remain uncultivated, and the valley in a large degree uninhabited. Still the Waldenses were not allowed openly to exercise their religion, but were fain several times in the year to traverse the glaciers to Vars, in the territory of France, to receive the communion and the benediction of a pastor.

Half a century later (in 1623) persecution recommenced. A Dominican monk, named Bouvetti, obtained from the duke of Savoy authority to proceed against the Waldenses of Barcelonnette, to whom he brought once more the alternative of abjuration or exile. The execution of this alternative was pitilessly prosecuted by the governor of the valley, Francis Dreux; so that after many fruitless endeavours to effect a modification of their fate, the Waldenses, unshaken in the faith of their fathers, had once more, and now without return, to abandon their native valley, and to seek an asylum in lands less afflicted. Some withdrew to Queyras and Gapencois, others to Orange and Lyon, others to Geneva, others still to the valleys of Piedmont, which seemed their mother-country.

The inhabitants of Frayssinières in France, whose laborious habits and pure life the illustrious De Thou has depicted in the most vivid colours, were also in their turn the victims of persecution; between 1056 and 1290 no fewer than five papal bulls demanded their extirpation, and so early as 1238 the Inquisition preyed upon them.

In 1344, most of the inhabitants of Frayssinières, being persecuted, took refuge in the valleys of Piedmont; but they afterwards returned thence with their barbas, resisted the inquisitors, and were soon stronger than before.

After the extermination of the Waldenses of Val-Louise, the bloody Cataneo undertook to deal with those of

Frayssinières, and summoned them to appear before him at Embrun. Knowing that the object was to obtain their abjuration, they did not attend; hereupon they were condemned, as contumacious rebels and heretics, to be burned, and their property to be confiscated to the Romish church. Such of them as were seized were accordingly sent to the stake without any further formality; and any one who interceded for them, though it were a son for a mother, a father for his child, was immediately imprisoned, and, in many cases, condemned also to the flames as abetting heresy.

Upon the death of Charles VIII., in 1498, delegates from almost all the provinces of the kingdom repaired to Paris to take part in the coronation of Louis XII.; and the inhabitants of Frayssinières took the occasion to depute one of their number to attend, and to lay their complaints before the new sovereign. Louis XII. referred the matter to his council, and after consultation with the pope, papal and royal commissioners were appointed to investigate the subject on the spot. Upon arriving at Embrun, these commissioners had all the documents of the processes against the Waldenses on the part of the inquisitors laid before them, and having investigated them, censured the bishop, and annulled all the condemnations pronounced against the inhabitants of Frayssinières.

After this, the Waldensian Christians in Dauphiny experienced various turns of fortune, some of them memorable indeed, but we have not space to dwell upon them more particularly. During the 17th century, they were permitted freely to exercise their religion, and had regular pastors at Restolas, Abries, Château-Queyros, Arvieux, Moline, and St. Veran.

The revocation of the edict of Nantes destroyed their

temples and proscribed themselves. Thousands of them went into exile. Those of Queyras withdrew into the valleys of Piedmont. Under Lewis XV. their faith being still interdicted, these poor people exercised their worship in the desert, like those of Le Gard and of the Cevennes. When a religious assembly was to take place, the villagers descended separately, by different paths, with spade on shoulder, as if repairing to their work, and all would meet in some solitary nook, where, taking their psalm-books from their bosoms, they would unite in prayer. Whole families were wont to traverse long distances to attend these meetings. Departing in the evening, they would travel all night, and at the entrance of villages the men would take off their shoes and walk barefoot, so that the sound of their steps might not betray them; the feet of the mules or horses, on which the women and children rode, were covered with linen, for the same purpose, and thus the pious procession would reach the secret place of prayer. Sometimes the gendarmerie, then called the maréchaussée, would suddenly come upon the assembled worshippers, and in the name of the king, arrest the pastor; but the assemblies of the desert, dispersed at one point, would rally at another. Where copies of the Bible had, by incessant seizures, become too few to supply the wants of each, societies of young persons were formed, for the purpose of learning the Scriptures by heart, and thus preserving it, in their memory at least, from the menaced confiscation. Each member of these societies was entrusted to retain exactly in his memory a certain number of chapters; and when the assembly of the desert assembled, these new Levites, standing beside the minister, in face of the faithful, would supply the reading of the interdicted volume, by successively reciting, each in his turn, all the chapters of the book indicated by the pastor, for the common edification. Descendants of these glorious men, who thus aided to preserve the protestant church in France through periods of storm, still subsist at Frayssinières, at Vars, at Dormilhouse, Arvieux, Molines, and St. Veran. A recent apostolate, worthy of representing the ancient Waldensian fervour, has connected with these districts the name of Felix Neff.

Chapter Seventh.

THE WALDENSES IN PROVENCE.

SEVERAL colonies of the Waldenses established themselves in Provence towards the close of the thirteenth century. For awhile adhering to a close reserve in their religious worship, and punctually paying all taxes, tithes, and seigneurial dues, they were not interfered with by the Romanists; but the German reformers having reproached them with cowardice and dissimulation in not more openly manifesting their faith, they ceased to practice their worship in private only. Forthwith the inquisitors were let loose upon them, and one of these, John di Roma, was so excessive in his cruelties and spoliations, during the ten years he acted in these valleys, that the king had him imprisoned. The persecutions, which he had commenced, were, however, none the less continued. In 1534, the bishops of Sisteron, Apt, Cavaillon, and other sees, each in his diocese, sought out the Waldensians, and filled the prisons with them. Having ascertained that these heretics were natives of Piedmont, information was transmitted of their apprehension to the archbishop of Turin; and a commissioner, appointed by him, wrote to the authorities in Provence, directing that proceedings should be suspended until full inquiry had been made by him. The bishop of Cavaillon, however, on the 29th of March, 1535, informed him that thirteen of these prisoners had been already burned to death. Others, he said, had died in prison. Thus the intervention of the commissioner was futile against the vehement zeal of these persecuting prelates.

Clement VIII., a year before his death, promised plenary indulgence to every Waldensian in the French territories who would enter within the pale of popery: not one of them accepted the offer. Thereupon the pope complained to the king of France, who wrote to the parliament of Aix; and the parliament ordered the seigneurs of the lands occupied by the Waldensians, to compel their vassals either to abjure or to quit the country. Upon their refusal, an attempt was made to conquer them by intimidation. Some of them were cited to appear before the court of Aix, to explain the causes of their disobedience: they did not attend, and, in default, the court condemned them to be burned alive. Their brethren thereupon took up arms, and delivered the prisoners. The authorities took up arms, and a civil war seemed inevitable. The case was laid before the king, Francis I.; and he, thinking to pacify all parties, published in July, 1535, a general amnesty, on the condition that the heretics should abjure within the space of six months.

The six months passed away, and there was no abjuration: thereupon every seigneur and magistrate of these districts assumed the right of exacting abjuration, or of inflicting punishment on the recusant, by means of confiscation and imprisonment. Many of the seigneurs used largely this new mode of enriching themselves. Menier d'Oppede grievously abused it. The descendant of a Jewish family, poor, of evil reputation, and remorseless in soul, he took advantage of this crusade against the faithful: collecting a force of armed men, he would issue forth, seize upon some Waldensian farmer, and command him to invoke the saints. "There is but one Mediator between God and man," would the Waldensian reply; "and that is he who is himself both God and man, even Christ." The heretic would then be dragged to the caverns beneath the chateau d'Oppede, and there remain until he paid a heavy ransom, or till death released him, in which case his captor confiscated all his property to his own use.

These revolting depredations especially disgraced the year 1536. In the following year, the attorney-general of the parliament of Provence, at the instance of the fanatic clergy, and of greedy spoliators, drew up a report, setting forth that the Waldensians were daily increasing. Upon this report the king commanded the court to suppress the rebels; in June, 1539, he further enjoined it to take cognizance of heresy, and in the following October the court ordered the seizure of one hundred and fifty-four persons, denounced as heretics by two apostates.

In the excessive fermentation to which such measures naturally gave rise, a mere spark would light up a flame; and this happened in the following manner.

The Judge of Apt, taking a fancy to a mill there, denounced the miller, Pellenc, as a heretic; Pellenc was burned alive, and his mill confiscated to the profit of the denouncer. Some young people of Merindol, whose Provençal veins still boiled with Italian blood, could not restrain their indignation at such iniquity, and in their ignorance or their despair of legal forms, they executed justice for themselves; they went by night, and destroyed the mill, so unrighteously possessed, at the price of their brother's blood, by his murderer. The judge made his complaint to the court of Aix, and named the persons whom he suspected to have taken part in this violence.

The court, though it was vacation time (July, 1540), held an extraordinary sitting, and decreed the arrest of eighteen persons.

The officer appointed to effect the arrest proceeded to Merindol; he found the houses all empty. "Where are the inhabitants of this village?" he asked, of a mendicant whom he met on the way. "They have fled to the woods, for they heard that the troops of the count de Teuda were going to kill them." "Go seek them," said the officer, "and tell them they shall receive no harm." A few Waldensians made their appearance, and the officer served the summons upon these, ordering them to appear before the court in two months.

On the 2d of September they assembled together, and addressed to the court a memorial protesting their submissiveness to its orders, and their fidelity to the king; and supplicating the court not to be influenced by their enemies, who had already misled it, since, in the summons which they were directed to obey, there were the names of some persons who were dead, of others who had never existed at all, and of infants who could not yet walk. The court, irritated at having its blunders pointed out by these simple mountaineers, replied that the living should appear before it without troubling their heads about the dead. The Waldensians consulted an advocate as to what course they should pursue. "If you desire to be burned alive," was the answer, "you will go before the court." They did not go before it, and, accordingly, upon the 18th of November, 1540, the court of Aix pronounced against them an inconceivable judgment, condemning to the stake twenty-three persons, seventeen out of whom were named, delivering up their wives and children to any one who could seize them, forbidding all persons to aid them in any way, and ordering Merindol, as a place notorious for heresy, to be burned to the ground, and utterly destroyed.

This decree aroused general indignation, not only in the populace, but in the generous hearts among the nobility and the advocates. The young count d'Allenc, one of the most distinguished members of the Arlesian nobility, waited upon the president Chassanée, made an appeal to his justice and humanity, and obtained a respite, during which the court, itself alarmed at the decree it had pronounced, referred the matter to the king, who directed Dubellay, to proceed to Provence, and inquire into the conduct of the Waldenses.

Upon the report of this nobleman that the Waldenses were retired and quiet people, reserved in their manners, chaste and sober in their lives, and laborious in their habits, but that they did not attend the mass, the monarch, by a letter dated the 18th of February, 1541, proclaimed a general amnesty, pardoning all the condemned on condition of their abjuring their errors of doctrine within three months. This amnesty was not published by the court of Aix till the middle of May, when there only remained two weeks of the stipulated time unexpired; but had there been but one moment, they would never have sought to save their mortal life, at the expense of their immortal soul, by abjuring the truth. On the contrary, they proclaimed more emphatically than ever their persecuted doctrines, in a confession of faith, dated 6th of April, 1541, which they transmitted to Francis I., and which the sire de Castelnau read to him. Each point of doctrine was supported by texts of scripture. "Well, what have our people got to say in reply to that?" asked the monarch, from time to time. But his fickle and superficial mind soon forgot the impression thus made upon him.

The illustrious and learned Sadolet, whose features Raffaelle has transmitted to us in a celebrated picture, heard of this confession of faith, and requested to be furnished with a copy of it. He was at this time bishop of Carpentras, and it was with him the Waldenses of Cabrières first appeared on the stage; for, being inhabitants of his diocese, it was they who laid before him a copy of the common confession. "We consent," said they, "not only to abjure, but to submit to the severest penalties, if it can be shown to us, out of the holy scriptures, that our doctrines are erroneous."

The cardinal replied to them with kindness, admitted that they had been the victims of black calumnies and false criminations, requested them to come and confer with him, and sought to make them perceive that, without departing from the spirit of their confession, they might modify its letter. He took no pains, indeed, to prevent their perceiving that he himself desired a reform in catholicism. Had the Waldenses encountered only such examiners as he, blood would not have flowed! He wrote to the pope to express his surprise that the Waldenses were persecuted, while the Jews were spared; but the poor folk soon lost his protection, for he was recalled to Rome, and thus, removed from his observation, the Waldenses remained alone in face of their persecutors.

The term of the amnesty indicated by the royal letter having arrived, the court of Aix ordered the Waldenses to send ten representatives, to declare whether they intended to avail themselves of it, and to conform. One representative alone appeared, named Estène. "We consent to abjure," he repeated, "if our errors can be demonstrated."

The cardinal de Tournon, excited against the Waldenses by the legate of the papal see, sent word to the king that the clergy had rejected the confession of faith which the sectaries had laid before him, whereupon the governor of the province was ordered to clear it of heresy. The bishop of Cavailln, deputed by the court of Aix, visited Merindol to inquire into the religious views of the Waldenses. On reaching the village, he summoned the principal inhabitants before him, and rejecting all question between them of doctrine, required them at once "to abjure their errors;" intimating that all he desired was a mere formality on their part, after which they would be left at peace, and at full liberty to place what interpretation they pleased on their abjuration. But the Waldenses were not Jesuits; they frankly refused compliance, and the bishop withdrew.

On the 4th April, 1542, he returned, and was equally unsuccessful. Two years then passed away, in suspense on the one hand, in hesitation to act on the other, and then Francis I., on 14th June, 1544, on the plaint of the Waldenses of Cabrieres, issued an edict suspending all proceedings against the Waldenses, restoring them to their social privileges, and releasing such of them as were in prison. The court of Aix, before publishing this edict, sent one of its officers to Paris, to procure, if possible, its revocation. On the 1st January, 1545, letters of revocation were, in the privy council, placed before the king for signature, and he signed them without reading them, or being at all aware of their purport. They were, however, effective for the purpose, and that purpose was the execution of the decree of the 18th November, 1540, and the destruction by fire and sword, not simply of the twenty inhabitants of Merindol, contemplated by the decree, but of the entire population of seventeen villages. The instant that this sanguinary order had been thus fraudulently obtained, it was despatched by especial courier to Oppede, the president of the court of Aix, who, as instantly upon its receipt, sent instructions to the governor of Provence, to assemble troops for its prompt execution. No notice was given to the doomed people, lest they should make their plaint before their sovereign, and thus lay bare the fraud of which he was the dupe and they were to be the victims. The soldiers were quietly collected, and they only awaited the arrival of captain Poulain, who was shortly expected from Piedmont.

He came on the 7th April. Between the 7th and the 11th all the preparations were completed for carrying into effect this retroactive sentence. The 12th was a Sunday, but nevertheless the court assembled at the summons of Oppede.

The inhabitants of Lourmarin were ordered to prepare billets for a thousand foot and three hundred horse. The inhabitants replied by taking up arms. The order was repeated; they required a delay of twelve hours for reflection. "Subjects do not make terms with their sovereign," was the rejoinder. The chatelaine of Lourmarin, Blanche de Levis, came herself to intercede for her people, but she was not listened to. All in tears, she then addressed her vassals, and entreated them to avoid certain destruction, by laying down their arms. "Our destruction would only be the more certain and the more prompt, were we to lay them down," was the reply. "But let us depart quietly, and we will abandon our goods to those who seek them by our death."

The poor chatelaine, however, could do nothing. The dame de Cental also wrote to Oppede, entreating him to spare her vassals. But already the troops, spread over the country, had begun to pillage and destroy.

Oppede began by setting fire to the houses in La Roque, Ville-Laure, and Trezemines, which had been abandoned by the Waldenses; he did the same at Lourmarin, where a hundred and fourteen houses were destroyed.

On the 18th of April, the combined troops appeared before Merindol; the inhabitants had retired, but a young man, named Maurice Blanc, who had been late in the fields, was seized by the pillagers. They tied him to an olive tree, and the soldiers, converting him into a mark for their arquebuses, fired at him from a distance. The fifth bullet terminated his sufferings.

They then set fire to the village, which was entirely consumed. Some women having been surprised in the church, they were stripped naked, subjected to indescribable outrages, and then compelled to hold each other by the hand, as in a dance, were urged, at the pike's point, up the castle-rock, whence, already severely wounded and suffering, they were precipitated, one after the other, into the abyss beneath. Elsewhere many were taken and sold. One father had to travel to Marseilles to ransom his daughter. A young mother, endeavouring to escape across the fields, with her infant in her arms, was overtaken and outraged by these ruffians, pressing all the while her nursling to her bosom.

An aged woman at Lauris, between Cabrieres and Avignon, whose years saved her from this particular brutality, became in their hands an object of insult to humanity and to their own religion. They cut her hair in the shape of a cross, and having covered this tonsure with some tinsel, they led her through the streets, singing psalms derisively, in imitation of a procession of priests.

Coming, at length, to a large oven, which was heated to bake a quantity of bread for themselves, the soldiers pushed their victim to the opening with their pikes, crying, "Enter there, you old devil!" The poor creature, exhausted with her sufferings, was about to enter without resistance, but the soldiers who had prepared the oven would not permit this use to be made of it.

Signalizing its march by a thousand similar brutalities, under the most various and most revolting forms, the army reached Cabrieres. This fortified town, being within the pope's territory, could not have been touched without the consent of the pontiff, but the vice-legate Mormoiran had furnished Oppede with full power to act as he should think fit. The army came to the town on the 19th of April, and though this was the Sabbath, at once commenced battering the walls. The Waldenses within, occupied in prayer, gave no indication of submission, and the firing continued all day and all night. On Monday morning it was stayed, and Oppede wrote to the besieged, that if they would open the gates of the town, they should receive no harm. The first troops which entered were those from Piedmont, trained and hardy warriors, who were to have begun the carnage; but, knowing the stipulations of the surrender, the soldiers declared that their honour was concerned in its observance. Meantime, Oppede sent for the principal men of the place, who came without distrust. They were eighteen in number; their hands were tied, and they were passed among the troops, to which they made no objection, thinking they were merely there as hostages for the tranquillity of the rest of the population. But as they were traversing the ranks of the Provençal troops, commanded by Oppede, the son-in-law of this man, named de Pourrieres, cut with his sabre the bald head of an old man, whose faltering steps had accidentally approached too near the officer's feet.

"Kill them all," cried Oppede, when he saw the old man fall; and instantly the cowardly and frantic troops whom he so fitly commanded, butchered the unhappy hostages, whose quivering limbs, as they lay in recent death, the same de Pourrieres and the sire de Faulcon savagely mutilated. The heads of the murdered men were raised on pikes, and the soldiers being thus excited, the signal for general massacre was given. A number of women, shut up in a barn, to which fire was applied, sought to save themselves from the flames by leaping from the walls; they were received on the points of pikes and swords. Others had retired to the castle. "Death! blood!" exclaimed Oppede, as he pointed out to his soldiers the path to the asylum of the victims.

But the most horrible scene took place in the church. Hither the great majority of the women had repaired for refuge: the soldiers seized them, stripped them naked, outraged them in the most brutal manner, and then threw some of them from the tower to the ground, while others, after being dragged forth to glut the ruffianism of other soldiers who came up, were finally despatched by being eventerated. The horrors perpetrated on this, and on many similar occasions, were such as it is impossible to describe. The abbé Guerin, who was present at this massacre, states in his deposition that in the church alone "four or five hundred poor women and girls were outraged and slain."

The prisoners who were not put to death, were sold by the soldiers as galley-slaves. The vice-legate, indeed, acting in the true spirit of popery, refused to grant any quarter whatever. Having ascertained that twenty-five women, most of them mothers of families, had concealed themselves in a grotto near Mys, he ordered a party of soldiers thither to exterminate them, though the place was not within the papal territory. On reaching the mouth of the grotto, a discharge of musketry was directed within; no one came forth, fuel was piled up inside, and a large fire lighted, and all these living creatures of God perished in the flames and the smoke. In this extermination, there were burned seven hundred and sixty-three houses, ninety-nine stables, and thirty-one barns. The number of persons slaughtered was upwards of three thousand.

While still at Cabrieres, Oppede received a message from the lord of the town of La Costa, entreating him to spare his vassals. This was on the Monday evening. "Let them make four breaches in their walls," replied Oppede, "and we will see." On the Tuesday morning these breaches were commenced, but when the inhabitants saw Oppede's troops advancing as to an assault, they hastily filled up the breaches they had made, and closed the gates. The troops were fain to content themselves that day with destroying the gardens of the castle, which stood outside the town; the next morning, 22d of April, Oppede wrote to the syndics of La Costa, undertaking that if the gates were thrown open, the inhabitants should receive full protection and justice; the gates were opened on the faith of this promise, and the furious soldiers rushing in, at once proceeded to the work of massacre, outrage, and destruction. There was a small warren behind the castle; hither the soldiers dragged their female captives to dishonour, before they slew them. One mother, after in vain seeking to defend her daughter from the brutal ravisher, stabbed herself, and then drawing the ensanguined knife from her wound, gave it to her child, as the last resource from dishonour.

An inquiry into these atrocities was instituted in September, 1551, by order of Henry II., who desired to free his father's memory from this stain of blood; the fraud by which the revocation of the king's pardon had been effected was laid bare, but though the advocate, Guerin, was punished with death, the great criminal, Oppede, not only escaped, but returned triumphant to Provence, where he was welcomed by the clergy, who had blasphemously offered up public prayers and Te Deums in the churches, "for the safety and speedy return of this illustrious defender of the faith."

The few Waldenses who had escaped death, retired for a while to the valleys of Piedmont.

Chapter Eighth.

THE WALDENSES IN CALABRIA.

THE first migration of the Waldenses of Piedmont from their own valleys, to the richer land of Calabria, took place in 1340. By a convention with the local seigneurs, ratified later by the king of Naples, Ferdinand of Aragon, they were permitted to govern their own affairs, civil and spiritual, by their own magistrates and their own pastors. Their first colony was near the town of Montalto. A half century later, rose the town of San Xisto, which afterwards became the capital of the colony; other towns and villages of theirs were named Vacaresso, L'Arguelena, San Vincenzo, Le Rosse, contributing to create prosperity in a district that was previously well nigh desolate.

The marquis di Spinello, struck with the ameliorations effected by these industrious and upright men in the territories which had been ceded to them, invited a number of their body into his own states, gave them lands, aided them to build a town, and authorized them to surround this town with a wall, whence it derived the name of La Guardia.

Towards the close of the fourteenth century, another migration of Waldenses took place, from Provence into Italy; these new colonists settling in Apulia, not far from their Calabrian brethren, built their several walled towns, which they named after those whence they had come: La Cellare, Faët, La Motte. Again, in 1500, other Waldenses from Frayssinières and Pragela, established themselves in Calabria, on the small river Vollurate, which runs from the Apennines into the Bay of Tarento, whence they, and new comers, spread over other portions of the kingdom of Naples, even to Sicily. Agriculture and the sciences flourished among them. Baarlam of Calabria, of whom Petrarch was a disciple, was himself a disciple of the Waldenses. The missionary pastors, whom the synod at home sent amongst these colonists, remained with them, two at a time, for the space of two years, and were then replaced by others, themselves visiting on their return to their villages all the chief towns of Italy, in each of which they had brethren, more or less numerous. The Waldensian historian, Gilles, relates that his grandfather, on one of these pastoral visitations to Venice, was assured by the faithful, when he conversed with them, that the city contained no fewer than six thousand members of that body.

Until 1558, the Waldenses of Calabria remained unmolested in their modest and tranquil retirement. In that year, having applied to the synod for the appointment amongst them of a permanent pastor, the application was granted, and there was nominated to the honourable, but perilous post, a young Piedmontese, a native of Conio, named John Louis Paschale, who, having quitted the career of arms to become a soldier of Christ, had prepared himself for the ministry by studies recently completed at Lausanne.

Paschale departed, accompanied by another pastor, Jacob Boveto, also a Piedmontese, and who suffered martyrdom at Messina, in 1560.

Upon his arrival in Calabria, Paschale began zealously to preach the gospel as publicly as it was preached at Geneva. Thereupon, there arose a report that a Lutheran had come, who was about to destroy everything with his doctrines; the ignorant murmured, and the fanatics vociferated that he must be exterminated with all his adherents. The marquis Salvator-Spinello, suzerain of the Waldenses, who was then at Foscalda, a small town near La Guardia, sent word that some of their body must appear before him and explain their new proceedings; and, accordingly, a body of them, headed by Paschale, waited upon the marquis. This was in July, 1559. But the zealous young pastor had not to combat, as he had expected, honest errors, in a fair controversy, with evangelical texts and arguments. His enemies sought, not the truth, but silence; and, accordingly, after listening to Paschale for a few moments, the marquis, finding that submission was not to be expected from the Waldenses, dismissed the flock with a menace, and placed Paschale, and a fellow pastor, Marco Ascegli, who had accompanied him, in the dungeons of Foscalda. Hence, after an imprisonment of eight months, they were, on the 7th of February, 1560, transferred to the dungeons of Cosenza, where Ascegli, after being subjected to the torture, was burned to death.

On the 14th of April, Paschale was removed from the castle of Cosenza, and in company with twenty-two prisoners, condemned to the galleys, conveyed, under circumstances of great cruelty, to Naples, which they reached on the 23d of April. On the 16th of May, he was taken in chains to Rome, and imprisoned in the Torre di Nona, in a deep, dark, damp dungeon, without the least furniture, or even straw to lie on, and where his arms were bound so tightly with small cords that they entered the flesh.

For three days several members of the holy office were engaged during four hours each day, in argument with

Paschale, endeavouring to bring him to retract, but in vain; and on the 8th of September, 1560, he was conducted to the Convent della Minerva, to hear his condemnation pronounced. On the following morning he was taken to the square in front of the castle of St. Angelo, and there, in the presence of pope Pius IV., was strangled, his body burned, and his ashes thrown into the Tiber.

The attention of the holy office having been thus called to the Waldenses of Calabria, cardinal Alexandrini was despatched to San Xisto, in company with two Dominican monks. These wolves in sheeps' clothing, assuming extreme mildness of demeanour, assembled the inhabitants, assured them that no harm was designed against them, and that if they would *merely* consent to hear no other preachers than those sent them by the Romish bishop, and dismiss the Lutheran pastors who were misleading them, they had nothing to fear. They then, in order to ascertain how many persons observed the practices of the Romish church, had the bell rung for mass, and invited the people to attend. Not one attended; on the contrary, the entire population of the town, with the exception of a few young children and aged persons, quitted the place, and withdrew to an adjacent wood. The popish commissioners, repressing their anger, performed mass, and then proceeded to La Guardia. Here, having had the gates closed, they assembled the people: "Dear and faithful friends," said they, "your brethren of San Xisto have abjured their errors and attended mass; we invite you to follow this prudent example, or we shall be compelled, much to our regret, to condemn you to death." The alarmed population, after some hesitation, consented to hear mass; and after the performance of this ceremony the gates were opened When, however, some of the people of San Xisto came and revealed the truth, the population of La Guardia, indignant at the deceit which had been practised upon them, and ashamed of their own culpable weakness, assembled in the market-place, resolved to join their brethren in the wood, and were only dissuaded from doing so by the representations of the marquis of Spinello.

The grand inquisitor now demanded that the public force should aid him in the complete execution of his mission; and two companies of soldiers were accordingly placed at his disposal. These he despatched to the wood of San Xisto, to seize the fugitives, but, instead of taking them prisoners, the fanatic troops no sooner discovered the unhappy Waldenses than they fell upon them, killed a great number, put to flight the rest, and pursued these like wild beasts. The fugitives at length attained some high rocks, where they entrenched themselves, and, as the soldiers came up, hurled upon them great stones, with such effect that many were slain, and more wounded, so that the officers deemed it expedient to retreat, and to communicate the result to cardinal Alexandrini. The legate thereupon applied to the viceroy of Naples for greater force, wherewith to suppress this rebellion, as he called it, of the Waldenses; the viceroy himself marched to San Xisto, at the head of his troops, and there denounced fire and sword against all who should not abjure their heresy. The Waldenses, on their part, fortified themselves on the mountain tops; and their position became at length so formidable, that the viceroy, not venturing to attack them with the troops he had brought, put forth a proclamation by which he offered a free pardon to all exiles, outlaws, and other criminals, who would aid to exterminate the Waldenses.

This proclamation, so characteristic of popery, had the

effect of collecting together a multitude of reprobates, marauders and bandits, many of whom were intimately acquainted with all the by-paths of the Apennines; and by these the Waldenses in the mountains were hunted down and slaughtered, some dying by the sword, some by fire, some by famine.

Meanwhile the inquisitor and the monks were not idle. By a foul stratagem, they induced the surviving population of La Guardia, in number seventy souls, to assemble together, and, so assembled, they were seized by soldiers, concealed for the purpose, loaded with chains, and taken as prisoners to Montalto, where they were all subjected to the most cruel tortures by the inquisitor Panza, for the purpose of forcing them, not only to forswear their faith, but to forswear themselves, by admitting against their brethren and their pastors the pretended abominations which the corrupt imaginings of popery had conceived and laid to their charge. To effect a confession of these crimes from the agony of the Waldenses, was a grand object with the inquisitors; and one unhappy man, Stephano Carlini, was, to this purpose, tortured in so horrible a manner, that his bowels gushed forth. Another prisoner, Verminello, having, in excess of pain on the rack, promised to attend mass, the inquisitor deemed him a likely person, under aggravated torture, to confess also to the crimes which the church of Rome so earnestly desired to bring home to the Waldenses; and the miserable man was accordingly kept for eight consecutive hours upon an instrument of suffering, aptly called *hell;* but he could not be brought to sanction the atrocious calumnies, an admission of which would have released him from torture. Bernardino Conto was covered with pitch, and burned alive in the market-place of Cosenza. Another martyr, Mazzone, was stripped naked, his body shredded with iron whips, and the mangled frame then beaten to death with lighted brands. Of this victim's two sons, one was flayed alive, and the other hurled from the summit of a tower. From the same tower was precipitated another young man, who, for his prodigious strength, was surnamed Samson. As his mangled frame lay, still breathing, on the flag-stones below, the viceroy passed. "What carrion is this?" he asked. "It is a heretic, who will not die." The viceroy kicked the wretched man's head aside. "Let the pigs come, then, and eat him," said he; and the barbarous order was executed, the prostrate body of the martyr palpitating with life for some hours, beneath the tearing teeth of the unclean brutes, which a human brute far more unclean and foul than they had set to the work.

Sixty women of San Xisto had ropes bound round their bodies and limbs so tightly that wounds were made, and these festering, engendered corruption that was removed with hot lime. Afterwards, some of them were burned alive, others starved to death in their dungeons, while the handsomer among them were sold to satisfy the passions of the highest bidder. At Montalto, eighty-eight Waldensian prisoners were crowded in a low, damp dungeon. By order of the marquis Buccianici, the executioner came, took the nearest prisoner, led him outside, bound a strip of linen round his head, made him kneel, and cut his throat. Then, placing his knife between his teeth, and holding the ensanguined linen in his hand, the executioner returned to the dungeon, withdrew the next prisoner, and in like manner dispatched him; and so with the rest, until on that blood-stained ground there lay the headless trunks of eighty-eight martyrs, gentle as lambs, and as lambs slaughtered. Other persons were sawed asunder. Others, eighty-six in number, having been first flayed alive, had their bodies cleft in two, and the ghastly portions were stuck on pikes along the high road, for the length of thirty-six miles. The preachers and elders of the Waldenses were burned alive, their bodies being covered with resin and sulphur. For two whole years did the fire and sword of antichrist devour this unhappy district, and sixteen hundred victims gratified with their blood the sanguinary thirst of Rome. A few of the Waldenses effected their escape, and regained, with infinite toil, the valleys of their ancestors.

Chapter Ninth.

HISTORY OF VARIOUS MARTYRS.

THERE is no town in Piedmont, under a Waldensian pastor, where some of the brethren have not been put to death. Jordan Terbano was burned alive at Suza; Hippolyte Rossiero at Turin; Michael Goneto, an octogenarian, at Sarcena; Villermin Ambrosio hanged on the Col di Meano; Hugo Chiamps, of Fenestrelle, had his entrails torn from his living body, at Turin; Peter Geymarali, of Bobbio, in like manner, had his entrails taken out at Luserne, and a fierce cat thrust in their place to torture him further; Maria Romano was buried alive at Roccapatia; Magdalen Foulano underwent the same fate at San Giovanni; Susan Michelini was bound hand and foot, and left to perish of cold and hunger on the snow at Sarcena. Bartholomew Fache, gashed with sabres, had the wounds filled up with quick-lime, and perished thus in agony at Fenile; Daniel Michelini had his tongue torn out at Bobbio, for having praised God; James Baridari perished, covered with sulphureous matches, which had been forced into his flesh under the nails, between the fingers, in the nostrils, in the lips, and over all his body, and then lighted. Daniel Revelli had his mouth filled with gunpowder, which, being lighted, blew his head to pieces. Maria Monnen, taken at Liousa, had the flesh cut from her cheek and chin bones, so that her jaw was left bare, and she was thus left to perish. Paul Garnier was slowly sliced to pieces at Rora; Thomas Margueti was mutilated in an indescribable manner at Miraboco, and Susan Jaquin cut in bits at La Torre. Sara Rostagnol was slit open from the legs to the bosom, and left so to perish on the road between Eyral and Luzerna; Anne Charbonnier was impaled, and carried thus on a pike, as a standard, from San Giovanni to La Torre. Daniel Rambaud, at Paesano, had his nails torn off, then his fingers chopped off, then his feet and his hands, and then his arms and his legs, with each successive refusal on his part to abjure the gospel. In March, 1536, Martin Gonin, pastor of Angrogna, was seized on his return from Geneva, at Grenoble, and, after a mock trial, taken from his prison at night, and drowned in the Isere. In June, 1556, Barthelemi Hector, of Poitiers, was burned at Turin, for having sold copies of the Bible to the shepherds of the Alps. In 1555, a pastor of Geneva, Jean Vernoux, one of the earliest fellow-labourers with Calvin, Antoine Laborie Quercy, who had quitted the magistracy in order to devote himself more actively to the cause of the gospel, and three friends of theirs, Batailles, Tauran, and Tringalet, were on their way to the Waldensian valleys, seized by the maréchaussée, in the gorges of the Col Tamis, and, after a lengthened interrogatory before the court of Chambery, were all burned in one fire.

Among the leaders who had signalized themselves by excessive ferocity in the crusade against the Vaudois, under Innocent VIII., was Captain Varagle, or Varaille. A son of this man, endowed with remarkable capacity, entered into holy orders in 1522, and took up his abode not far from the Waldensian valleys, in the little town of Busque, one of the most retired in Piedmont. Here his rapid progress in literature and theology, and his eloquence in the pulpit, attracted the attention of his superiors.

The influence of the Reformation was now making itself everywhere felt; and the Romish church comprehended the essential importance of strengthening its power, which the synod of Angrogna had just aided to weaken. Young Geoffrey Varaille, selected to operate as a counterpoise to the impulse of reformation, received the difficult mission to visit the principal towns of Italy, and raise up the credit of the Romish church by his eloquent preaching. He was to be accompanied by an Observantine monk of the convent of Monte Fiascone, named Matteo Baschi, the founder of the Capuchin order, and by ten members of the secular clergy.

These twelve being assembled together, proceeded, with a view to the accomplishment of their mission, to examine for themselves the arguments of the reformers against catholicism. It was not long ere their enlightened minds recognized the force of these arguments so fully, that, becoming themselves objects of suspicion to the popish authorities, they were all imprisoned at Rome, where they remained captives for five years. At the expiration of this period, Varaille, released from his dungeon, entered the service of the papal legate at the court of France, and abode with him at Paris for a considerable time. Here the rays of the Reformation fell upon his soul with still greater power than in Piedmont; and the massacre of the Waldenses of Merindol and Cabrierés, which became the subject of inquiry before the court of peers, so filled up the measure of his indignation and disgust against a church imbrued in the blood of the just, that he resigned the high position he occupied at Paris, and repaired to Geneva, to investigate, at the fountain-head, the *new doctrines*, as they were called, but which he, to his delighted surprise, soon learned to recognize, on the contrary, as the ancient, the primitive doctrines.

Varaille was now nearly fifty years old, but faith makes a man young again; and full of an ardour he had never known before, he unhesitatingly cast off his past life, to commence a new one, with more of moral force than he had ever yet possessed, and was received among the ranks of those evangelical pastors whom, theretofore, he had approached as an adversary. The Waldensian churches required at this epoch a pastor who could preach in Italian. Geoffrey Varaille was selected for the duty, and was installed in the parish of San Giovanni, amid those very valleys against which his father had led a crusade. In 1557, on his return from a visit to his birthplace, Busque, he was denounced at the foot of Monte Viso, by the prior of Starffade, and apprehended by the nephew of the archdeacon of Saluzzo. He was treated with respect; handsome apartments were assigned him as a prison, and he was even permitted to go at large on parole. How many ordinary prisoners would have profited by this liberty to escape! But the Christian is not one, with whom it is lawful to break faith with an enemy. Nay, having learned that the reformers of Bubiana, a portion of his flock, were about to rescue him by main force, he desired them to abstain, and to leave him in the hands of God.

After various interrogatories he was conducted in chains to Turin. His replies to his judges, and the written propositions which he laid before them in support of his faith, are a monument of his talents, learning, and piety. During his detention, Calvin wrote thus to him from Geneva:— "Very dear and beloved brother; Though the news of your imprisonment has deeply grieved us, yet the Lord, who can shed light from darkness, has furnished us with joyful consolation, in the fruits already produced by your trials. Let the glory which sustained St Paul also inspire you with courage; for though you are captive, the word of God is not captive, and you can render testimony of it to many who will spread abroad the seed of life they have received from your lips. Jesus Christ requires this testimony from all; but especially from such as you, under the seal of the ministry you received to preach the doctrine of salvation, which is now assailed in your person. Hesitate not, then, to confirm with your blood, if need be, the words which you have taught with your lips. Our Lord has told us that the death of the righteous is precious to him: let this reward suffice for you. I will not dwell on this point, persuaded that you repose firmly on him in whom, whether we live or die abides our eternal happiness. My companions and brethren salute you.—Geneva, 17th Sept. 1557."

When the sentence of death was announced to the heroic pastor, he replied calmly to his judges,—"Be assured, you will sooner want wood wherewith to burn us, than we ministers ready to burn in seal of their faith: from day to day they multiply; and the word of God endureth for ever."

Geoffrey Varaille, having been previously strangled by the humanity of the executioner, was burned at Turin, on 29th March, 1558.

Chapter Tenth.

THE WALDENSES IN THE VALLEY OF THE PO.

THE most ancient establishments of the Waldenses in the province of Saluzzo were around Paesano, and in the deep valleys of Cruzzol and Onzino, where the sources of the Po flow from Mount Visol. It has been stated that their origin in these localities was contemporaneous with that of the other Waldenses who dwell on the left bank of the Po; but Gilly informs us that the inhabitants of Praviglelmo, Biolet, and Bietonnet, came from the valley of Luserne. This emigration must have taken place at a very remote period, since it was its descendants who peopled the marquisate of Saluzzo; and we find Waldenses there so early as the thirteenth century. In 1308, inquisitors were sent there "to destroy heresy:" but they were compelled by the population to withdraw, ere they had even begun their "pious labours." A similar attempt, a few years afterwards, had for its sole result the courageous martyrdom, at Saluzzo, of the barba, Martin Pastre.

It was not until 1499 that violence against the Waldenses in these districts assumed anything of a systematic form. At this period, Marguerite de Foix, marchioness of Saluzzo, the slave of her confessor, became, in the hands of fanaticism, the facile instrument of persecution. Under the direction of the clergy by whom she was infested, she issued a decree, commanding the Waldenses, under penalty of death, either to adopt within her borders Romanism or to quit the country. They adopted the last alternative, and withdrew among their co-religionists into the territories of the seigneurs of Paesano. Hither, the marchioness, "having purchased the right to pursue them," had them assailed by two hundred soldiers. Most of them fled to Barges with their herds, but some were taken and thrown into prison. They were tried, *with torture*, and on the 24th of March, 1510, five of them were condemned to be burned alive on Palm Sunday. The pyre was raised in a field opposite the house of the father of one of the victims, named Maynard; but when the day of execution came, there was so heavy a fall of snow and rain that the wood would not burn, and the ceremony was posponed until the next day. In the meanwhile, however, a friend having conveyed a file to the captives, they effected their escape, and took refuge with their co-religionists at Barges. Three of the prisoners who remained were, however, burned alive on the 2d of May; others died under the bastinado; others perished slowly in the dungeons of Paesano; a few escaped with exile; but the property of all was confiscated, and two-thirds of the proceeds went to the marchioness of Saluzzo, who was thus infinitely more than repaid the outlay she had undergone in the persecution.

On the 18th of July, 1510, the Inquisition demolished the church of the Waldenses. This "*synagogue* of the heretics," says a contemporary manuscript, "was white and beautiful without, but within full of windings, like a labyrinth." In the year following, five more Waldenses were burned alive at Saint Frons. Meanwhile, all who escaped the fire and the sword, had taken refuge amongst their brethren in the valley of Luserne, by whom they were fraternally supported for five years. From time to time, during this period, negotiations were essayed by them with the marchioness of Saluzzo, with a view to their return home; but their letters received no reply. It became necessary that they should no longer be a burden on their charitable brothers, and in 1512 they assembled, armed, in the valley of Rora, and, departing at night, traversed the mountains of Cruzzol, descended into the valley of the Po, reached their homes, fell like a thunderbolt on their despoilers, drove them from the district, and established once more, by their daring resolution, their own position and the faith of their ancestors.

For some years the churches of the valley of the Po were tranquil. The breath of the Reformation then began to arouse men's minds; and in the province of Saluzzo, the seigneurs of Montroux, of Villanova-Solaro, and others, opened their castle halls to meetings of the new reformers. The disciples of these rapidly increased; and until pastors of their own came, they repaired with zeal to the preachings which now took place regularly in the valley of Luserne. The duke of Savoy made every effort to check this progress of protestanism, but in vain; and on the 6th of June, 1563, the church of Dronero, one of the most flourishing in the marquisate, obtained, under the edict of pacification which the king of Navarre had procured in favour of his co-religionists, letters-patent authorizing it to open a protestant church at the gates of the town. These letters were by the influence of Mary de Medici, withdrawn in the same year, but the courage of the protestants was not quelled; and in the following years, favoured by the intestine agitations of France, they organized themselves throughout the marquisate on the footing of the reformed churches, with pastors, deacons, consistories, and a regular, and even general, public worship.

Chapter Eleventh

THE WALDENSES IN THE PLAIN OF PIEDMONT.

IN the space between Turin and the Waldensian valleys, there is probably not a single town in which the reformation of the sixteenth century did not find adherents and sympathy. Romanism had fallen into utter degradation. Cornelio d'Adro, an inquisitor of Raccoms, writing to the holy office, on the 22d of October, 1567 says:—"I cannot adequately depict the decay with which our religion is struck in this country; the churches are in ruin, the altars stripped, the sacerdotal vestments in rags, the priests ignorant, and everything connected with the church in utter contempt." In this juncture the abler partisans of Rome saw that their most efficient course for stemming the torrent of the new opinions, was in affecting to share them. "Reform is necessary," said they, "and the church herself will undertake it; do not, therefore, separate from her, or needlessly and unfilially assail her." The Waldenses however, would admit no concessions, insisting upon this declaration of our Saviour: "Whosoever shall confess me before men, him will I confess also before my Father which is in heaven: But whosoever shall deny me before men, him will I also deny before my Father which is in heaven." The papists at length (15th February, 1560) procured, from the duke, an order that none, save the inhabitants of the Waldensian valleys themselves, should exercise the

Protestant worship, and that none should visit the valleys merely for the purpose of attending that worship. The inquisitors forthwith commenced their persecutions throughout Piedmont, and two martyrs were burned alive at Carignano. The Protestants, alarmed like a flock of sheep suddenly assailed, dispersed. The archers then proceeded to the valley of Meano, where they seized a number of Waldenses, and among them their pastor, Jacob, who, upon his reiterated refusals to abjure, was led to the stake, his mouth gagged and his arms bound, and burned alive by a slow fire.

The city of Turin belonging at this time to France, the catholic clergy obtained (17th February, 1561) from Charles IX., an order for the suppression, in and about the city, of the reformed worship. The Protestant pastors were, in pusuance of this order, banished from Turin. The assemblies of *The Religion*, for such was the admitted designation of Protestantism, were, first ordered to be watched by the authorities, and then, shortly after, to be altogether suppressed. All who were found guilty, in the very act of common prayers and biblical meditations, were treated as high criminals. The reformers of Conde, of Ozasc, and Frossac, rather than attend mass, renounced their homes and their property, and took refuge among their brethren in the valley of Lucerne.

The churches of Conio and Caragli had acquired large extension. Men of the higher ranks were prominent in their flocks; and so long as their valour had been necessary to the duke of Savoy, in his wars as an ally of Spain against France, these seigneurs were permitted the free exercise of their religion.

But peace was concluded; and the clergy superseding these war-men around the person of the sovereign, urged upon him that his glory was concerned in re-establishing, in its integrity, the religion of his ancestors. The duke assented; and first, the protestants were forbidden to exercise their worship beyond the limits of the Waldensian valleys; and then, (28th September, 1561), all the inhabitants were required to place in the hands of the magistrates any books *of the Religion*, which they might possess. At the same time, the duke ordered all his subjects to attend the preachings of the missionaries he was about to send amongst them. The preaching of one of these missionaries informed the auditory that "God had given them a mild winter that year, that so they might economize wood for burning the Lutherans in the spring." It may be readily conceived that such eloquence as this produced no great effect. On the 28th of December, 1561, a fresh edict commanded all persons whosoever to attend mass without further delay; but scarcely any of the Protestants obeyed the injunction, and the number of recusants being so great, no steps were taken, at the time, to enforce the decree.

In 1565, however, the duke having ordered the Waldenses of the valleys—to whom, in 1561, he had granted the free exercise of their religion—to abjure, within two months, the Protestants of Conio were imperatively enjoined forthwith to attend before the magistrates, and make a declaration of Romish orthodoxy, under penalty of the severest punishments. Fifty-five families were found daring enough, in the presence of the authorities, to repudiate popery, and declare themselves protestants. The humbler among these, knowing the consequences of their recusancy, at once sold their little property and departed elsewhere. A few only, of the more powerful, obtained permission, on the guarantee, in each case, of a

Roman Catholic proprietor, to retain their lands and their religion, on the condition that they should not exercise that religion either in their own houses or elsewhere, under penalty of the total confiscation of all they were worth. Thus disappeared the church of God from the banks of the Stura.

The church of Caragli underwent much the same vicissitudes with those of Conio. In March, 1565, a list of the Reformers there was required from the magistrates, and the number returned was nearly 900. In April, the duke of Savoy sent to Caragli a missionary, and with him an order for all the inhabitants to attend his preachings. The great majority of the Reformers paid no attention to this order: thereupon the duke menaced all who should persist in their heresy "with his severest displeasure;" and on 10th June appeared an edict, ordering all Protestants who would not, within the space of two months, abjure, to quit the territory. The duchess of Savoy, and the seigneurs of Villanova-Solaro, under whose protection the reformers had hitherto prospered, essayed to procure a revocation of this impolitic and cruel edict; but the influence of the Catholic clergy prevailed, and on 30th November, the decree was carried into execution, popish charity taking the further precaution of prohibiting any of the surrounding populations from giving harbour or aid to the proscribed families who thus preferred exile to abjuration. The noble family of Solaro itself, which now consisted of six brothers, all Protestants, was, upon its pertinacious adherence to the faith it had adopted, banished and dispersed some years afterwards, and its property confiscated.

Meanwhile under the French rule, the churches of Saluzzo enjoyed toleration; but their pastors were for the most part foreigners—Swiss, or Piedmontese; and, taking advantage of this circumstance, the popish clergy induced the duke of Savoy to demand (1567), from the French lieutenant of the province of Saluzzo, the extradition of any of his subjects who might have taken refuge there; and the governor of Saluzzo accordingly ordered all foreigners to quit the territory within three days, and not to return, except upon special permission, under penalty of death and confiscation of goods. By the intervention, however, of Henry of Navarre, this decree was withdrawn, and these churches seemed to have a chance of tranquillity.

When the massacre of St. Bartholomew took place, Biragne, the governor of Saluzzo, received orders to slaughter all the Protestants within his jurisdiction. Appalled at these sanguinary instructions, he submitted them for consideration to the Chapter; and although several of its members were in favour of complete and immediate execution of the order, the majority, headed by the excellent archdeacon of Saluzzo, Samuel Vacca, insisted that so cruel a decree must be the result of some misconception or misrepresentation; and a delay was thus obtained, which saved the lives of the menaced brethren until the reprobation which speedily visited the cowardly slaughter that had taken place, ensured their safety.

For a while the churches of Saluzzo remained peaceful and flourishing; but in 1597, Charles Emanuel, having taken possession of the marquisate, called upon the churches of Saluzzo to come into the bosom of Catholicism. The churches respectfully declined the invitation, and the duke did not further press the point at the time; but, becoming undisputed master of the territory under the peace of Lyon (17th Jan. 1601), he issued (June, 1601) a decree, ordering all Christians of the evangelical party to quit his states within two months, unless they abjured within a fortnight. The refractory were to be punished with death, and the confiscation of their goods. The Reformers addressed humble but urgent memorials to the duke for the revocation of this decree; and in the hope that the storm would pass over, permitted the two months asigned to elapse without making any preparations for their departure. At the expiration of that period, they received orders at once to depart, or at once to abjure ; and thus taken by surprise, solicited with urgent entreaties and promises on the one hand, and menaced for themselves and their families on the other, many of them, with hearts well-nigh broken, consented to enter the Romish church. The rest withdrew, some to Geneva, some to France, some to the Waldensian valleys.

As yet, no menace had been directed against the Waldensians of Praviglelmo and of the upper valley of the Po, where the evangelical worship had been exercised from time immemorial. When the Waldensians of the plain, however, were all banished or dispersed, the Waldensians of the hills were in their turn, enjoined to abjure or to depart. But these hardy mountaineers, full of indignation at this invasion of their long-undisputed rights, assembled in arms, and having first menaced the Catholics among whom they lived, with fire and sword, if during their absence any evil should happen to their wives and children, descended into the plain, took possession of the market-place at Château-Dauphin, and threatened to devastate the whole district if the edict against them was not withdrawn. The Catholic population, who had ever found in the Protestants good and peaceful neighbours, assembled, addressed a memorial to Charles Emanuel, the edict was revoked, and for awhile the Waldensians of Praviglelmo escaped the proscription which fell so heavily upon their brethren.

9*

Chapter Twelfth.

THE SECOND GENERAL PERSECUTION OF THE WALDENSES OF PIEDMONT.

AFTER the first general persecution of the Waldenses by Cataneo, which is related in the fourth chapter, the course of the present narrative diverged from the history of the Piedmontese valleys, to give a brief account of the Waldenses of the adjoining valleys in Dauphiny and Provence on the French side of the Alps, in the valley of the Po, in the plain of Piedmont, and in Calabria. In each of these places numerous Waldenses were formerly to be found, either indigenous or colonists from the mother-valleys. These places, as we have seen, were signalized by some of the earliest as well as some of the bloodiest persecutions of this poor people. Having given as full an account of them as our space permits, we now return to the main thread of the narrative.

At the time of which we now write, the Waldenses of Piedmont were included within the dominions of the king of France. The Pope, in negotiating a treaty with the French king, Henry II., took occasion to demand the institution of severe measures against the Waldenses. Henry accordingly directed the parliament of Turin to proceed against the so-called heretics. The parliament appointed two commissioners, San Juliano and Della Chiesa, to re-

CLUSE, IN SAVOY.

pair to the valleys, to make investigation and report thereon, and to take what course they should think fit for converting the Waldenses to Romanism. These delegates, attended by a numerous suite, reached the valleys in March, 1556, and commenced proceedings by menacing with the severest punishment all who should offer any resistance to their measures. After visiting Perosa, Angrogna, and other places, the commissioners repaired to Luzerna, whence they issued (23rd of March, 1556,) an edict ordering the Waldenses to abjure, and no longer to receive foreign preachers, other than such as should be deputed to them by the archbishop of Turin. One-third of the goods of all contraveners of this decree was to go to the denouncers of them. The Waldenses replied with a profession of faith, based on the Bible, in the spirit of which they declared their resolution to persevere, after the example of their ancestors. The commissioners, by order of the parliament, then proceeded to France, and laid a report of their proceedings before the king, in order to receive his further instructions. It was not until the following year that they returned to the valleys, when they informed the Waldenses that the king commanded them forthwith to embrace Romanism. Three days only were granted them for deliberation; but briefer space would have sufficed. "Prove to us," replied the faithful, "that our doctrines are not conformable with the Word of God, and we are ready to abandon them; if not, cease to demand from us abjuration." "We don't ask you for discussion," returned the commissioners; "we only want to know whether you will turn Catholics: yes, or no!"

"No!" replied the Waldenses. Thereupon (22nd of March, 1557), forty-six of their principal men were cited to appear before the court of Turin, on the 29th, under penalty of a fine of five hundred gold crowns for each disobedience. Not one of them appeared. A month afterwards, fresh citations were served upon them, and also upon all their pastors and schoolmasters. These citations were equally fruitless. The syndics were ordered to arrest them, but the order was not obeyed; and the war of Spain and England against France, the mediation in favour of the Waldenses of the Swiss cantons, and the resumption of his states by Philibert Emanuel, who, in 1559, married the sister of Henry II., a lady favourable to Protestantism—combined, for a time, to restore peace and security to the Waldensian valleys. The manly firmness, tempered with mildness and christian meekness, with which the persecuted Waldenses used to touch upon their wrongs, cannot be more thoroughly illustrated than in the following petition, presented by them to Philibert Emanuel:—

"A supplication of the poor Waldenses, to the most serene and most high prince, Philibert Emanuel, duke of Savoy, prince of Piedmont, our most gracious lord.

"Festus, governor of Judea, being required by the chief priests and elders of the people, to put to death the apostle Paul, answered no less wisely than justly, that the Romans were not wont to put any to death, before they had brought his accusers face to face, and given him time to answer for himself. We are not ignorant, most gracious prince, that many accusations are laid against us, and that many calumnies are cast upon us, to make us objects of abomination to all the Christians and monarchs in the Christian world. But if the Roman people, though pagans, were so equitable as not to condemn any man before they knew and understood his reasons; and if the law condemns no man (as it is testified by Nicodemus, John vii.) before he hath been heard, and before it is known what he hath done, the matter now in question being of so great concernment, namely, the glory of the most high God, and the salvation of so many souls, we do implore your clemency, most gracious prince, that you will be pleased to lend a willing ear to your poor subjects, in so just and righteous a cause.

"First, we do protest, before the almighty and all-just God, before whose tribunal we must all one day appear, that we intend to live and die in the holy faith, piety, and religion of our Lord Jesus Christ; and that we do abhor all heresies that have been, and are, condemned by the Word of God.

"We do embrace the most holy doctrine of the prophets and apostles, as likewise of the Nicene and Athanasian creeds: we subscribe to the four councils, and to all the ancient fathers, in all such things as are not repugnant to the analogy of faith.

"We do most willingly yield obedience to our superiors; we ever endeavour to live peaceably with our neighbours; we have wronged no man, though provoked; nor do we fear that any can, with reason, complain against us.

"Finally, we never were obstinate in our opinions; but rather tractable, and always ready to receive all holy and pious admonitions, as appears by our confessions of faith.

"And we are so far from refusing a discussion, or rather a free council wherein all things may be established by the Word of God, that we rather desire the same with all our hearts.

"We likewise beseech your highness to consider, that this religion we profess, is not ours only, nor hath it been invented by man of late years, as it is falsely reported; but it is the religion of our fathers, grandfathers, and great grandfathers, and other yet more ancient predecessors of ours, and of the blessed martyrs, confessors, prophets, and apostles; and if any can prove the contrary, we are ready to subscribe, and yield thereunto. The Word of God shall not perish, but remain for ever; therefore, if our religion be the true word of God, as we are persuaded, and not the invention of men, no human force shall be able to extinguish the same.

"Your highness knows that this very same religion hath, for many ages past, been most grievously persecuted in all places; but, so far from being abolished and rooted out thereby, that it hath rather increased daily; which is a certain argument that this work and counsel is not the work and counsel of men, but of God, and therefore cannot be destroyed by any violence. Therefore, we beseech your most serene highness to consider what it is to undertake anything against God, that as you may not imbue your hands in innocent blood! Jesus is our Saviour; we will religiously obey all your highness's edicts, so far as conscience will permit; but when conscience says nay, your highness knows we must rather obey God than man: we unfeignedly confess that we ought to give Cæsar that which belongs to Cæsar, provided we give also to God what is due to him.

"There want not those who will endeavour to incite the generous mind and courage of your highness, to persecute our religion by force of arms. But, O magnanimous prince, you may easily conjecture to what end they do it, that it is not of zeal to God's glory, but rather to preserve their own worldly dignities, pomp, and riches; wherefore, we beseech your highness not to regard or countenance their sayings.

"The Turks, Jews, Saracens, and other nations, though never so barbarous, are suffered to enjoy their own religion, and are constrained by no man to change their manner of living and worship: and we, who serve and worship in faith the true and almighty God, and one true and only sovereign, the Lord Jesus, and confess one God and one baptism, shall we not be suffered to enjoy the same privileges?

"We humbly implore your highness's goodness, and that for our only Lord and Saviour Jesus Christ's sake, to allow unto us, your most humble subjects, the most holy gospel of the Lord our God, in its purity; and that we may not be forced to do things against our consciences; for which we shall, with all our hearts, beseech our almighty and all-good God to preserve your highness in prosperity."

The pertinacious solicitations, however of the nuncio, the prelates, the king of Spain, and several of the princes of Italy, so far prevailed with the duke, that on the 15th of February, 1656, he issued a decree prohibiting all persons who were not actually inhabitants of the Waldensian valleys from repairing thither to hear the reformed preaching; and immediately afterwards commissioners were appointed to prevent the biblical worship from being celebrated beyond the confines of these valleys. These commissioners were, the duke's brother, Philip of Savoy, count de Racconis, George Costa, count de la Trinité, and the grand inquisitor of Turin, Thomas Jacomel, an iron-hearted, profligate, grasping man. The count de la Racconis soon retired in disgust from the commission, leaving the two others to pursue their career of blood.

The monks of the abbey at Pignerol hired a band of marauders, whom they sent forth to pillage the Protestants, and to bring them, women and men, to the monastery, where the poorer sort were burned alive, or sent to the galleys, and the richer imprisoned until they paid ransom. The valley of San Martino was ravaged by the seigneurs of Perrier, Charles and Boniface Truchet. On 2nd April, 1560, before daybreak, they assailed the village of Rioclareto, killed many of the inhabitants, drove forth the rest, without clothes or food, to suffer cold and hunger on the snow-clad mountains, and took possession of their dwellings, vowing that no one should re-enter them until he had promised to go to mass. It was not until three days afterwards that the despoilers were expelled from the village by its surviving population, with the aid of four hundred Waldenses from Pragela, who had marched to reinstate their brethren.

Meanwhile, the count de Racconis, who repaired to the valley of Luzerna, attended one day the preaching of the pastor of Angrogna, and was so much struck with it, that he obtained from the Waldenses a detailed statement of their doctrines, which he promised to lay before the pope in the hope that it might tend to a discontinuance of persecution. But the pope, Pius, IV., replied—"I will never permit any discussion on points canonically determined. The dignity of the church demands that all should submit, implicitly and without question, to its constitutions; and it is my duty to proceed, with the utmost rigour, against all who will not so submit." All that the pope would concede was, that a legate should proceed to the village, to absolve "from their past crimes," all who would apostatize, and instruct them *without* dispute, that is to say, without examination, in their new duties. Accordingly, the commander Possevino, was appointed legate by Emanuel Philibert, with instructions to establish, in the Waldensian churches, *Brothers of Christian Doctrine*, under whose influence intellectual servility would soon have produced that abject submission so essential to the Romish church.

Possevino proceeded first to the castle of Cavour, whither

he summoned the Waldenses of the valley of Luzerna to attend him, by deputies. Three deputies were sent accordingly, and to these the commander, having notified his powers, put the question, whether they would attend the preachings which he himself proposed to address to the population of the valleys? "Yes," replied they, "if you preach the word of God; but if you preach the human traditions that destroy the word, No!" Possevino, without any appearance of being offended with this freedom, replied, that he would preach nothing but the pure gospel.

At this moment a Waldensian of San Germano appeared before the commander, to complain that the Romanists of Miradol, having first despoiled him of his cattle, had despoiled him also of a hundred crowns, which with much pains he had collected for their ransom, keeping both cattle and money too. "If you had gone to mass," insolently replied Possevino, "this would not have happened to you. I shall do nothing for you. This is but the commencement of what has been reserved for the heretics!" Such was the first example of justice and pure evangelical doctrine furnished by the representative of the Romish throne and church!

The next morning he ascended the pulpit of the great church of Cavour, and, in a fervid harangue, announced that he was about to convict all the Waldensian pastors of heresy, to expel them, and to re-establish mass in the villages. Two days afterwards, he preached at Bubiana, denouncing terrible menaces against the hardened, and making magnificent promises to such as would abjure. At San Giovanni he invited the heads of the Waldensian churches to a conference.

"Here," said he, "is the statement of the doctrines which you profess, which you yourselves have delivered to his highness. Do you abide by it?" "We see no reason to depart from it." "You undertake therein to repudiate your errors when they shall be demonstrated to you as such?" "We renew the undertaking." "Well, then, I will demonstrate to you, that the mass is found in Scripture. The word *massah* signifies *sent*, does it not? "Not precisely."* "The primitive expression, *Ite, missa est*, was employed to dismiss the auditory, was it not?" "That is quite true." "Well, then, you see, gentlemen that the mass is found in the Holy Scripture!"

To this ludicrous argument the Waldenses replied, that even had the term *massah* the meaning in Scripture which the commander supposed—which it had not—it would in no degree prove the divine institution of the mass; and that assuredly private masses, transubstantiation, and other points contested by them, were in no such way justified by his proposition.

"You are heretics, atheists, reprobates!" exclaimed Possevino, furiously. "I came not here to dispute with you, but to drive you from the country, as you deserve;" and he forthwith sent orders to the syndics of the various communes of the valleys, to expel their pastors, and to provide for the support of the priests whom he should send in their place. The syndics replied that they would only dismiss their pastors in the event of their being convicted of errors in doctrine or conduct; and that they would not provide for the support of the other persons announced, unless they were equally irreproachable in conduct and doctrine.

The intercession of the good duchess Marguerite in favour of the Waldenses, was ineffectual against the machinations of the nuncio and the prelates: and in October, 1560, the duke levied troops in Piedmont, and offered free

***Massah*, in Hebrew, means burden, decree, or present.*

pardon to all convicts, outlaws, and vagabonds who would enrol themselves as volunteers to serve against the Waldenses. The faithful seemed menaced with total and inevitable destruction: their foes rejoiced, their friends trembled. Among the latter, count Charles of Luzerna, then governor of Mondovi, urgently entreated the Waldenses, both by letters and in person, to yield to circumstances, at least so far as to send away their pastors until the storm should have passed over; but the zealous folk refused, saying, that were they to be ashamed of God's ministers, God would be ashamed of them.

War was accordingly declared. The Waldensian families hastily occupied themselves in collecting together such things as were indispensable to life, in order to be ready to retire with their herds into the mountains. The zeal and fervour of the pastors were redoubled. Never had the religious assemblings of the faithful been more numerous. The hostile army approached: the Waldenses fasted, prayed, celebrated the Lord's Supper, and then prepared, without fear, nay, with joy, to receive from the hands of God, all the trials to which he might think fit to expose them. The mountain paths resounded with the psalms and hymns of those who were conveying the aged, the infirm, the women, the children, household goods and provisions, to the surest retreats among the hill tops. The counsel of the pastors, indeed, was that they should not attempt to defend themselves with arms, but simply retire from aggression, or await martyrdom amid their families.

On the last day of October, 1560, a proclamation was posted in all the villages of Angrogna, that the Waldenses would be destroyed by fire and sword, unless they were converted to the Romish church; and on the 1st of November, the popish army, under the command of the count de la

Trinté, encamped at Bubiana. Levied in haste, and from all classes of desperate adventurers, these troops, wholly destitute of discipline, gave way to every sort of excess, pillaging before they had struck a blow, and making no distinction, even, between Papist and Protestant. The former, to preserve the chastity of their daughters from the gross brutality of these ruffian soldiers, adopted a course involving the highest testimony ever rendered to the virtues and generosity of the Waldenses. Knowing the austere purity of Waldensian manners, the strength of their retreats, the valour of the defenders of those retreats, these retreats appeared to them the surest asylum for their children, and accordingly, at the very moment that Romanism was marching in arms against the Waldenses, the Waldenses were made the depositaries of the menaced honours of the daughters of the Romanist population. And nobly was this confidence justified: the Waldenses defended the sacred deposit thus confided to them, with the same courage and respect as their own families, exposing themselves equally in their defence, and when the danger was over, restoring them to their parents, without a thought of recompense.

On the 2d of November, the army crossed the Pelice, and encamped in the meadows of Giovanni. Thence it advanced towards Angrogna, displaying its wings on the hills of Le Cotiere. Several skirmishes took place at this point with about equal advantage, though many of the Waldenses had only slings and cross-bows; but the small defence-parties left of the Waldenses, were too distant one from the other, to act with vigour. They accordingly retired, fighting as they went, to the higher grounds. The enemy followed, but evening had now set in, and both parties were wearied with the day's skirmishings.

On the summit of Le Cotiere, towards Roccamanante, the Waldenses halted. The enemy, thereupon, also halted, a short distance below, and lighted their fires for the bivouac of the night. The mountaineers, on the contrary, threw themselves on their knees, to offer up thanks and supplications to God, a proceeding which excited infinite laughter and jests on the part of the persecutors.

At this moment, a Waldensian child who had got hold of a drum, and carried it off to a ravine near at hand, beat it; and at the sound, the Romanist soldiers, conceiving it to announce the approach of fresh enemies, rose in disorder and seized their arms. The Waldenses observing this movement, and apprehending an attack on themselves, dashed down to repel it. The popish troops, fatigued and taken by surprise, gave way, and on being more closely assailed, threw down their arms, and fled down to the valley, thus losing in half an hour, all the ground it had taken them a day to acquire. The Waldenses, after thanksgiving to God, took possession of the abandoned arms, and made their way to Pra-del-tor.

Next morning, the count de la Trinité, having rallied his troops, encamped at La Torre, repaired its fortifications, and placed a garrison there, who behaved so outrageously, that the Romanists of the place were fain to send their wives and daughters away, and to place them under the safe-guard of the Waldenses.

The small fortresses of Villar, Perosa, and Perrier, were, in like manner, garrisoned with troops. On Monday, the 4th of November, a detachment from La Torre, augmented on the way by the garrison of Villar, attacked Tagliaretto, but were defeated with considerable slaughter. A similar attempt upon Pra-del-Tor was similarly unsuccessful; and on the 9th of November, the popish general announced that if the Waldenses would lay down their arms, he would go with a small train to celebrate mass at Angrogna, and then apply his utmost efforts to obtain peace for them. The Waldenses passed a whole night in deliberation whether they should consent; the desire to manifest their pacific tendencies, to give no pretext to their enemies for violence, and to omit no chance of terminating the war, prevailed, and they determined to accept the count's proposition.

The count de la Trinité having celebrated mass at Angrogna, without calling upon any of the Reformers to attend, intimated a desire to visit Pra-del-Tor, a place celebrated among the Waldenses as the ancient school of their barbas; and as the count consented to leave his troops behind him at Angrogna, the Waldenses assented to the visit.

Pra-del-Tor is situated in a verdant hollow, surrounded by rugged heights, looking from above, like a crater, but below, like an oasis around the desert. The sole acess is a narrow, tortuous path along the edges of the rocks. The population received the count with respect, and he appeared affected by their reception. On his return, at Serres, he had a soldier hanged for having stolen a fowl, but at Angrogna, once more surrounded by his troops, he felt it unnecessary to wear the aspect of over-clemency, and accordingly took no notice of many outrages which, during his absence, had been committed by his men, but returned to La Torre, leaving his secretary at Angrogna to receive the memorial which he had desired the Waldenses to draw up for presentation to their sovereign. This memorial, which protested the loyalty of the persecuted folk, and entreated the duke to leave their conscience free, in order that his own might not stand laden with the weight of their death before the judgment seat of God, was conveyed to Vercelli by several Waldensian deputies, to be laid before the duke.

During their absence the count de la Trinité called upon the people of Tagliaretto to lay down their arms, his intention, doubtless, being to avail himself of their defencelessness, to turn that bulwark of the Pra-del-Tor. The people of Tagliaretto went to deliberate on this proposition with those of Bonneto, and while they were absent on this mission, the enemy, eager for violence, attacked their village, plundered and burned their houses, and carried off as prisoners their wives and children. The men assembled at Bonneto, on hearing what had taken place, hastened in arms after the marauders, rescued the captives, and dispersed the enemy. One aged Waldensian, assailed by a popish trooper, fell on his knees to implore mercy; the soldier raised his sword to strike, but, at the instant, the old man seized him by the legs, threw him down, and himself leaping from a precipice, dragged the enemy with him into eternity. All the Waldenses had quitted the lower portions of the valley for the mountains. The troops of the count de la Trinité having mercilessly ravaged the deserted villiages, ascended to Villar, where a few inhabitants still remained, whom they took prisoners. It was here that a popish soldier of Mondovi ferociously exclaimed; "I'll take some heretic's flesh home with me!" rushed upon a Waldensian, and biting a large piece of flesh from his cheek, swallowed it.

The Waldenses sought the count de la Trinité, and respectfully, but with firmness, remonstrated against these acts of violence. "Is it not the custom," they asked, "to abstain from hostilities pending a capitulation? We have laid down our arms, relying upon your word, and now, doubtless against your intentions, your troopers commit all sorts of excesses upon us." The count assured them that had he been present, these things should not have happened, and he returned the prisoners. The booty, however, he kept.

The irritation of the Waldenses was aggravated by incessant harassings; at length, the count de la Trinité, having assembled their leaders "to discuss the basis of a solid accommodation," promised to withdraw his army, on condition that the Waldenses would undertake to pay a sum of 20,000 crowns.

"I will get the amount reduced to 16,000 crowns," said the worthy secretary of this worthy master, "if you will give me 100 crowns for myself." The bargain was made, and the Waldenses consented to pay 16,000 crowns ($10,000.) The duke abated one-half of this sum; the Waldenses, who had nothing left them but their herds, were compelled to sell these, in order to raise money for the payment of the tribute; but here again they were defrauded. The general, for a sum of money, sold to a few monopolists the right of purchasing the herds, which thus, in a restricted market, were sold for much less than their value. By this sacrifice of their last remaining means, the Waldenses raised 8000 crowns, which were duly paid to the duke. The army should now have withdrawn; it did not stir; the Waldenses remonstrated to the general. "You must give up your arms," said he. Some arms were surrendered. "And now," said the general, "before we go, you must give me an undertaking to pay the other 8000 crowns; you engaged to pay 16,000, and you have only paid 8000." "But the duke exempted us from paying the remainder." "That is no affair of mine; you promised to pay 16,000 crowns, and you shall pay it." The obligation to pay the further 8000 crowns was signed. "Now, then, you will remove your troops?" "Not till you have sent away your pastors: it was principally for that object I came." The Waldenses, in despair, impoverished and defenceless, had no alternative but to make this agonizing concession also. They resolved to conduct their pastors to Pragela, which at that time belonged to France, hoping, ere long, to bring them back again. The road by the plain being infested by maurauders and assassins, and especially by those in the pay of the monks of Pignerol, it was determined to traverse the Col Julien. This plan having become known to the enemy, an ambush was laid for the pastors near Bobbi; the pastors escaped, and the maurauders indemnified themselves by pillaging all the houses in the locality, under pretence of seeking the fugitives.

The count de la Trinité withdrew his army, indeed, but it was only into the valley between Briqueras and Cavour; and he left strong garrisons in La Torre, Villar, Perrier, and Perosa, whom the Waldenses were compelled to support—sheep nourishing wolves.

A party of the garrison of La Torre, commanded by one Bauster, proceeded one day to a village on the road to Angrogna, and ordered the inhabitants to entertain them. The poor Waldenses produced the best provisions they had; after eating and drinking their fill, the troopers closed the doors of the court-yard in which they were seated, seized the men who had been waiting upon them, bound them, and carried them away prisoners to La Torre. The unhappy creatures were released a few days after, on payment of ransom; but they had been so cruelly maltreated by the papists that one of them died in agony the day after his return home, and another only survived to endure a long martyrdom, from the sufferings he had under gone. The flesh of his feet and hands torn away by torture, hung in shreds, the bones fell off one after the other, and he remained a cripple for life. The same party, under the same leader, surprised in like manner the village of Bonneto, and carried off two brothers, John and Odar Geymeto, whom they put to a cruel death.

I speak not of the young women and girls who were seized and taken into these dens of iniquity; the atrocious outrages to which they were subjected may not be described.

The deputation sent to Vercelli did not return until January, 1561. Their mission had proved wholly futile. After harassing them, day after day, for more than six weeks, with a succession of monks and priests, who essayed to win them over to the mass, they were dismissed with the assurance that unless they and those they represented, forthwith abjured, they should be all exterminated, and they learned that whole troops of idolaters, monks, and priests, were about to be let loose upon their valleys. Such intelligence as this might well have been expected to spread depression and despair through these valleys; but, on the contrary, no longer fearing to compromise their deputies, who were returned, or their goods, which were gone, or peace, which was manifestly impracticable, the Waldenses reinstated, in each parish, the pastor whom they had removed, raised up their levelled churches, and resumed everywhere the songs, the labours, the duties, the joys, and the occupations of their wonted biblical life, fully resolved to defend these and each other. At the same time came letters from Switzerland and Dauphiny, wherein their brethren exhorted them to maintain their courage, placing all their confidence in God. These brethren themselves furnished a signal example of what they taught; for the reformed in France were now furiously persecuted by the duke of Guise and the cardinal of Lorraine, whom the feeble Francis II. had placed, the one at the head of his armies, the other at the head of his council. Dangers bring men closely together; the valley of Pragela, which then belonged to France, was menaced with the same calamities that threatened the valley of Luzerna. Thereupon took place one of those grand and solemn scenes, which, at once heroic and religious, seem rather adapted for an epic poem than for grave history.

Deputies of the valley of Luzerna repaired to the valley of Pragela, to renew, in the presence of God, the alliance which had ever existed between these primitive churches of the Alps. This alliance was sworn by the combined people, assembled on a plateau of snow, facing the mountains of Sestrieres and the chain of the Gunivert. Then the inhabitants of Pragela sent, in their turn, delegates and pastors into the valley of Luzerna.

They reached it on the 21st of January, 1561. The evening before, there had been published throughout the valley, a ducal proclamation, that, within twenty-four hours, the inhabitants were to decide upon going to mass, or were to be subjected to all the punishment reserved for heretics: to fire, to sword, to cord, the three arguments of Romanism. The expiration of this term coincided exactly with the arrival of the Pragalese pastors at Puy, a hamlet built on a verdant slope at a short distance from Bobbi. The pastors, elders, deacons, and faithful of Bobbi and the contiguous hamlets, at once ascended to Puy, to inform the new comers of the sad calamities to which they were reduced; and there, after earnest prayers to God, for his counsel and aid, considering that no Waldensian would abjure, that it was impossible for them to procure an asy lum elsewhere, that it was absolutely determined to crush them, a thing which even a worm will not endure without resistance, it was resolved, with solemn enthusiasm, that they would defend themselves and one another to the death.

Such was the opening of the most brilliant campaign ever accomplished by persecuted heroes against persecuting fanatics.

The delegates of Pragela and of Luzerna, standing erect in the centre of the kneeling and enrapt people, pronounced these words :—

"In the name of the Waldensian churches of the Alps, of Dauphiny, and Piedmont, which have ever been united, and of which we are the representatives, we here promise, our hands on the Bible, and in the presence of God, that all our valleys shall courageously sustain each other, in matters of religion, without prejudice to the obedience due to their legitimate superiors.

"We promise to maintain the Bible, whole and without admixture, according to the usage of the true apostolic church, persevering in this holy religion, though it be at peril of our life, in order that we may transmit it to our children, intact and pure, as we received it from our fathers.

"We promise aid and succour to our persecuted brothers, not regarding our individual interests, but the common cause, and not relying upon man, but upon God."

The pastors had scarcely done speaking, when several of the people simultaneously exclaimed: "To-morrow they require from us an ignominious abjuration of our faith: well! let us, to-morrow, make a signal protestation against the persecuting idolatry that would impose that oath upon us."

The next morning, accordingly, before daybreak, instead of going to mass, they rushed, in arms, to the protestant church, which the papists had already decked out with the frippery usual in their worship. Images, flambeaux, rosaries, were thrown into the street and trampled under foot. The minister, Humbert Artus, ascended the pulpit, and selecting for his text, the verse of Isaiah (xlv. 20): "Assemble yourselves and come; draw near together, ye that are escaped of the nations: they have no knowledge that set up the wood of their graven image, and pray unto a god that cannot save," pronounced a discourse that confirmed and encouraged the resolution of his auditory, who marched thence to purge the church of Villar also from the gross fetiches of Roman idolatry. On their way they met the garrison of Villar, leisurely marching to make, as it is thought, a facile prey of the Waldensian recusants. It assailed the reformers, who repelled it and drove it back to whence it came. The judges, the monks, the seigneurs, and the podesta, who had all complacently assembled to receive the abjuration of the heretics, had scarcely time to take refuge with the fugitive soldiers in the menaced fortress. The Waldenses laid siege to the place, posted sentinels and videttes, levied stores, and firmly awaited events.

The garrison of La Torre came next day to deliver the besieged; but the Waldenses met and routed them on the plain of Teynan; they returned next day in greater numbers, and were again repulsed. Three bodies of troops presented themselves on the fourth day, and underwent the same fate. For ten days the Waldenses occupied themselves in making powder, in digging mines, in forming casemates, and in other preparations for taking the citadel. The garrison, at length, reduced to extremities, without ammunition, without provisions, without water, surrendered, on condition that their lives should be spared, and that in departing they should have the escort of two pastors, thus manifesting that they had more confidence in these persecuted ministers, than in any other protection. The terms were granted, the garrison marched out, and the fortifications of Villar were forthwith destroyed by the conquerors.

This advantage gained by the Protestants, suggested to the count de la Trinité the expediency of preventing union among them. He drew up his army between Luzerna and San Giovanni, and sent word to the inhabitants of Angrogna that they need fear nothing from him, if they would take no part in the affairs of the other valleys. But the people, rendered cautious by the treachery of which they so often had been made the victims, made no other reply, than the preparing more actively than ever for the common defence.

They threw up entrenchments, they established posts and signals; every house became a manufactory of pikes, bullets, and other weapons; the best marksmen were formed into a body, called the *Flying Company*, it being their part to hasten wherever danger most menaced. They were always to be accompanied by two pastors, to prevent excesses, unnecessary effusion of blood, and the relaxing in religious exercises. Each morning and evening, and before every engagement, these ministers offered up prayers in the encampment.

The advanced post of the Waldenses, that of Sonnaillette, was attacked on the 4th of February, 1561, and the combat lasted till night. Three days after, the popish army marched upon Angrogna in several separate corps, which united on a steep and rocky ascent called Le Coste. But the Waldenses, who occupied the heights, rolled down huge rocks on their ranks, and dispersed them.

The severest struggle, however, that had yet occurred, took place on the 24th of February. The count had brought to bear all his forces, and all the resources of his strategy, the object being to surprise Pra-del-Tor, where the entire population of Angrogna had assembled, and where they had constructed mills, ovens, houses, and all the appurtenances of a fortified post. This citadel of the Alps was protected, not only by rocks, but also by heroic fighting-men. An attempt had been made to reach it by Tagliaretto, but this access was defended by the conquerors of Villar. Two bodies of troops were accordingly directed against it from other quarters. The one, commanded by Charles Truchet and Louis de Monteil, advancing by the valley of San Martin, the other, under La Trinté, by that of Pramol. These two bodies were to attack Pra-del-Tor, the one by the Col du Laouzon, the other by the Col de la Vachera. On the morning they were to act, a third body appeared at the extremity of the valley of Angrogna, burning and pillaging, in order to draw the defenders from the principal post. But the manœuvre did not succeed. The troop coming by La Vachera advanced first; the Waldenses assailed and dispersed it. The second troop was then discovered, slowly descending the mountain side. It was allowed to involve itself in the ravines, and the guides had reached an opening whence they could look down into the valley, and had cried out, "Haste! haste! Angrogna is ours!" when the Waldenses, rushing upon them from the rocks, and exclaiming, "It is you who are ours," attacked them with energy. The enemy, confiding in their numbers, turned upon this small force, but now came up the Waldenses who had defeated the first comers, and who assailed the enemy on their left. The latter still resisted, but suddenly the Flying Company appeared on the right, and the papists, assailed on three sides, turned and retreated, as best they might, up the arduous ascent. Charles Truchet was prostrated by a stone, and his head was cut off with his own sword: and Louis de Monteil, after he had attained the other side of the mountain was overtaken and slain. All their soldiers would have been slain with them, had it not been for the pastors of the Flying Company, who hastened to the field of battle to save, and to dismiss those who could no longer save themselves. This victory supplied the Waldenses with store of much-needed arms and armour, taken from the enemy.

To avenge his defeat, the count de la Trinté burned the village of Rora, whose inhabitants, after a long and vigorous resistance, retired, over the mountain snows, to Villar.

It was the next occupation of the Waldenses to construct, with trees, stakes, great stones, and snow, barricades at the narrowest points of the valley. These were scarcely completed, when the count de la Trinté advanced, having divided his army into three corps, two of which, infantry, were to march along the two heights of the valley, while the third, cavalry, followed its centre. A company of pioneers was in front, to level the barricades. The Waldenses, on their part, advanced on the left bank of the Pelice, till they came opposite Chiabrol, and fired on the cavalry as soon as it appeared; then, retreating from tree to tree, and from rock to rock, they continued to harass it, until they came to the first barricade, above Villar. Here they halted, and swelled the ranks of the Flying Company, who defended this post. Much of the day was spent in skirmishes, at and about the barricade, upon which the enemy made no impression. Meanwhile, the infantry, who had advanced along the heights, passed, towards evening, beyond the line thus heroically defended. It became, therefore, necessary for the Waldenses to separate, in order that a portion of their body might repulse these new-comers. The first of these who appeared had already crossed the torrent Respart, and were ascending the vine-covered hills which overlook Villar, when the Waldenses, who had hastened up the opposite ascent, met them, assailed them, and, after a long struggle, compelled them to retreat upon La Torre, with considerable loss.

In the following week, the Waldenses occupying the heights, the count attacked the hamlet of Boudrina, with a body of 2000 men, and for a while this large force seemed triumphant; but the Flying Company came up, with the men of Angrogna, and turned the fortune of the day, so that the enemy were routed, and driven back once more to La Torre. The count de la Trinte then retired to Luzorna, and thenceforth left both Villar and Bobbi unmolested.

But there remained Angrogna, the central position of the valleys, approachable on all sides except from the west; and having collected a new army of not fewer than 7000 men, the count resolved to vindicate his military honour by the taking of Angrogna.

On Sunday, 17th March, 1561, the Waldensian families, assembled with their defenders at Pra-del-Tor for the worship of God, saw, as they quitted the church, three long trains of soldiers advancing in parallel lines—the one along the heights of La Vachera, the other by the road from Foreste, and the third by that from Serre.

The approaches to Pra-del-Tor, to which the first two lines of attack were advancing, were defended by a bastion of earth and rock-work, which the Waldenses had taken the precaution to construct, but the lower path had not been barricaded, though it might have been far more easily so closed than any other access, by reason of the narrowness of its path. Indeed, the natural difficulties of the approach, which the Waldenses had considered a sufficient impediment, were so great, that the enemy's column which used it was the last to arrive in sight of Pra-del-Tor. Upon perceiving it, the Waldenses descended to attack them, leaving at the bastion above only a few defenders; but these were armed with long pikes, with which each assailant, as he appeared on the escarpment, was forthwith thrust down the precipice. After a long struggle, however, which cost the lives of two of their number, this little band was about to give way, when the Flying Company, having routed the assailants below, dashed up to the bastion, whose garrison, thus reinforced, at once assumed the offensive. The enemy, furiously attacked, turned and fled. The captain of the band, Sebastian di Virgile, was slain; and the number of the soldiers killed was so great, that the Count de la Trinitê actually sat down and wept when he beheld the heaps of bodies. At the other bastion, the Waldenses were equally successful: they had awaited in firm silence the approach of the enemy, till they came within gunshot, and then, with a general discharge, took the papists by surprise; at a second discharge, the enemy gave way. The Waldenses rushed forth, attacked and decimated the enemy, and dispersed the survivors. As the captain of the battalion afterwards stated, the catholic troopers seemed panic-struck in the presence of these raw mountaineers, and there ran among them this cry—"God must be with these men!" It was a matter of no small astonishment with the papists generally at this time, that the Waldenses, thus triumphant, and familiar with the locality, had not followed up their victory by pursuing the enemy and completely annihilating them, as they might readily have done; but the chiefs, as Gilly observes, and especially the ministers, would not permit this, having resolved, at the outset, that while, under necessity, they would do their best to defend themselves by force of arms, they would never transgress the limits of absolute self-defence, alike out of respect for their superiors, and out of a desire to spare human blood, using every victory granted them by the God of battles with the utmost possible moderation.

The Romish chiefs attributed these repeated defeats of their troops to the circumstance that they had not been accustomed to warfare in the mountains, asserting that, could they encounter the Waldenses on the plain, they would scatter them like chaff. It so happened that in a few days afterwards an encounter did take place on the plain; but it was the papists who were scattered like chaff—not the Waldenses. Victory, as Gilly remarks on the occasion, depends not on the greater or smaller number of men, not on the greater or smaller space of battle-field, not on the higher or lower elevation of the ground, but wholly on the merciful aid of the Lord, who, when it so pleases his wisdom, gives the will and the power to triumph to those who support a just cause.

After these numerous engagments, in which the Waldenses only lost fourteen men, the count de la Trinité sent persons to open negotiations with them; but while the parley was proceeding, and the attention of the Waldenses thus lulled, he assembled his troops, and marched them, in the night of 16th of April, against the two strongest points in the country—Pra-del-Tor and Tagliarette. Tagliarette, assailed first, was occupied at day-break by a number of attacking parties, who threw themselves simultaneously upon all the scattered hamlets which constitute the district. The inhabitants, surprised in their sleep, were some slain and some taken prisoners; and the rest, escaping in their night attire, owed their lives to their agility, and to their knowledge of the mountain paths. The assailants, after plundering the abandoned cottages, descended by Costa-Rossina to the slopes overhanging Pra-del-Tor, to co-operate with the other troops in the projected extermination of the Waldenses.

Now the first proceeding of these, with the opening of each day, was to offer up a prayer to God in common. It was day-break, and they had just terminated this religious exercise, when the first rays of the sun lit up, on the mountain tops, the helmets and cuirasses of the advancing enemy. Six resolute mountaineers, dashing up the ascent, posted themselves in a defile where only two persons could march abreast; and here they kept in effectual check the long file of the foes who were accumulating behind this obstacle. As each two of the enemy turned the rock, they were shot down by the two foremost Waldenses; the two next were shot in like manner by the two next Waldenses, firing over their comrades' shoulders: the two last Waldenses loaded the weapons as they were discharged. Thus, for a quarter of an hour, the passage was closed. Meantime, other Waldenses ascended to the rocks which, higher up, overlooked the defile in which the enemy's forces were collecting. All at once, upon this armed mass, there rained angular rocks, which crushed whole ranks in their fall, and then, bursting into splinters, rebounded from the bodies like grape-shot, and prostrated fresh victims. Unable to advance, or to deploy, or even to fight, the unfortunate troops retrograded in disorder and but a portion escaped. The other corps, who had advanced by La Vechera to aid in the attack on Pra-del-Tor, finding their comrades already defeated, joined the survivors in their flight.

The Waldenses, doubly indignant at being thus basely assailed pending the armistice which they had generously accepted, furiously pursued the fugitives, and harassed them with stones and bullets, up to the plateau of Campo-la-Rama near La Torre. Here the papists, facing about, hastily formed in battle array, hoping to surround the Waldenses, with the aid of fresh troops from La Torre; but the protestants, giving them no time, either to form or to receive succours, dashed upon them, slew, among the first victims, their leader, Cornelio, and drove them, discomfited and in utter disorder, up to the very gates of La Torre. The same evening, the count de la Trinité raised his camp, and retreated to Cavour. It was announced that he was gone to fetch cannon. "Let him bring them," cried the Waldenses; "he'll not take them back with him." But he came not; and the victors, returning to Pra-del-Tor, covered it, towards La Vachera, with a bastion so large, that it was visible at Luzerna, three leagues off.

At this period there arrived in the valleys a new legion of defenders. The Waldenses of Provence, who had escaped from the massacres of 1545, doubly inured to warfare by their misfortunes and by the savage life they had led on the rude slopes of Leberon, issued from their retreats, on hearing that their brethren of the Piedmontese valleys were undergoing persecution; and either because the climate of Provence had generated in them more violent passions, or that the monstrous cruelties of Menier d'Oppede had infuriated them against all catholics, these auxiliaries were far from imitating the moderation of the Waldenses with regard to the papists. Animated with a spirit of vengeance, explained, though not excused, by the terrible sufferings they had endured, they scoured the country about the valleys, ravaged the possessions of the catholics, rendered carnage for carnage, and diffused that insurmountable terror which is created by the fury of despair. The surrounding population, victims at once of the hostile army and of the devastating incursions of these implacable avengers, loudly demanded that this war, so disastrous for all parties, should be concluded. On the other hand, desertion manifested itself in the papist army; the soldiers would not fight against such adversaries, nor even march towards those formidable mountains, where, as they said, the death of one Waldensian cost the lives of more than a hundred catholics. At last the count de la Trinite fell ill, while the Waldenses, so far from becoming weaker, had defenders more resolute, more powerful, more numerous than ever.

It was considered, therefore, expedient to make terms with them. The first overtures offered merely peace, and this on condition that the Waldenses would send away their pastors, and ransom their brethren who were prisoners. These conditions were at once rejected. The count de Racconis the (5th of May) wrote to the Waldenses, inviting them to send delegates to Cavour, to arrange with him the basis of a definite arrangement. The delegates were sent, and on the 5th of June 1561, a decree was issued, granting to the Waldenses, almost every thing which they had asked. It became to them in fact the charter of their liberties.

The pope, the nuncio, the catholic clergy, raised a vehement outcry against this convention, and did their utmost to frustrate it; but the cause of truth prevailed, and the convention of the 5th of June afforded a solid basis to the Waldenses for the ulterior defence of their liberty of conscience, which, though it underwent thereafter many rude assaults, triumphed over them all, for all the persecuted ones placed their trust in Him who said "Call upon me in the day of trouble. I will deliver thee, and thou shalt glorify me."

Chapter Thirteenth.

CONDITION OF THE VALLEYS UNDER CASTROCARO.

AFTER so protracted an interruption of agricultural labours, after such multiplied pillagings, and burnings, and losses of every description, undergone by the Waldenses, there was utter poverty throughout their valleys. The confiscated lands, houses, &c., had been stripped of every movable appurtenance, before they were restored; and many were not restored at all. The monks of Pignerol continued their depredations upon the surrounding protestants; and, from time to time, Waldenses escaped from the massacres in Calabria, made their way, hungry, naked, and utterly destitute, to the valleys, and became an additional burden upon the impoverished mountaineers, ever prompt to share with their brethren the little that remained to themselves. Their distress became known, and collections were made for them in Switzerland, in Germany, and even in France.

They were just recovering from their depression, when Castrocaro, a man who had been their prisoner, and whom they had generously released, professing to the duchess of Savoy, their protector, the most friendly intentions towards them, obtained the appointment of governor of the valleys. But, treacherous both towards his benefactress and towards his benefactors, he was faithful only to the archbishop of Turin, to whom he had promised that he would gradually withdraw from the Waldenses all the liberties which had been granted to them, and do his utmost for the complete annihilation of their church. His mode of effecting this object was by successive restrictions; and first, in 1565, he demanded a revision of the treaty of Cavour, concluded in 1561.

The Waldenses rejected the proposition. He then pretended that they had transgressed it. The Waldenses applied to the duke to maintain its provisions. Castrocaro proceeded to Turin, and returned with new conditions, which he laid before the Waldenses for their signature. But these conditions were not signed by the duke, and the Waldenses refused to subscribe them. Castrocaro menaced them with a war more cruel than the preceding. A conference was established at which some concessions were extorted from the representatives of the Waldenses; the Waldenses disavowed their representatives. The parties were growing embroiled, and this was precisely what the popish governor desired.

He had a body of troops placed under his command, on pretence of maintaining order, and established himself with this garrison in the castle of La Torre. He thence issued orders to the people of Bobbi to dismiss their pastor, Humbert Artus; and to those of San Giovanni, no longer to admit the protestants of the plain to their religious meetings.

The Waldenses, by the medium of the duchess, obtained the abrogation of these orders; but Castrocaro, nevertheless, on the 10th of September, 1565, issued a proclamation in the valley of Luzerna that all who did not conform should be put to the edge of the sword; and at the same time wrote word to the duke that the Waldenses were in open rebellion against his authority; whereupon the duke, indignant, ordered the people to obey their governor. The latter forthwith persecuted the faithful under all sorts of pretexts; he removed the learned Scipio Lentulus, pastor of San Giovanni, on the pretext of his being a foreigner; he arrested Gilles des Gilles, pastor of La Torre, on the pretext, utterly futile, that he had been to Grenoble and Geneva to invite foreign troops against his sovereign. This was the pastor who, in the late war, had, by his energetic interposition, saved the life of Castrocaro, as well as those of a multitude of catholic soldiers. This vital service, which would have inflamed noble minds with eternal gratitude, engendered absolute hatred towards his benefactor in the base soul of Castrocaro, who having, in February, 1566, seized his liberator, threw him into prison, treated him there, as his grandson relates, "worse than the worst brigand," and had well-nigh effected his death by burning, when the excellent pastor was released on the mediation of the elector Palatine.

Castrocaro next published an edict commanding all protestants, not born within his jurisdiction, to quit it, under penalty of death and confiscation; but the duchess of Savoy procured the abrogation of this barbarous order. The perfidous governor then essayed to interdict the Waldenses from assembling in Synod; but he failed. "At all events," he declared, "he would be present at these synods, in order to prevent plots against the safety of the state;" but the Waldenses protested against this innovation, fearing, not his presence, but the precedent.

In the following year, the wars of religion were rekindled in France; the duke of Cleves, marching at the head of an army of Spaniards against Flanders, was to traverse Piedmont, and his first exploit, it was announced, was to be the extermination of the Waldenses. The fanatics rejoiced, the Christians mourned, anxiety once more spread through the valleys, and a solemn fast was observed there towards the end of May, to avert the menaced visitation. It was averted; the storm passed on one side, and while all the rest of Europe was in combustion, the Waldenses enjoyed, for a few years, comparative peace.

Castrocaro availed himself of this respite, to construct, or rather to complete, the fort of Miraboco, an erection especially obnoxious to the people of Bobbi, by reason of the obstacle it established on the road to Queyras, the free passage of which created some resources for their *colayers*, or hawkers, who, by that route, conveyed their produce, for sale or exchange, to Upper Dauphiny. Castrocaro, however, had a special hostility to the people of Bobbi; and his next step was to require from them the surrender, into the hands of the papist pastor of La Torre, of the protestant church of Bobbi, and the land appropriated to the support of its minister. The Waldenses refused, and were, thereupon condemned by Castrocaro to pay a fine of one hundred gold crowns, within twenty-four hours, and a further penalty of twenty-five gold crowns for every day that the one hundred crowns should remain unpaid. Upon an appeal to Emanuel Philibert, this demand was withdrawn, but the Waldenses, seeing the system of persecution once more in such active operation, deemed it necessary to renew among themselves that oath of alliance and Christian combination which had been instrumental to their late triumphs; and they accordingly, on the 11th of of November, 1571, signed, by their representatives at Bobbi, the following convention:—

"When any one of our churches shall be impeached, individually, all the rest, combined, shall reply, as with one mouth, in assertion of the common rights. No one of us shall adopt any determination, in such a matter, without consulting his brethren. All of us solemnly promise and swear to adhere perseveringly to the ancient union transmitted to us by our fathers, never to abandon our holy religion, and to remain faithful to our lawful sovereigns."

Amid the vexations which now harassed the Waldenses, especially those of Lower Piedmont, there is a circumstance of a very singular nature to be noted: Charles IX. of France actually wrote a letter of the most pressing nature to the duke of Savoy, in favour of the persecuted. "I have a request to make," wrote he, "of no ordinary kind, but as earnest a one as I could possibly put to you, and it is this: that having, under the influence of passions excited by war-troubles, treated your subjects with extreme harshness, you would, for love of me, and at my prayer and special recommendation, receive them into your good grace, and re-establish them in their confiscated properties." This letter, written at Blois, bears date, 28th September, 1571, Charles IX. being then twenty-one years old.

"Charles IX." say the Benedictine authors of the *Art de Vérifier les Dates*, "had received from nature an excellent disposition and rare talents; he was brave to intrepidity, endowed with marvellous penetration, vivid conception, sure judgment, and expressed himself with a noble facility. But the seductions by which he was surrounded perverted this favourable disposition; the queen-mother herself formed him in the arts of feigning and dissimulation; the marshal de Retz taught him to laugh at oaths; and the Guise, by their sanguinary counsels, converted the natural impetuosity of his character into cruelty." And there is no doubt that, under other circumstances, he would have been one of the most accomplished and excellent princes in the annals of French royalty. But ill example and sinister counsels produced their wonted result; on the 23rd of August, 1572, within a year after the transmission of this letter, took place the massacre of St. Bartholomew

Upon the occurrence of that monstrous event, the hopes which the reformed churches had conceived were succeeded by the most agonizing apprehensions. Castrocaro, among the foremost persecutors, alarmed the Waldensian valleys with his menaces of extermination. "Sixty thousand Huguenots have perished in France," he exclaimed, with malignant vehemence, "and do you, miserable handful of heretics, think you are to escape?" The papist population already congratulated each other on the approaching abolition of the Waldenses. The latter began to prepare for the worst; the women and children, conveying the household goods, sought the securest caverns of the upper mountains; the men, remaining behind, prepared their weapons, and, until compelled to make use of them, continued to watch and pray.

But the cry of horror which resounded throughout civilized Europe at the enormous assassination of August, 1572, had its effect upon the duke of Savoy, whose heart was touched, whose intelligence was confounded, at so monstrous an atrocity. He protested energetically against the cruelties which had been perpetrated, vowed that no similar crime should ever sully his life, and assuring the Waldenses that they were in no danger, induced them to return once more to their dwellings.

A relation of the troubles which, at this epoch, befel the Valley of Perosa will more fitly be introduced later, in connection with the history of the valley of Pragela; but there is one episode which may find its place here, as coming within the general movement of the districts under consideration.

Amid the almost universal fury now prevalent against the protestants, the pastor of San German, named Francis Guerin, did not hesitate to go forth, himself, alone, to combat catholicism with that bloodless but most potent weapon—reasoning. One day, in 1573, he proceeded to Pramol, where papism was rampant. It was Sunday, the people were assembled in church, and the curé was celebrating mass. Francis Guerin mingled with the auditory, and waited, in silence, until the service was terminated. No one suspected that, amid the crowd, there was a knight of Christ, who, armed with the shield of faith, the hemlet of salvation, and the sword of the Spirit, which is the word of God, was about to make that word triumph, by the power of love and of courage, over the servile forces of superstition.

The cure having concluded his service, the pastor rose, and asked him whether he had finished. "Yes," replied the cure. "What have you been doing?"—"I have been celebrating mass." "What is the mass?" asked the pastor in Latin. There was no answer. "What is the mass?" asked the pastor in Italian; but the poor curate could not answer. Thereupon, relates the Capuchin, brother Augustin, in a contemporary manuscript, the protestant minister mounted the pulpit, and began to preach against the mass and against the pope, and, among other things, said: "O poor folk! See what you have here—a man who knoweth not what that is he doeth. Every day he says mass, yet he knows not what mass is; every day he does that which neither he understands, nor you, whom he calls about him. But behold here the Bible, and hear the words of God;" "and thereupon," adds the Capuchin, "with his gimcracks, he perverted the whole district, so that now there is neither cure nor mass to be found there."

For five years, Francis Guerin acted as pastor of the district thus gained over to the gospel; he then, at the head of the Waldensian militia, penetrated into the marquisate of Saluzzo, then an object of contention between Savoy and France, and, after the respective armies had withdrawn, remained to consolidate there the evangelical churches.

At length, the Waldenses were relieved from the oppressions of Castrocaro. Emanuel Philibert having died in 1580, Castrocaro announced that his successor was about to march an army for the extermination of the Waldenses. The latter having, hereupon retired to the mountains, the treacherous governor sent word to the duke that the Waldenses were preparing to resist his authority, and solicited permission to take rigorous measures against them. A commissioner, however, being sent to investigate the matter on the spot, soon satisfied himself, at once of the innocence of the Waldenses and of the odious vexations practiced on them by their calumniators. He found that Castrocaro, himself living in pampered luxury in the castle of La Torre, where "he had grown fat and rich," permitted, and not unfrequently ordered, his soldiers to perpetrate every description of excess upon the people around. He had in his palace a breed of ferocious bloodhounds, of unusual size and strength. His son, Andrew, was so profligate a debauchee that no modest woman could quit her house unless with an escort. His three daughters went indifferently to mass and to the protestant church, having no sense of religion whatever, but merely eager to display the frippery in which they delighted. The duke of Savoy, upon being made acquainted with the facts, ordered Castrocaro to appear before him at Turin; but, under various pretexts, the governor withheld obedience to the mandate. His highness thus finding that rebellion at La Torre was not on the part of the Waldenses, but on the part of their oppressor, ordered the count of Luzerna to arrest Castrocaro. This, however, was no easy matter, by reason of the fortifications, the desperado soldiers, and the ferocious dogs, who guarded the governor. Treachery, however, aptly did its work upon the treacherous. A captain of the garrison, one Simon, came to an understanding with the count of Luzerna, and by his means Castrocaro was seized in bed on the 15th of June, 1582, and taken to Turin, where he died in prison. His son also expiated his excesses in a dungeon; the three daughters, with the mother, were left to subsist in obscurity upon a small pension reserved to them out of the father's ill-acquired gains, the residue of which was confiscated to the state.

Chapter Fourteenth.

CONDITION OF THE WALDENSES DURING THE REIGN OF CHARLES EMANUEL.

In 1585, Charles Emanuel, who had ascended to the throne of Savoy in 1580, married the daughter of Philip II. of Spain; and the latter being one of the league against the protestants, it was assumed that his son-in-law would not delay to follow his example. Thereupon the monks and the Jesuits exalted their horns, and menaced the faithful with extermination, unless they should consent to a prompt conversion. The fear of the faithful became great, not so much by reason of the immediate vaunts and menaces of the monks, but by reason of the great papist league which they knew was forming throughout Europe; and they saw that they must prepare, if not to avert, at least to meet calamity, by more than ordinary recurrence to Almighty God.

A solemn fast of four days was accordingly observed in the valleys, on the 15th and 16th, and on the 22d and 23d of May, 1585, according to the usage of the primitive church in similar emergencies; and as if to show that the blessing and the favour of God are ever granted to the fervent prayer of man, the Waldenses speedily learned that throughout Dauphiny the Reformers had defeated the soldiers of the league; and as one-third of the Waldensian valleys appertained to that province, the advantages obtained by these greatly contributed to strengthen the position of all.

In 1595, Charles Emanuel, on his return from recovering the fort of Miraboco, which had been taken by the French, halted in the market-place at Villar, and said to the Waldenses who had assembled to congratulate him on his victory: "Be good subjects to me, and I will be a good prince to you—a good father. With regard to your freedom of conscience, and the exercise of your religion, I will make no innovation upon the liberties you have enjoyed hitherto; and if any one molests you therein, come to me, and I will see to it."

The catholic clergy, irritated at this gracious intimation, and unable to effect anything, by violence, against the Waldensian church, attacked it by indirect means. First, it obtained permissson to establish, in all the valleys, catholic missionaries, who were to be entitled to the protestant churches whenever they thought fit; and, pursuant to this permission, the archbishop of Turin himself installed a body of Jesuits in the valley of Luzerna, and one of Capuchins in that of San Martin. Several conferences were held between the Jesuits and the pastors, but without the least result. Indeed, there was no one by whom the result of such discussions could be decided. The conference at Appiaso, for example, was presided over by the count of Luzerna: at the close of the discussion, the pastor having replied to the Jesuit, requested the president to decide with whom the advantages of argument rested. "Gentlemen," replied the count, "if you had disputed the qualities of a good horse or a good sword, I could give you my opinion, for I know something about both matters; but as to your controversy, I make neither head nor tail of it." On the 2d of August, 1598, there was a special conference between the pastor of San German and the Capuchin Berno. The arguments on both sides were printed, but the Inquisition prohibited their being sold; the inference from which is, that, in the opinion of the Holy Office, the victory in argument was not on the side of Romanism. Defeated in discussion, the Jesuits had recourse to such acts of violence as were practicable, and imprisonment, fine, and torture effected a few venal conversions. In 1599, there came to La Torre a curé, very bold and blustering, and who seemed much fitter to create disturbances than to conduct a church. His name was Ubertino Braida. His first proceeding was to demand tithes, which the protestants had never paid; his demand was rejected. He then proceeded to outrage the Waldenses with all sorts of insults, and, like another Goliah, offered to fight any one of them, hand to hand. But despite his assumption of extreme valour, he always wore a shirt of mail, under his cassock. One evening, some young men, after supper, went to the curé's house, resolved to test his courage, and made a disturbance The curé ran out at the back door, and took to flight. The young men did not pursue him at all, contenting themselves with a laugh at the result of their experiment. The podesta of La Torre, stimulated by the friends of the fugitive, cited the young men before him, and sentenced them to remain prisoners for a few days, in the house of a gentleman, whom he named. The Waldenses repaired to the house; but learning next day that a troop of archers had been despatched to take them to Turin, and cast them into the dungeons of the Inquisition, they took to flight during the night. Next day, they were again summoned to attend before the podesta; and not appearing, were condemned to banishment from the states of Savoy, under penalty of the galleys, if they were ever found within its limits.

The poor young men withdrew into the mountains, where, having provided themselves with arms, they wandered about from place to place, and lived upon the contributions, voluntary or enforced, of the population. Here these *banditti* (banished men) lived for some years, their number constantly increasing. Prohibition was proclaimed, by sound of trumpet, from affording them aid, food, or shelter; but they became all the more formidable, imposing black-mail not merely on individuals, but on whole towns. The podesta of La Torre marched against them with some troops, but he was so thoroughly defeated, that, ashamed to show his face again in La Torre, he abandoned his charge there, and retired to Luzerna.

In the commencement of February, 1602, the archbishop of Turin, the governor of Pignerol, and the count of Luzerna, came into the valleys, attended by a troop of Jesuits and Capuchins, and caused infinite disquietude to the protestants, who daily expected to see the Waldensian valleys become the theatre of some catastrophe. The catholics charged all the excesses committed by the banditti on the Waldenses as a body, and loudly demanded of the duke of Savoy to destroy, once for all, this focus of heresy and den of brigands. The Waldenses appointed special ministers to seek out, censure, and exhort the banbitti; and a universal fast was observed throughout the valleys, on the 11th and 12th of August, to conciliate the divine pardon and mercy. The women and children once more sought their mountain retreats; the men once more, preparing their weapons, assiduously watched and prayed, knowing that the only secure defence is that of our Lord.

Meanwhile the governor Ponte repaired to La Torre,

whither he convoked the syndics of all the Waldensian communes, and ordered them to deliver up the banditti. Protesting earnestly their entire fidelity to the sovereign, the syndics replied by attributing the recent calamities to unjust proscriptions, and admitting that some of these wretched outlaws had been guilty of excesses, pointed out the difficulty of separating the guilty from the innocent, and the injustice of punishing all alike, and concluded with an emphatic appeal for amnesty and peace. The governor rejected this proposition, and renewed the order that the banditti should be delivered up, dead or alive; but a few days afterwards, the governor was himself arrested and deprived of his office, on the charge of having maintained secret relations with the French generals.

Thereupon count Charles of Luzerna, who enjoyed great influence at court, offered to mediate in favour of the valleys with the duke, pursuant to a promise he had recently made to that effect, to the elector of Saxony, at Dresden.

On the 19th of November, 1602, Vignaux and Gillis, deputies, the one for the valley of Luzerna, the other for that of San Martin, waited on the count in his palace at Luzerna. Every one was anxious to have the matter settled, for the force of the banditti had been lately augmented by a great number of protestants who had been driven from the marquisate of Saluzzo, and the plain of Piedmont. The result of the conference was the appointment of a Waldensian deputation to the duke, at Turin, the count promising the support of his utmost influence. The duke, however, while disposed to make some concessions, would not grant an amnesty, and the Waldenses would not accept the former without the latter. At length, after protracted negotiations, the duke issued, from Cunio, on the 9th of April, 1603, a decree granting substantially what the Waldenses had asked, including an amnesty for the banditti, so called.

There still remained, however, the banditti belonging to Saluzzo, Fenile, Bubiana, Villafranca, and other districts of Piedmont. For the extirpation of these, the duke organized a body of special troops, who were to be maintained by the Waldenses, and whom he placed under the command of one captain Galline. This officer, however, under pretext of pursuing the outlaws, committed various outrages upon the persons and property of the peaceful inhabitants. One day in July, when the people of Bobbi were all engaged in the fields, he entered the village with his bravoes, killed a young man who, for some reason, had been unable to quit his home, drove out the pastor, and was about to pillage the place, when the villagers, having received an alarm, rushed home. Galline, finding himself surrounded by superior numbers, pusillanimously threw down the sword yet reeking with murder, and entreated for mercy. It was granted, and the Waldenses, taught to observe the great lesson of good for evil, even proffered to escort the band of marauders back to Luzerna, in order to save them from the indignation of the other hardy mountaineers, who, on hearing of Galline's outrage, were hastening down to aid their brethren. When the affair reached the ears of the duke, he sent the grand provost to Luzerna, to inquire into the circumstances, and take measures accordingly. The provost announced to the other Waldensian communes that, whatever the result, they would not be affected, on the understanding that they should take no part with the people of Bobbi; but all without hesitation not only declared that they entirely took part with the people of Bobbi, but that henceforward they would not contribute, in any shape or degree, to the support of Galline and his men. The provost returned to Turin, having effected nothing. Count Charles of Luzerna then interposed, and the result of his mediation was an edict, dated 29th of September, 1603, which on the one hand, required the valleys to pay a fine of fifteeen hundred ducatoons, but, on the other, granted a general amnesty for the past, permitted all outlaws to return home without being liable to prosecution, authorized the Waldenses to retain any property they possessed beyond the limits of their valleys, and even to make open profession of their faith in presence of catholics, when desired so to do, (whereas hitherto they had been prohibited from avowing it,) and merely forbade them to defend it by polemical discussions, a prohibition manifestly recognizing its force. These concessions were especially favourable to a great many of the people of Saluzzo, who had taken refuge in the valleys, and who were thus permitted to abide there. Large collections made for them at about this time in France and Switzerland, enabled them to recover somewhat from the effect of the confiscations to which they had been subjected.

During the few years of tranquillity which the Waldenses now enjoyed, their numbers daily increased; and the church of Copiere was, in 1608, enlarged to its present dimensions. Towards the commencement of 1611, however, the court of Rome, which had succeeded in establishing fresh persecutions against the reformed churches of France, and had procured a regiment to be sent into the valley of Barcelonette, for the conversion, in the manner of Rome, of the Waldenses in that locality, sought to effect the employment of similar means of conversion in the Piedmontese valleys. In all great emergencies, the Waldenses have ever been accustomed, before and above all things, to recur to fasting and prayer, to penitence and supplication: in the present emergency, a public fast was ordered, 20th of January, 1611. On the morning of that day, a violent earthquake shook all the Waldensian mountains: it seemed an omen; for, eight days afterwards, the regiment of the baron de la Roche arrived, from Barcelonnette, in the valley of Luzerna, and immediately proceeded to ravage the district, and put the men and cattle and goods they seized to arbitrary ransom, notwithstanding every effort was made to appease their insolence. The exactions and oppression of these troops continued for nearly a month; they were then removed to new cantonments, where, attempting to renew the excesses they had perpetrated in the valley of Luzerna, they were all slain by the peasants.

In 1613, a large portion of the Waldensian militia took part in the war of Montferrat, under the command of the count of Luzerna, and upon the special condition that they should be at full liberty to assemble every night and morning for the celebration of their own religious services, wherever they might be. Their conduct in this campaign obtained for them the grateful praises of their sovereign. In the following year, they were again levied, to take part in the war against Spain, and on this occasion marched in the direction of Vercelli, accompanied, as before, by their pastors. These expeditions gave them opportunities of destroying many prejudices which had been spread abroad against them, and of comforting and strengthening many secret friends of their doctrine who made themselves known to them in various places.

In 1620, various troubles befell the churches of Saluzzo and other districts contiguous to the Waldensian valleys. Deputies from the latter, who put themselves forward as mediators, were seized and imprisoned, and the sum of six thousand ducatoons was imposed, as the price of their release, and of the cessation of the vexations by which the protestants were persecuted. The six thousand ducatoons were, by the numerous exactions of the courts of justice, swollen to nearly eighteen thousand this heavy amount the valley of Luzerna advanced, in the expectation that, being a payment for the common interest, the other valleys (Perosa and San Martin) would afterwards contribute their proportion of it. When, however, the 'application for these quotas was made, the two valleys, under the influence of evil counsellors, refused to comply with it, disavowing all share in the arrangement. This disavowal was precisely what the popish plotters wanted. "If you have no share in the arrangement," said the magistrates, "you do not participate in its advantages, and you do not come within the amnesty. Let justice take its course." Justice—popish justice—did take its course. The richest inhabitants of Pinache, Clots, and Prali, were immediately arrested, under the pretext of their having taken part in the late troubles, and made to pay for their release ransoms amounting to a much larger sum than the two valleys would have had to contribute as their share of the money paid by the valley of Luzerna for the tutelary edict which they had so imprudently disavowed. Nor was this all: the persecution of these two valleys still went on; and to effects their cessation, the inhabitants had to pay, in addition to the sums paid by individuals for individual ransom, a fine of three thousand ducatoons to the duke. Nor was this all: they were ordered to demolish six of their churches. This they absolutely refused to do, and thereupon seven regiments of infantry were sent to treat them in all respects as a conquered country; these troops demolished the churches, and ravaged the whole district in its length and breadth.

Various attempts were made, in like manner, between 1620 and 1624, to persecute the valley of Luzerna; but the privileges which this valley had so highly purchased were not wholly without effect in mitigating oppression. In 1625, the presence of Lesdiguières in Piedmont, whither he had been invited by the duke of Savoy to act against the Genoese, interposed in favour of his co-religionists, gave respite to the valleys. In 1626–7, one father Buonaventura, a monk of great note among his own people, was employed as missionary among the Waldenses. When he prayed, he was sometimes, his admirers said, raised from the ground by a mysterious force. Some took him for a saint; others for a sorcerer. During his progress, several boys of from ten to twelve years old disappeared; these, it was afterwards ascertained, had been carried off by *bravoes* in the employment of the worthy monk, and shut up, with a view to their *conversion*, in the monastery of Pignerol. On the 9th of June, 1627, several heads of protestant families were arrested simultaneously at Luzerna, Bubiana, Champiglone, and Fenile, and taken prisoners to Cavour, with the result which has been already related in this work.

In 1628, a French army, under the marquis d'Uxel, presented itself at the entrance to the Alps, on its way to Montferrat to serve against the troops of Charles Emanuel. The Waldenses were called upon to defend their mountains, and acquitted themselves valiantly of this charge. The duke himself twice visited them, at this time, and paid due homage to their patriotism; for they received no pay, but only bread. This, indeed was a great point; for the harvest had failed in Piedmont in 1626, and in the spring of 1628 the poor folk had been compelled to sell everything they possessed, in order to purchase food at Queyras. The presence of the French army on the frontiers aggravated their misery by impeding this barter; and, by and bye, the people of Queyras, growing alarmed at the quantity of provisions that were leaving their district, prohibited any further exportations, and even imprisoned the famished wretches who came in search of supplies.

The monks of Pignerol and their acolytes availed themselves of these circumstances to seek to purchase, from the starving Waldenses, abjuration at the price of a loaf of bread. In this good work especially signalized himself Marc Aurelio Rorengo, the son of a gentleman of La Torre, who, having quitted the magistracy for the popish church, had been appointed prior of Luzerna on his undertaking to employ his utmost efforts in the suppression of heresy. Having procured a religious corporation to purchase his father's house, he immediately converted it into a monastery of reformed Franciscans; and the brethren, on being installed (23rd June, 1628), at once proceeded to distribute food amongst the famished population, with brilliant promises to the protestants who would consent to abjure. But, faithful to the example of the primitive church, the Waldenses, rejecting these insidious proffers, made a common store of all their possessions, and distributed daily bread to all who asked for it. The monks, frustrated in this direction, applied their efforts at conversion by famine to the Waldensian communes, but with as little success. At Bobbi, the Waldenses would not even permit the monks to perform mass, and they accordingly proceeded to Villar, where they fitted up an old ruined palace, which has since become the catholic church of the place. At Rora, two monks were located in a deserted house. The language of these ecclesiastics was at first exceedingly mild and conciliating; but on the 29th December they showed the scorpion's tail, in the shape of an edict, published by count Bighem, which "forbade all persons to trouble or vex, in any way or degree, the very reverend Observantine fathers, whatever they were pleased to do, under penalty of death to the offender, and of a fine of ten thousand gold crowns upon the commune in which the offence should be committed; every informer receiving two hundred gold crowns, and his name being kept secret." Next, count Philip of Luzerna denounced the most terrible menaces against the people of Bobbi and those of Angrogna, who had absolutely refused to permit under any pretext, any Observantines to settle in their districts.

The governor of Pignerol, count Capri, then proceeded into the valleys, assembled all the syndics and pastors, and informed them that the pope and the duke were resolved that the monks should be established in the mountains; and that if the Waldenses would not admit them voluntarily, force would be employed. "To-morrow," he said, "I will have mass performed at Bobbi."

On the morrow, accordingly, he proceeded with the Romish ecclesiastics to Bobbi; but every door and window was closed, and not a single person was visible. He summoned the syndic, and ordered him to have a stable, at all events, opened for his service; but the syndic replied, that his authority ceased at the threshold of private houses. "Well, then," exclaimed the count, "I will force open your own house."—"Your Lordship will reflect before you act thus," returned the syndic, with respectful calmness. The count did reflect, that the defenders of the village, though not visible, were none the less near, and he accordingly contented himself with performing mass on the high road, after which he withdrew. Two days afterwards he proceeded to Angrogna on a similar mission, and had precisely the same reception, with the same result. Towards the close of January, 1629, he went to La Torre, in company with a French gentleman, M. de Serres, convoked the syndics, and attempted to intimidate them into receiving the monks, but to no purpose. On the contrary the Waldenses shortly afterwards assembled in arms, surrounded the habitations in which the monks had established themselves, and called upon them to withdraw. They refused; whereupon, it being prohibited to the men to lay hands upon them, the women approached, forced open the doors, and some of these robust mountaineers, accustomed to carry heavy burdens, shouldering the poor ecclesiastics like so many bundles of wood, carried them off. Their furniture, goods, copes, reliques, &c., were then packed in carts, and transported beyond the limits of the commune after the owners. The clergy complained to the court, and the Waldenses sent deputies to defend them. The result was an edict, dated 22d February, 1629, by which the former concessions to the Waldenses were confirmed, and the vexations practised on them ordered to be discontinued.

On the 16th July, 1630, Charles Emanuel died, aged sixty-eight years and a half, after a reign of half a century; and at his death, France took possession of Savoy and part of Piedmont.

Chapter Fifteenth.

THE PLAGUE AND OTHER CALAMITIES.

In 1629, the year after the famine, the poor inhabitants of the Waldensian valleys, who, having no harvests of their own, were in the habit of repairing to the rich domains of Piedmont, and giving their services in exchange for a certain quantity of corn, were deprived of this resource, by the popish priests, who, from the pulpits, forbade their congregations to employ a single protestant labourer, and even themselves threatened to kill any follower of the "religion" whom they should find in their fields.

On the 23d of August, of the same year, at eight in the morning, a formidable storm of rain, suddenly fell upon the Col Julien, and created an inundation on both sides of the mountain. The villages of Prali and Bobbi were so suddenly invaded by the torrent, that the inhabitants had scarcely time to escape, and many houses were utterly destroyed. In September, there came a wind of intense coldness, accompanied by a dry cloud or mist, and the chestnut crop was utterly annihilated; then there came a second inundation of rain, which destroyed all the grapes. On the 12th of that month, the Waldensian ministers assembled in solemn synod, in testimony of their fraternal union, little deeming that they would never again meet in this world, and that of those fifteen pastors two only would, ere a few months elapsed, survive their brethren.

In 1630, a French army, placed, by cardinal Richelieu, under the command of three marshals of France, De Schomberg, De la Force, and De Crequi, to oppose the projects of Savoy on Montferrat, made its appearance in the Waldensian valleys. The Waldenses, having in vain appealed to the duke for succours, sent deputies to the marshal de la Force, who was encamped with a detachment at Briqueras. "Yield yourselves to the king," replied he, "and we will protect you; otherwise, we will kill, burn, exterminate you." Left without resource, the Waldenses capitulated (5th April), on the assurance that all their privileges should be respected, and that they should not be required to serve against their sovereign.

Towards the close of April, the king of France set out from Lyon, with all his court, to march upon Savoy. A deputation of Waldenses waited upon him at Moutiers, and obtained the confirmation of their privileges. By the treaty of Ratisbon, which terminated this war, the valleys of Luzerna and San Martin were restored to Piedmont. but those of Perosa and Pragela, with Pignerol, remained in the dominion of France.

In this same deplorable year, 1630, a scourge still more terrible than war deprived the Waldensian valleys of nearly two-thirds of their population. The heat was excessive at the time when the army of Richelieu entered the valleys; in that army were many volunteers, who had fled from France to escape the plague, which then raged in that country; but, in their flight, they had still brought the seeds of the pestilence with them. In the first week of May, this terrible malady manifested itself in the village of Porte, near Perosa. Next it appeared at San Germano, then at Prali, and soon it spread throughout all the valleys. The pastors immediately, pursuant to the custom of their church, assembled together to consult the Lord, to seek inspiration from prayer and meditation, and to discuss, one with the other, the course they should pursue in this alarming conjuncture. This meeting took place at Pramol. In a few days afterwards, the pestilence broke out at Pramol also, and the pastors began to hold their preachings in the open fields. In June, the commune of Angrogna was invaded by the pestilence, and on the 11th of July, there fell beneath its stroke the pastor of San Giovanni, and the pastor of Meano; on the 12th the pastor of Prali; on the 24th, the pastor of Angrogna. Before the 1st of August, seven other Waldensian ministers died. On the 2d of August, the six surviving ministers met on Mont Saumette, an isolated eminence in the centre of the three valleys, near La Vachera. Here, after weeping and praying, they distributed among themselves the care of the vacant churches; but, in a little while, three of the six followed their brethren; and the three survivors then held a conference on the heights of Angrogna, with deputies from all the parishes of the valleys, to determine upon the means of providing for the celebration of worship. Letters were despatched to Constantinople, recalling Antony Leger; to Geneva, for a supply of protestant clergy; to Grenoble, imploring the pastors of Dauphiny to come and console and strengthen the Waldensian church, thus cruelly tried.

There remained but one pastor for each of the three valleys; Peter Gilles in that of Luzerna; Valerius Gros, in that of St. Martin; and John Barthelemy, in that of Perosa. But on the 22d of April, 1631, the plague seized upon John Barthelemy also, and on the 25th he died;

so that upon the venerable ministers Gilles and Gros, already worn down by years and infirmities, devolved the care of all the churches of the Waldenses.

The mysterious and terrible scourge, which had subsided during the winter, rose up again, with renewed force, in the spring of 1631, and extended its ravages to the hills of Angrogna and Bobbi, which it had before spared. More than 12,000 persons died in the valleys; in La Torre alone, upwards of fifty families became completely extinct. The crops rotted in the fields, for there was no one to reap them; the fruits fell from the trees, for there was no one to gather them. During the summer heats, horsemen were seen to fall from their saddles to the ground, seized with sudden death. "The highways," says Gilles, "were so encumbered with the dead bodies of men and animals, that they were almost impassable. Many estates were abandoned, for want, not merely of cultivators, but of proprietors. Towns and villages, lately full of life and occupation, of merchants, artisans, labourers, became silent and desert. Whole families, in numberless instances, disappeared; there was no family which did not lose some of its members. The venerable minister, Gilles, lost his four elder sons, and being, with the exception of Valerius Gros, the sole surviving pastor of the valleys, found his duties augment with his afflictions; but God gave him strength to bear his double burden of calamity and labour. He went through all the parishes, preached twice every Sunday, and once at least, every other day; visited the sick, and consoled the afflicted, calm and serene amid his dying flock, to whom he communicated his own unshakable confidence in Him who raises up the fallen and heals those whom he had wounded. His indefatigable devotedness carried him through every danger; and he was preserved to the Waldensian church, and with him that most complete monument of the ancient Waldensian history, which he has transmitted to us in his chronicle, so rich in details respecting an epoch otherwise but little known.

The pastor Brunet was the first who hastened from Geneva to succor the valleys; he arrived in December, 1630, the month before the cessation of the plague. Other ministers of the gospel followed; but none of them could administer divine service in the Italian tongue, which had hitherto been the language of Waldensian preaching and spiritual instruction. It was necessary, therefore, to have the service performed in French; and as the ancient language of the Waldenses is a dialect between French and Italian, the people soon became accustomed to the new formulary. From this period date the regular relations which have ever since been maintained between the Waldensian church and that of Geneva.

The most urgent functions which the new pastors had first to accomplish in the valleys was the re-organization of their churches, so cruelly decimated. "It was a marvel unprecendented in these countries," says Gilles, "to see the multitude of marriages that took place at this time. Everywhere the plague had taken from parents their children, from children their parents, from the husband his wife, from the wife her husband; so that all being desolate, each sought out a brother or a sister with whom to raise up the fallen habitations and to create a new home."

War, the other scourge from which the valleys had suffered so grievously, disappeared shortly after the plague. On the 6th of April, 1631, Victor Amadeus signed, at Queyras, a treaty of peace, by which he resumed possession of all his states, and obtained some towns in Montferrat, as an equivalent for Pignerol and the valley of Perosa, which remained in the hands of France.

On the eve of his return to Turin, he received, at Carignano, a deputation from the Waldenses, whom he received with much kindness, saying to them; "Be good subjects to me, and I will be a good prince to you." The prior of Luzerna, Rorengo, and the superior of the monastery of La Torre, Fra Paolo, no sooner heard of this favourable reception, than they applied themselves to counteract it, and all sorts of offences were alleged at court against the Waldenses; so that, when another deputation of these waited on the prince (8th September, 1632), to solicit from him the formal ratification of their privileges, he informed them that an officer of state was about to proceed to the valleys to inquire into the offences which had been laid to their charge, and that to this officer they might state their grievances. Soon afterwards, accordingly, a commissioner, accompanied by Rorengo, visited all the valleys, collected information, and received complaints. The nature of his report is unknown; but, in the following year, another commissioner, Christopher Fauzon, summoned a meeting of Waldensian delegates at La Torre, and proceeded first to harangue and then to question them. He told them they were charged with having recently established themselves at Luzerna and Bubiana; they proved that they had been established in both places from time immemorial. He contested the right of the parishioners of San Giovanni to ring a bell for the purpose of summoning the faithful to church; they showed that this custom had been also immemorial. Ultimately, he demanded from the Waldenses a written statement of the proofs by which they assumed to establish their right to celebrate the protestant worship, in each of their parishes. After some hesitation, for the Waldenses feared a new snare, the document was furnished, and the commissioner quitted the valleys. No communication was made with reference to the written statement supplied by the Waldenses, and things remained in their previous condition.

Chapter Sixteenth.

MORE MARTYRS.

In the time of the Reformation, the Christians of Provence and of the valleys placed themselves in communication with the reformers. The consequent animadversion of the church first assailed the Provençals, about Avignon. The Rome of the west found it necessary to combat the religious awakening which menaced her predominance, and the inquisitor Giovanni de Roma raised the first martyr-pyres on the slopes of Leberon. The proceedings against these victims made known the presence, among the heretics of Provence, of many persons who had come from the valleys of Piedmont. Hereupon the count of Aix wrote to the senate of Turin, and the senate appointed a commissioner, Pantaleone Bersori, to proceed to Provence, and inquire further into the matter. Bersori returned from Provence with numerous and precise data as to the leading Waldensian families in Piedmont, and the high antiquity and extensive ramifications of the ministry of the barbas, accomplishing its work in silence and obscurity, that it might bear more fruit.

Bersori, furnished with the information he had collected in Provence, proceeded to the valleys, and continued there the inquisitorial proceedings begun in Provence by the court of Aix. There was no want of witnesses ready to testify to the evangelical faith. One of these, Bernardino Fea, of San Segonzo, upon being interrogated by the judge as to the communications he had had with the heretics, replied:

"When I was at Briqueras, in 1529, I met Louis Turin, of San Giovanni, who took me with him to his house. There, another inhabitant of San Giovanni, Catalan Girardet, who came in, invited us to go to La Torre, where, he said, we should hear good things; Louis Turin also requested me to go, and we went.

"On arriving at La Torre, Catalan conducted us to the house of Chabert Ughet, where, in a large room, we found a number of persons assembled. A barba, named Philip, was preaching, and, after his sermon, he questioned me, and then instructed me in various points of their religion."

"What did he say?"

"That there is no salvation except in Jesus Christ, and that we ought to do good works, not in order that we may be saved, but because we have been saved."

As this witness had not ceased to attend mass, he was not prosecuted; but Catalan Girardet was arrested, and, on his refusing to apostatize, was condemned to be burned alive. He died firm and serene, his forehead radiant, amid the flames that were devouring him, with the blessed assurance of the salvation he had received, and of the eternal happiness he was about to receive.

Shortly after the count de la Trinité had put the Waldensian valleys to fire and sword, the pastor of Prali, Martin, was visited by two men who had been in the service of the seigneurs du Perrier, those malignant foes of the Waldenses, the cruel and treacherous Truchets. The pastor of Prali was a Frenchman; his two visitors announced themselves as also Frenchmen; and Martin received them as countrymen. They expressed a desire to enter the reformed church, and the good pastor invited them to remain his guests, till he had shown them the way of salvation. The parishioners, who distrusted these two men, partly from instinct, partly from the fact that they were recognized as having not long before borne arms against the Waldenses, entreated Martin to be on his guard; but the simple and excellent man believed in the sincerity of his guests' conversion, and appealed to the Christian sentiments of his flock for a more charitable construction. The population of Prali, however, remained full of anxiety, and saw with regret and apprehension the two men still abiding with their beloved pastor, who had no family, and lived in a retired spot. At length, the pastor did not make his wonted appearance at the church for the celebration of divine service. The people, in a state of fearful suspense, hastened to his house. The door was closed; they knocked; no one replied. Some of the parishioners forced their way into the cottage through a window, and in an instant their cries of anguish announced a deplorable catastrophe. The pastor Martin lay lifeless, bathed in his own blood. The monsters, whom he had treated as children, had cut his throat, stripped the house, and fled. The Waldenses hastened in pursuit of the assassins, but could discover no traces of them. Some time afterwards, however, they audaciously returned to the valleys in the service of the seigneurs du Perrier, who thus manifested themselves the accomplices, and who had probably been the instigators of this odious murder.

So fierce was the hostility of the persecutors, that Barberi, the duke's commissioner, absolutely arrested and imprisoned the secretary of an embassy sent by the elector palatine to Emanuel Philibert, for the purpose of interceding with him in favour of the Waldenses. The only pretext for seizing the secretary was, that he was a protestant pastor; he was, of course, immediately released. In a letter which this official addressed to the Waldenses, he states—"The chancellor Stropiano, in reply to our intercession for you, accuses you of being disturbers of the public peace; says that the Waldenses are conspiring against the state; and cites, in support of this accusation, the case of nine Waldenses who lately assembled in a frontier town, and whom he arrested as conspirators." Now the simple fact, as to this pretended conspiracy, is, that a a few Christians having met for worship in a private house at Bourg, in Bresse, were engaged in prayer, when a number of archers surrounded the house, and took them prisoners. As it was necessary to devise some charge to justify this gross violation of private right, the Waldenses were accused of being suspected of meeting to conspire against the state; and as they could not disprove that they were suspected, they were sent to the galleys.

The Waldenses of Dauphiny and Provence paid at this time, in like manner, their tribute of martyrs to the constant testimony of the Christian church against antichrist.

The valley of La Grave, which slopes from Mont Pelvoux in direction opposite to Val Louise, had been enlightened by some wandering rays of the evangelical light, the focus of which was in the centre of the Waldensian valleys. A pedlar of Villar, a remote village of this valley, after having taken his family to Geneva, to be there instructed and led in the ways of the Lord, himself returned to France in pursuit of his trade. Being a skilful worker in coral, Romeyer proceeded towards Marseilles, for the purpose of purchasing a supply of that article, and on his road endeavoured to dispose of the coral ornaments he had with him.

At Draguignan, he showed them to a goldsmith of the town, named Lanteaume, who greatly admired them, and was desirous of purchasing them; but the parties, not being able to agree about the price, separated. There was at this time at Draguignan, the baron de Lauris, son-in-law of Menier d'Oppede, whose name is written in letters of blood in the history of the Waldenses. Lanteaume, loath to see the property quit the place, insidiously counselled Romeyer to show it to the baron de Lauris, who, being a rich seigneur, might be disposed to purchase it. The cupidity of the baron having been aroused by a sight of the ornaments, Lanteaume went and informed him that the owner was a Lutheran; and as confiscation of goods always accompanied a sentence of death, the two accomplices came at once to an understanding. Romeyer was arrested by order of De Lauris, in April, 1558. After various private interrogatories, in which he made no secret whatever of his religious faith, the tribunal of Draguignan assembled for his trial. An Observantine monk, on the preceding day, celebrated a mass to the Holy Ghost, "in order," as he said, "that the Holy Ghost might inspire the judges to condemn the cursed Lutheran to the flames." But his mass did not produce the effect he desired; for a young advocate, addressing the tribunal, pointed out that Romeyer had been guilty of no legal offence; that he had neither preached nor dogmatized in France; that he was a foreigner; was only occupied in Provence with his trade; and that justice, instead of condemning, ought to protect him. The whole bar supported this argument. The judges were half of them for an acquittal, half for condemnation, and the prisoner was relegated to his dungeon. One of the judges, who had voted for condemnation, had previously been with the prisoner in his cell, seeking to intimidate him, and failing therein, had pronounced against him from the bench.

Upon the decision of the judges being made known, the Observantine monk, who had made a sort of personal matter of the case, and who saw the credit of his masses and his prayers singularly compromised in public opinion by this result of the trial, had the bells of his monastery rung, harangued the mob who assembled at the sound, and insisted that good catholics should not permit an infamous heretic, a Lutheran, an accursed soul, to pollute, with impunity, the devout town of Draguignan with his presence. Having thus excited the populace, the worthy monk proceeded to the official and consuls of the town, representing that their honour was concerned in preserving intact the excellent reputation of their dear city; and then, all together, followed by the infuriated mob, went to the magistrates, vociferating that unless they condemned the heretic to be burned alive, they themselves would denounce them to the parliament, the king, the pope, and to all the powers of the earth, to procure their destruction. Such is the religious fervour of popery!

The lieutenant of the king, who, at this time, was the representative, in each district, of the administration, invoked the respect due to judicial forms, which ought not to be set aside, even against a heretic.

"Kill him! kill him!" cried the people. "Burn him! burn him!" cried the people.

The magistrate, unable to appease the tumult, promised to proceed to Aix, and lay the matter before the parliament.

The populace was, thereupon, about to disperse; but the monk, not satisfied, required that four persons should go to

Aix, at the expense of the town, and urge the condemnation of Romeyer. As these four deputies were on their way, they met one of the presidents of the court of Aix, who said to them: "Surely you need not so many formalities to burn a heretic!" The deputation, upon this hint, turned back, and proceeded to expedite the sentence of death. The lieutenant, who pursued his way to Aix, laid the matter before the court, and the court issued an order that the court at Draguignan should not try the prisoner; but fanaticism was not to be baulked of its prey; Barberi, the attorney-general, repairing to Aix, procured the withdrawal of the prohibition, and permission for the judges at Draguignan to try the prisoner, or in other, words, judicially to assassinate him.

He was condemned to be first racked, then broken on the wheel, and, lastly, burned to death by a slow fire. He might have relieved himself from all these tortures, by abjuration; but the monk, who was sent to make this proposition to him, returned with the announcement that he had found him *pertinax*, infallibly accursed. Forthwith, from all the pulpits round about, it was announced that, on the 16th of May, there would take place the public execution of an atrocious Lutheran; and in the town of Draguignan itself, proclamation was made by sound of trumpet, that every good catholic should bring a billet of wood to form the funeral pyre.

On the appointed morning, the deputy-lieutenant, several judges, lay and ecclesiastic, and the consuls of the town, proceeded to the dungeon of the prisoner, to apply the torture. They displayed before him the rack, the cords, the wedges, the iron bars, all the instruments of torture invented by the successors of the martyr-apostle.

"Denounce your accomplices, abjure your errors, and save yourself these torments," said the deputy-lieutenant

"I have no accomplices," replied Romeyer; "and I have nothing to abjure, for I profess only the law of Christ. You call my profession perverse and erroneous; but, in the day of judgment, God will proclaim it, against its transgressors, just and holy." Thereupon, relates Crispin, he was put on the rack, and cruelly stretched by the cords: in his anguish, he called unto God to have pity on him, for the love of Jesus. "Implore the Virgin," cried the idolaters. "There is but one mediator," replied the sufferer, "even Jesus: oh, God, mercy!" and he fainted; for, upon his refusal to invoke the Virgin, the tormentors had wrested his limbs more cruelly than before. Fearing that he might die before he was burned, the monks and priests disengaged his mangled frame from the wheel; the bones of his legs and arms were broken, and their fractured points came through his flesh. Some cordial was given to him to restore animation, and he was then carried to the place of final execution, and fastened by a chain to the post which rose amid the pyre.

"Invoke the Virgin and the saints," thundered a monk. The poor pedlar could only reply by a faint movement of the head, in the negative. The executioner, thereupon set fire to the pile. At first, being chiefly composed of branches and brushwood, it flamed furiously; but soon subsiding into a mass, the martyr hung suspended from the stake over the devouring heap; his lower limbs were scorched, his entrails came forth, and his poor frame was already consumed below, when his lips were still seen moving, emitting, indeed, no sound, but testifying, within, a last invocation of the martyr to his God, a last appeal to that Christ who had died for him.

I may here give an illustration of the arrogant opposition which the Inquisition, from time to time, manifested towards even the crowned heads who sought to save its victims.

According to the convention at Cavour, in 1561, between Emanuel Philibert and the Waldenses, the latter were in no sort to be proceeded against for any acts which had taken place during the war of 1560. A man of San Giovanni, named Gaspar Orselli, having been taken prisoner at that epoch, had, to save his life, promised to catholicize; but, upon peace being concluded, he had returned to the open profession of the faith which, at heart, he had never abandoned. The inquisitors thereupon had him seized, and confined him in the dungeons of the holy office at Turin. The Waldenses claimed him, in the name of the amnesty, and the duke ordered the inquisitors to release him; but they refused to obey. The edict of Cavour was recalled to them. "Our order is not subject to the secular power," replied the worthy Dominicans, who yet were ever ready to make use of the power they refused to recognize. Philibert, indignant at this insolent rebellion, sent them word that all the frocked legions in the world should not make him break his word, and that, unless they forthwith released the captive, he would batter their house down upon their heads.

At this unexpected menace, the holy office forthwith gave way. Orselli was released, and the duke, to whom all honour is due for his firmness on this occasion, wrote (20th of November, 1570) to the Waldenses, assuring them of his continued protection.

When liberty of conscience was suppressed in Piedmont, the noble family of Bazana, among others retired to the valley of Luzerna, where the evangelical worship was still permitted. A member of this family, Sebastian Bazana who had received his spiritual training from the lips of the pastor Gilles, destined afterwards to become the narrator of his martyrdom, had, after the death of his father, settled with his aged mother, his two brothers, and their families, at La Torre. There his zeal for the Christian faith drew upon him the animosity of the monks, who, watching for the occasion, had him seized at Carmagnola, 26th of April, 1622, and threw him into the dungeons of the castle there, whence, after an imprisonment of four months, he was transferred to those of the senate at Turin. The courageous captive was not without intercessors to solicit his pardon, nor Christian brethren to console him. The latter alone were successful.

"Greatly doth God favour me by your letters and your prayers," he wrote to Gilles on the 14th of July, "for all good comes to us from him, even friendship itself." From the dungeons of the senate he was transferred to those of the Inquisition, at whose gates, as at those of the lower hell, those who enter may leave all hope behind. At first his reception was of the most flattering description, so far as honied words and professions of intense interest in his welfare might go; but the adopted son of the valleys knew these wolves in sheep's clothing too thoroughly to heed their allurements, and the firm calmness with which he adhered to his convictions soon aroused the wrath of the persecutors. The wolves showed their teeth. Menaces of the most cruel character were soon followed up by still more cruel execution: after threat came torture; but the victim yielded not. Many powerful intercessions were made in favour of poor Bazana. Among others, Lesdiguières himself, though he had, some time before, become a papist, wrote thus (15th February, 1623) to the duke of Savoy: "I solicit from your highness the life and liberty of one Sebastian Bazana, a prisoner in your city of Turin. He is a man against whom there is no reproach, save his religion; and if all who profess that religion are to be punished with death, the great Christian princes, with your highness yourself, would have some difficulty in repopulating their states. The king of France has taken all his subjects professing that religion into his peace, and I would counsel your highness to do the same. It will be the surest way of firmly establishing tranquillity throughout your dominions." Lesdiguières followed up this letter by two others to the same purpose, and the duke of Savoy called upon the Inquisition to comply with their benevolent request; but the inquisitors answered, with unctuous humility, that the matter was no longer in their hands, having been submitted to the decision of Rome.

Several months passed away; for a year and a half Sebastian Bazana protested, by his earnest and energetic resignation, against the violence with which the Christian faith was struck in his person. On the 22d of November, 1623, his sentence was announced to him: he was condemned to be burned alive. "I welcome my death," he answered, with courageous gentleness, "since it is the will of God, and will, I trust, be for his glory. But as to men, they have pronounced an unjust sentence, and they will soon have to render their account for it." I know not whether by fortuitous coincidence, or by the judgment of God, but certain it is, that he who had pronounced the iniquitous judgment, was, that very night, struck with death in his own house. His victim followed him the next morning, 23d of November, 1623.

As Bazana was quitting the gates of his prison, on his way to execution, they fastened a bandage over his mouth, in order to stifle his evangelical voice even at the pyre. But as the executioner was tying him to the stake, the bandage fell off, and the martyr thus proclaimed the cause of his death:—"People," he said, "it is for no crime I die, but for seeking to act in conformity with the word of God; to sustain truth against error; to ——." Here the inquisitors stayed him, by putting light to the pile: Bazana set up the song of Simeon, as versified by Theodore Beza, that touching canticle, sung by the faithful of his church after the sacrament:—

"Laisse-moi désormais,
Seigneur, aller en paix,
Car selon ta promesse,
Tu fais voir à mes yeux
Le salut glorieux
Que j'attendais sans cesse!"

But his voice was soon silenced by the flames.

BRIDGE OVER THE GUILL.—(HIGH ALPS.)

Chapter Seventeenth.

THE PROPAGANDA.

CHARLES EMANUEL II. acceded to the throne of Savoy on the 4th of October, 1638, being at that time but four years and some months old. It was under his reign that the most terrible persecutions that ever ensanguined the Waldensian valleys took place, yet we cannot justly make him alone responsible for the crime, since, up to his majority, it was his mother who governed in character of regent. This was Christine of France, daughter of Henry IV. and of Mary de' Medici, who inherited all the hard and haughty attributes of her grandmother, so that it was the spirit of the Medicis, rather than that of the house of Savoy, which presided over the carnage of 1655.

From 1637 to 1642, Thomas and Maurice of Savoy, brothers of the late king, disputed, with his widow, the regency of his states, a struggle which occasioned the most disastrous troubles to Piedmont. Then, from 1642 to 1659, there was the war with the Spaniards, to eject whom from her dominions Christine found herself necessitated to call in the troops of France. All this while, the fomenters of Rome were pursuing their work against the Waldensian valleys; and in these pious labours they were now materially aided by the *Congregatio de Propagandâ Fide*, a society composed of both priests and laymen, established at Rome in 1622, by pope Gregory XV., for the purpose of propagating the catholic faith. This association soon overawed by its influence the secular clergy, who had imprudently admitted it as an ally; and, ere long, the torch of conflagration in one hand, the sword of death in the other, and its feet in blood, it proceeded to the savage extermination of all doctrines not accordant with its own. Nothing was forgotten in its work, except the gospel: and what has it gained? that which persecution ever gains—the burden of crimes committed, the responsibility of blood poured forth, the execration of mankind. It was the prior of Luzerna, Marc' Aurelio Rorengo, who planted in the Waldensian valleys the first shoot of this powerful tree, the branches of which were soon to overspread Piedmont, and cover it with the ensanguined fruits of the most odious fanaticism. A member of the Roman propaganda, a preaching monk, named Placido Corso, noted for his polemical talent, was despatched to the valleys to labour at the conversion of the Waldenses. On arriving, 10th of November, 1637, at La Torre, his first proceeding was to invite the pastor of the place, Gilles, the historian, to a discussion, which was at once accepted. The monk committed to paper all the arguments and data upon which the Roman catholic church arrogates for itself the titles of apostolical and sacred; Gilles refuted these; numerous letters were exchanged in continuation of the controversy, until, at length, Placido Corso left his antagonist's last response unanswered.

Hoping to be more successful in a conference *vivà voce*, where his adversary would not have time for selecting and weighing his arguments, the popish propagandist next applied to Antony Leger, who, recently returned from Constantinople, where he had filled the office of chaplain to the embassy, was now performing the modest duties of pastor in the ancient parish of San Giovanni; and it was agreed that a public conference should take place at La Torre, on the 4th of December, 1637; Rorengo, at his own desire, acting as president, Scipio Bastia, the younger, as secretary for the protestants, and the Capuchin, Fra Lorenzo, as secretary for the catholics.

The first conference was occupied entirely with one of the most difficult questions of canonical theology, that of the apocryphal books. The second conference, which took place on 1st January, 1638, at San Giovanni, lasted till nightfall; after this the propagandist refused to have anything further to say to a set of dogmatists who he affirmed, made a pope of the bible. The bible was to the Waldenses far more than a pope; but the servile slave of the holy see could conceive no similitude more effective. The next controversialists who undertook to combat the Waldensian pastors was a Minorite, brother Hilarion; but after a few letters exchanged with the pastor of Bobbi, Francis Guerin, he also gave up the contest. The victor, however, had subsequently to pay the penalty of his victory, in being (1651) driven from his country by the Inquisition. The weapon of dialectics failing them, the papists had recourse to assassination and abduction. A young man, the servant of an English protestant, Mr. Moreton, was assassinated at La Torre; a girl of Bubiana was carried off by the monks; her brother, who hastened to her assistance, was slain, and the girl herself taken off to Turin, was never afterwards heard of by her friends.

In the contest for the regency, the Waldenses armed in support of the duchess Christine, and, opening a way through the Alps to the French succors under Turenne and D'Harcourt, were the means of restoring to the regent one of the most valuable provinces of her realm. The return for this eminent service was the cruellest ingrati tude. Antony Leger, who had taken the lead in asserting the claims of Christine, was driven from his parish by persecution, under the most frivolous pretext, and compelled to take refuge at Geneva, where he long lived an honoured professor of the Academy. The next act of arbitrary rule on the part of the regent, in her anxiety to win over the popish clergy from her competitor, the cardinal Maurice, of Savoy, was to issue an order (3d November, 1637) for all the Waldenses who had settled out of the precise limits of their valleys, to return within those limits in three days. At about the same time, instructions were communicated to the magistrates in favour of the Capuchin missionaries, upon whose denunciation the magistrates were commanded forthwith to arrest all suspected persons. In the following year (9th November, 1638), another royal decree was published against any territorial extension on the part of the Waldenses, whc were prohibited from purchasing or even farming lands beyond their own narrow limits, on pain of confiscation and death. This prohibtion was renewed in April, 1640; and with it came orders to the prefect of the province, Rossano, to interdict the protestant worship at San Giovanni, and to close the Waldensian church there. To superintend the execution of this edict, there was sent from Turin a special delegate, a doctor of laws of Moncaliere, and auditor of state, noted for his Romish zeal, one Gastaldo. The first proceeding of this official, after having established himself at Luzerna, was to cite before him (14th January, 1641) all such Waldenses as had property beyond the limits that were assigned to them, which limits had just previously been still further narrowed, by interdicting to the Waldenses the right bank of the Pelice. The persons so cited having refused to appear, their property of every description was forthwith confiscated to the public exchequer. Next, in January, 1642, came an edict ordering among other matters, that the Castellans in the Waldensian valleys should lend gratuitous aid to the Capuchin missionaries in all cases where so required by them, should attend all meetings held by the Waldenses, and, were they thought fit, dissolve them. The Waldenses on their part, were prohibited from meeting, except in the presence of the said Castellans, under penalty of fifty golden crowns for each offence and each offender; the edict winding up with promise of exemption from all public charges whatsoever, during the space of five years, to every protestant who would consent to catholicize. On February 17th, 1644, was proclaimed a prohibtion to the Waldenses to quit their limits at all, even for a few hours, except on fair days. On the 18th of September, 1645, the magistrates of the surrounding districts were enjoined to seize all Waldenses found in their localities; the official celebration of the catholic worship was ordered in all the protestant parishes; an establishment, which proved an utter failure, was formed at Luzerna, to receive and endow young Waldensian girls who would consent to abjure. On the 20th of February, 1650, the propagandists obtained an edict suspending all the privileges which had been granted to the Waldenses, until they should have demolished the eleven churches they possessed beyond their own special limits, had dismissed all their foreign pastors, had closed all their numerous trans-territorial schools, and consented to the universal celebration of the catholic worship throughout the valleys. On the 15th of May, in the same year, Gastaldo was directed to restrict the limits of the Waldenses, above San Giovanni and La Torre, and to compel all such as were settled in those communes, and in those of Luzernella, Bubiana, Fenile, and San Segonzo, to quit them within three days, under pain of death, and to sell their properties therein within fifteen days, under penalty of confiscation. The wholly protestant communes of Bobbi, Villar, Angrogna, and Rora, were ordered to maintain each a mission of Capuchins; and foreign protestants were probibited from settling in the valleys, under pain of death themselves, and a penalty of one thousand golden crowns upon the commune that should receive them. Gastaldo, however, little sympathy as he had with the Waldenses, saw the utter monstrosity of this Draconian decree, and by his intervention it was, after a while, withdrawn.

Meanwhile, the propaganda had acquired large development, by the jubilee, which, in 1550, brought to Rome the rich tribute of the superstitious of universal Europe; a sort of popular enthusiasm arose for this work, access to which was open to all catholics, of whatsoever rank, and which procured plenary indulgence for all, princes and peasants alike, who there met, for once, on a common level. Hence, the propaganda made rapid progress, not only in Italy, but in France, having special councils in all the towns of those countries; and it was at this time that it added to its original title, *de propagandâ fide*, the further designation, *et extirpandis hereticis.* The councils were composed of both laymen and ecclesiastics, and there being plenary indulgence for all propagandists, women also took part in the proceedings, so that there were councils of men and councils of women. At Turin, where the institution became established (31st of May, 1650) under the distinguished sanction of a royal ordinance, the male council was presided over by the archbishop of the city and by the marquis di San Tommaso, and the female by the marchioness di Pianeza, who thus sought, in a mistaken religious zeal, to expiate the sins of a dissipated youth.

Every means was resorted to by the propagandists to achieve the aim of their society. "The lady propagandists," writes Leger, "distributed the towns into districts, and each visited the district assigned to her twice a week; suborning simple girls, servant-maids, and young children, by their flattering allurements and fair promises; and doing evil turns to such as would not listen to them. They had their spies everywhere, who, among other information, ascertained in what protestant families domestic disagreements existed; and hither would the propagandists repair, stirring up the flame of dissension in order to separate the husband from the wife, the wife from the husband, the children from the parents; promising them, and, indeed, giving them great advantages, if they would consent to attend mass. Did they hear of a tradesman, whose business was falling off, or of a gentleman who from gambling or otherwise was in want of money, these ladies were ever at hand with their *dabo tibi*, on the condition of apostacy; and the prisoner was, in like manner, released from his dungeon, who would give himself up to them. To meet the very heavy expenses of this proselytizing, to keep the machinery at work, to purchase the souls who sold themselves for bread, regular collections were made in the chapels and in private families, in the shops, in the inns, in the gambling-houses, in the streets—everywhere was alms-seeking in operation, for the extirpation of heresy. The marchioness of Pianeza herself, great lady as she was, used every second or third day to make a circuit in search of subscriptions, even going into the taverns for that purpose. Twice a week the councils assembled to receive an account of what the members had respectively done, to consult what measures should next be taken, and to arrange for securing the aid, where necessary, of the secular arm—an aid, for that matter, never refused to them. The councils in the market towns were in subordination to those of the metropolitan towns; these to those of the capital, and these to that of Rome, the great spider that held the threads of all this mighty web."

All the Waldensian children whom they could abstract from their parents' houses, were considered by these misguided zealots as so many innocents rescued from the jaws of perdition; the greatest sacrifices were incurred, the vengeance of man and the decrees of the laws alike braved, in the abduction of these children, who were then placed with rich catholic families, who undertook their maintenance, or in convents, which undertook to wean them gradually from the world, from their country, from the pure affections of the heart, and from the biblical faith, natural and revealed law being alike scorned by the barbarous spirit of catholicism.

Another *modus operandi* adopted was the establishment at Luzerna, Pignerol, and Perrier, of *Monts de Piété*,* to which the distressed Waldenses eagerly resorted. Confiscations, the continuous billeting of troops upon them, for the last few years, deficient harvests, and several tremendous conflagrations, had gradually reduced the Waldenses to the last stage of penury. These establishments supplied the wretched population with corn, clothing, money on the security of their houses, furniture, land: when a Waldensian was known to have in this way pledged his last resource, to save his family from famine, the propagan-

* Pawn-broker shops.

dists would come to him, offering full and free restitution of all he had pledged, and quittance for the amount borrowed, on condition of his entering the Romish church; or they would have him first thrown into prison for the debt, and then assail him with their treacherous proposals. These means were effective with a few, but the work was found to proceed too slowly.

The marchioness di Pianeza died: when she had given up all hopes of this world, she bethought herself of her husband, whom she had not seen for many years: she sent for him, and said—"I have much to expiate, as towards man and towards yourself; my soul is in danger; aid me to save it, by labouring for the conversion of the Waldenses." The husband gave the promise required: and, as a soldier, sought to fulfil it by soldierly means—by fire and sword. He had a further reason for obeying: his wife left him considerable sums, to be received by him only on the condition of obedience.

It only remained to create a pretext for violence, and this was not difficult to devise. The monastery of Villar had been destroyed by fire in 1563, and the Waldenses had been charged as the incendiaries. At all events, they had been compelled, in the following year, to rebuild the edifice, so that this matter had nothing to do, as has been alleged, with the persecutions of 1655. Some other ground had to be sought. The curê of Fenile had been assassinated; the assassin being arrested, the propagandists promised him a free pardon, if he would make a public confession that he had killed the priest at the instigation of the Waldenses, and, in especial, of Leger, then pastor of San Giovanni. Berru, who had not shrunk from crime involving capital punishment—he had committed two other murders beside that of the curé—did not shrink from a perjury that was to save his life; and upon the denunciation of this reprobate, the pastor of San Giovanni was, without trial, without even citation, condemned to death as instigator of the assassination, while the real murderer was set at liberty.

Just at this time, the troops of Louis XIV., which had been succouring the duke of Modena, were on their return home through the valleys, and it was at once resolved to canton them among the Waldenses, so that they might be ready at hand to aid the persecution.

Chapter Eighteenth

THE MASSACRES OF 1655.

THE various provincial councils *de extirpandis hæreticis* addressed to the metropolitan council at Turin incessant complaints against the Waldenses, and these complaints were as incessantly laid before the duke by the archbishop of Turin and the ministers of state, all of whom were members of the propaganda. It was not until January, 1655, however, that Charles Emanuel, a prince of clement and amiable character, would take any measures in the matter, and he then merely consented to order Gastaldo to carry into effect the edict of May, 1650, for restricting the limits of his Waldensian subjects. The military operations which ensued are not chargeable against the memory of this prince, who, alike with the Waldenses themselves, was made the dupe of the insidious machinations of the propagandists. The Waldenses fell in thousands, victims of systematic and cruel carnage, and the duke found himself put under the ban of the civilized princes of Europe by reason of that carnage.

On 25th January, 1655, Gastaldo issued an order that all the protestant families domiciled in the communes of Luzerna and Luzernella, Fenile, Campiglone, Bubiana, Bricherasio, San Segonza, San Giovanni, and La Torre, should transport themselves into the valley and confines of Bobbi, Villar, Angrogna, and Rorata, the only places in the valley in which his highness would tolerate their religion, and this in the space of three days, under pain of death and of confiscation of goods. They were, besides, directed to sell their lands in the said districts within twenty days. All those who would consent to catholicize were exempted from the decree. Further, it was ordered that the catholic worship should be celebrated in all the protestant communes, the Waldenses being prohibited, under heavy penalties, from in any way impeding or disturbing such celebration; and the pain of death was denounced against any person who should dissuade a protestant from turning catholic. This order directed that all the members of the families indicated should remove; but Gastaldo, at first, contented himself with requiring the removal of the heads of these families. They obeyed, and retired to the upper portions of the valley, whence they addressed an earnest remonstrance to their prince, who, on his part, seemed well disposed to clemency, saying to count Christopher of Luzerna, who interceded for the remonstrants—"I am willing they should remain at San Giovanni and La Torre, provided they will withdraw from the other localities nearer the plain; for their adversaries will not let me have any peace till they have got some such concession." The propogandists, meanwhile, were not idle; they sent a statement to the duke that the Waldenses were in a state of revolt, and had already caused the curé of Fenile to be assassinated. In consequence, when the deputies from the Waldenses again presented themselves at the palace, they were not received, but were ordered to settle the matter with the council of the propaganda. The council, in their turn, refused to receive them, on the ground of their being protestants, and intimated that what they had to say, they must say by the mouth of a popish attorney. The popish attorney was sent; and then the council ordered that deputies must be appointed, competent to subscribe engagements in the name of the whole people. These deputies were sent; but their instructions bearing that they were to sign nothing in diminution of the privileges from time to time conceded to their constituents, the council refused to receive them, until they had procured unlimited powers. The month of March was occupied with the transmission of protocols, memorials, and supplications from the Waldenses to the duke and to the marquis di Pianeza, and with replies on the part of the latter, full of that tone of moderation which is so easily assumed by men of his cold, hard, calculating temperament. At length, in the beginning of April, 1655, a third Waldensian deputation, consisting of two delegates only, repaired to Turin, furnished with full powers, enabling them to accept whatever conditions his highness might be pleased to impose, provided only that their liberty of conscience was not assailed; in which case they were to request from the duke permission for the Waldenses to withdraw altogether from his states.

This was putting the question courageously and unambiguously, so that any answer given could not well be otherwise than also unambiguous. The marquis di Pianeza announced that he would give his answer on the 17th April. The deputies repaired to the palace at the appointed hour; they were told to come at a later period of the day; they returned—his excellency was still not visible; they returned a third time, and were then directed to come next day but one. "What does this mean?"

asked the deputies, the one of the other, filled with impatience and anxiety. They soon learned what it meant.

On the 16th April, the day preceding that on which they had been directed to appear before the marquis, the marquis had quitted Turin, at nightfall, to join the troops who had been directed to await him on the road to the valleys; and on the 17th, while the deputies, full of good faith and confidingness, were repairing to his palace at Turin, Pianeza, in whom Jesuitism had annihilated at once nobility of blood and soldierly honour, was on the threshold of their valleys, at the head of troops about to subject those valleys to devastation and death. These troops were numerous. Besides those already quartered in the valleys, there were the regiment of Grancey, commanded by Du Petit Bourg, which was quartered at Pignerol; the city regiment, commanded by Galeazzo; the regiment of Chablais, commanded by the prince de Montafon; and that of Saint Damian, commanded by captain Saint Damian; the marquis de Pianeza acting as general-in-chief.

On the 17th April, he sent a messenger to La Torre, to order the Waldenses to provide for the entertainment of eight hundred foot and three hundred horse, whom his royal highness had ordered to be quartered in their commune.

"How can his royal highness require us to lodge his soldiers in a place where his last edict has forbidden us ourselves to live?" asked the Waldenses.

"Then why are you here?" retorted the messenger.

"We are here for our affairs; but we have removed our permanent habitation within the limits that have been prescribed to us."

The messenger returned. Towards evening, the marquis, after having passed, without resistance, the line of Bricherasio, Fenile, Campiglone, Bubiana, and San Giovanni, whence the Waldenses had withdrawn, arrived under the walls of La Torre, with the city and Damian regiments. It is readily conceivable that this concentration of troops in the valleys, the avowed designs of the propaganda, the high rank of its supporters, the general excitation of popular fanaticism, the warnings of their friends, the menaces of their enemies, had by this time clearly opened the eyes of the Waldenses to the hostile intentions of the popish party, though they knew not to what extent they had to keep off their guard, or how far they were to trust their sovereign, for the deputies whom they had sent to Turin had not returned. What were they to do? They had prayed to God for counsel, they had advised with their pastors, they had written to Geneva for instruction; the general voice told them to defend themselves; but the uncertainty of their position precluded them from concerting any definite plan. They saw clouds gathering, but they could not imagine the malignity of the tempest that was about to pour down upon them. Had they done so, all hesitation would have disappeared, and the energy of their combined resistance would have been co-equal with their violated rights. In this state of ignorance and indecision, wishing to obey their sovereign and quarter his troops, yet uneasy at seeing in command of those troops one of the chiefs of that propaganda which had vowed their destruction, not venturing either upon confiding compliance or upon determined resistance, they resorted merely to half measures, futile in this case as in all others. Gianavel alone, so early as February, foreseeing the terrible persecution about to befall his co-religionists, had collected together a small body of resolute men, with whom he was prepared to act energetically; but the rest of his countrymen then regarded his proceedings as too distrustful—too violent!

The marquis di Pianeza had arrived under the walls of La Torre at ten o'clock on the night of Saturday, 17th April; his whole army encamped on the plain which extends from Les Appiots to Pra-la-Fera and Les Eyrals. The general-in-chief called upon the Waldenses to entertain his troops; the people in the town, in number not more than three or four hundred, replied that it was impossible for them to provide entertainment for such an army; that there was nothing prepared, and that they must be permitted time for considering the matter. All delay was refused; and the townspeople were ordered forthwith to receive the troops, who would otherwise take forcible possession of the place. Thereupon the Waldenses entrenched themselves behind the barricade which they had hastily constructed at the entrance to their town, opposite the bridge of Angrogna. The marquis di Pianeza attacked this bastion; but the besieged resisted so valiantly, that after three hours' fighting, the enemy had made no progress. But about one in the morning, count Amadeus of Luzerna, who was acquainted with the locality, put himself at the head of the city regiment, and while the other popish troops continued to engage the attention of the besieged, turned the town by the Pelice, advanced silently through the meadows and orchards, and then, entering La Torre by the Strada del Bruni, attacked the Waldenses in the rear. The latter at once faced about, pierced the ranks of the new-comers, and made good their retreat to the hills, having, in the whole engagement, lost only three men. It was now two o'clock in the morning: the Romanist, masters of the town, repaired in a body to the church of the mission, where they chanted a Te Deum, amid vehement vociferations of *Long live the holy Roman church! Hurrah for the holy faith! Down with the Barbetti!* At five o'clock in the morning, the marquis di Pianeza entered the town, "with all his nobility," and took up his quarters in the house of the mission.

It was now Sunday morning—the morning of Palm Sunday, the opening of Holy Week, and the spirit of antichrist burned to signalize this Christian festival by a grand massacre of Christians. That very Sunday, accordingly, immediately after mass, a body of soldiers, under the command of Mario di Bagnolo, departed, by way of diversion, or appropriate preparation for the coming festival, on a "heretic hunt," that is to say, to shoot all the Waldeneses they could find, and burn their houses. In the evening, fresh troops arrived at La Torre, and by Monday, 19th April, the army consisted of not fewer than fifteen thousand men. There was no longer any room for doubt: that ancient project, the extermination of the Waldesens, so maturely prepared and so unhesitatingly avowed by the more zealous partisans of the Romish church, was now, at length, to be effectually executed, and thus did popery design to celebrate the Easter of 1655.

The Waldenses, beholding, from the heights between Angrogna and Tagliarette, devastation and conflagration extending over the plain, put themselves on the defensive, placing sentinels at the advanced points, and small bodies of their militia in the more important passes. But they were poorly armed and inadequately organized, for they had formed no conception of the extent of the perfidy to which they were to be subjected. On the 19th, the troops of the marquis attacked these poor mountaineers simultaneously on the heights of San Giovanni, of La Torre, of Angrogna, and of Bricherasio. The Waldenses contented themselves with defending their posts. They were one against a hundred, but a powerful support sustained them—confidence in God. All the attacks upon them failed: the enemy could not drive them from any one of their entrenchments. The campaign, ultimately so disastrous to them, opened with a victory in their favour.

On the 20th (Tuesday), two attacks only were essayed, one upon the Waldenses of San Giovanni, entrenched at Castello, the other upon the protestants of Tagliarette. Both resulted in favour of the assailed. The former was repulsed with marked success by Captain Grayero; the latter was equally fatal to the assailants, for the Waldenses lost only two men, while of the enemy fifty were killed. Leger, who relates these details, took part in this engagement.

The marquis di Pianeza, finding the large army he commanded thus unavailing against determined resistance occupying advantageous positions, had recourse to a means which, but too often successful against the Waldenses, because they were ignorant of its use, has ever been successful with the Romish church, much of whose power is based on its exercise: he had recourse to perfidy. On the morning of the 21st, two hours before daybreak, he announced, by sound of trumpet, at each of the Waldenses entrenchments, that he was ready to receive deputies, with whom to treat for an accommodation, in the name of the duke of Savoy.

Deputies from all the communes of the valley waited upon him accordingly; he received them with infinite urbanity, entertained them at dinner, and conversed with them for a considerable time. He assured them of the most friendly views towards them, said that the order issued by Gastaldo, on the 25th of January, referred only to the inhabitants of the lower valleys, whom it was deemed expedient to remove into the mountains, but that the communes of the upper valley had absolutely nothing whatever to apprehend. He expressed the utmost regret for the excesses which had been committed by his soldiers, and, imputing them to the difficulty of enforcing discipline upon so large a body of troops, insidiously took the occasion to say that it was for the very purpose of effecting a better command over them that he had wished to distribute them; then, representing to the deputies the personal favour they would confer upon their sovereign by receiving, for a while, each commune a single regiment, he expressed his conviction that the duke, touched with so great a mark of confidence, would be induced to recall the decree which affected the Waldenses of the plain.

The deluded deputies promised their best assistance, and accordingly, despite the energetic opposition of Gianavel and Leger, the communes consented to receive the troops of the marquis di Pianeza. That very evening they took possession of all the roads, installed themselves in the villages and houses, and, regardless of the order given them to behave with caution, did not even await the morning to massacre several of the heretics.

Their impatience betrayed them. In their eagerness to secure the strong positions in the mountains, while two regiments took the ordinary road to Villar and Bobbi, and a third that of Angrogna, a special detachment began the ascent of Campo La Rama and of Costa Rossina, in order to arrive the more speedily at Pra-del-Tor. This detachment, on its way, set fire to the scattered village of Tagliarette; the smoke of the burning houses was seen, the cries of the fugitives and the shouts of their pursuers were heard, on the hill of Rorata, where a signal of distress was immediately lighted, and almost as immediately perceived from the heights of Angrogna, whither most of the inhabitants of the plains, expelled from Bubiana, Campiglone, &c., by the order of Gastaldo, had taken refuge. The inhabitants of Angrogna, thus aroused, saw in their turn, the approach towards them of the invading detachment, which, on its way to Pra-del-Tor, was triumphantly descending the opposite hill. On the other side, towards Le Porte d'Angrogna was seen advancing the regiment of Grancey. Thereupon the people of Angrogna lighted also their signal fires; and cries of—*To Perosa! To Perosa! To La Vachara! Treachery!* and so on, spread, like electric flames, along the mountain slopes, whence all the men capable of bearing arms hastily withdrew to the heights of La Vachera, and thence by the valley of Pramol, to those of Perosa and Pragela, which at that period belonged to France.

At Bobbi the alarm was raised less promptly, for the regiments of Bagnolo and of Petit Bourg, the former of which was to be quartered at Bobbi, and the other at Villar, arrived quietly by the ordinary road. Some apprehensions were, indeed awakened when it was found that the soldiers, instead of confining themselves to Bobbi, extended their occupation to Sarcena and Villanova; but still the officers declared their resolution to maintain the strictest discipline, and the isolated murders which had been perpetrated by the soldiers on the way had not, as yet, reached the knowledge of the Waldenses.

At Angrogna even, where they found only a few women, children, and old men, feeble guardians of the deserted village, the soldiers abstained, at first, from any excess. Di Pianeza contented himself apparently, with taking up merely his temporary abode there, in order to refresh himself and his men for a few days; and meanwhile sought to gain the confidence of the Waldensian children and women, whom he urged to recall their fathers and husbands, on the assurance that no evil was designed them. Some few returned accordingly: woe to them! *Non servanda fides hæretics*, said the council of Constance: *Ad extirpandos hæreticos*, cried the propaganda. In a day or two, the length and breadth of the valley, its villages, its houses, its roads, and its rocks, were occupied by the assassins in the pay of the propaganda; and now these assassins were called upon to do their work. On Saturday, 24th April, 1655, at four o'clock in the morning, the signal for a general massacre of the Waldenses was given to the traitorous troops, from the tower of the castle of La Torre. The soldiers, forewarned, had risen early, fresh with the sleep they had enjoyed under the roofs of those they were about to slaughter. The men whom, under the solemn engagement of security and protection, the Waldenses had fed and housed, were now on foot, throughout the valley, converted, by the arts of Rome, from brave soldiers into cowardly assassins.

To give an adequate idea of the horrors that ensued, one's eye must, at a single glance, comprehend the entire valley, take in each house, each room, view every act of death and torment, distinguish, amid the immense voice of aggregate anguish and desolation, each particular cry of destroyed honour, of parting existence. Literally, indeed, did the unhappy Waldenses suffer the things of which the apostle speaks: "They were stoned, they were sawn asunder, were tempted, were slain with the sword: they wandered about in sheepskins and goatskins; being destitute, afflicted, tormented; (of whom the world was not worthy:) they wandered in deserts and in mountains, and in dens and caves of the earth." Young children, writes Leger, were torn from their mothers' arms, dashed against the rocks, and their mangled remains cast on the road. Sick persons and old people, men and women, were burned alive in their houses, or hacked in pieces, or mutilated in horrible ways, or flayed alive, or exposed bound and dying to the sun's noontide heat, or to ferocious animals; some were stripped naked, bound in the form of a ball, the head forced down between the legs, and then rolled over precipices; some of these poor creatures, torn and mangled by the rocks, but stayed in their downward progress by the branch of a tree, or other prominence, were seen, forty-eight hours after, still lingering in all the torments of pain and famine.

Women and girls, after being fearfully outraged, were impaled on pikes, and so left to die, planted at angles of the road; or they were buried alive; or, impaled as above, they were roasted before a slow fire, and their burning bodies cut in slices, by these *soldiers of the faith* as by cannibals. After the massacre, such children as survived, and could be seized, were carried off, and cast, like lambs into a slaughter-house, into the monasteries and convents and private abodes of the propagandists. Next, after massacre and abduction, came incendiarism: monks and priests, and other zealous propagandists, went about with lighted torches and projectiles, burning down the houses, previously ensanguined by the soldiers with the blood of their owners and their families. The terrible narrative given by Leger of these atrocities, was prepared by him from the testimony of eye-witnesses, who gave their depositions before two notaries, who accompanied him from commune to commune for that purpose. The pen, he says, well-nigh fell from his hand, as he transcribed the horrible details. Here, a father had seen his children cut in pieces by the sword, or absolutely torn limb from limb by four soldiers; there the mother had seen her only daughter cruelly massacred before her face, after having been as cruelly outraged; there the sister had seen her brother's mouth filled with gunpowder, and the head then blown to atoms; there the husband had seen his wife, about to become a mother, treated in a manner which it would outrage humanity to describe. Of these, the eyes were torn from the head; of those, the nails from the fingers; some were tied to trees, their heart and lungs were cut from them, and they were thus left to die in anguish. The universal conflagration of the Waldensian houses succeeded the massacre of their inhabitants. In several communes, not a single cottage was left standing; so that this fair valley of Luzerna, as Leger expresses it, resembled a burning furnace, whence cries, fewer and fainter, attested that a people had lived.

All these victims might have lived, had they consented to abjure their faith. Some who were saved from immediate death, were thrown into prison, and there subjected to continuous torturings to compel them to apostacy. James and David Prins, of Baudena, near Villar, were taken to the prison of Luzerna, and there, having resisted the utmost solicitations of the priests, their arms, from the shoulder to the elbow were first flayed in strips, which, the upper end remaining uncut floated on the living flesh beneath; then, the arms, from the elbow to the hand, were flayed in like manner; then the thighs to the knee, and then the legs, from the knees to the soles of the feet; and in this condition they were left to die. These Prins were two of a family of six brothers, who, having married six sisters, lived with their families altogether on one farm, having no separation of goods, but each having his particular task; some in the vineyards, some in the cattle-yard; and all the forty persons of whom this combined family consisted, living together without the least discord, the eldest brother and sister, being as it were, father and mother to the rest. Yet these scenes, so patriarchal, so pure, so touching, so simple, so Christian, were made a prey to the demon of popery, cruel in its superstition beyond the cruelty of the most barbarous savages.

A farm servant of Bobbi, refusing to apostatize, had the palms of his hands and the soles of his feet pierced with dagger thrusts; he was then barbarously mutilated, and suspended over a fire, in order that the flame might stay the effusion of blood. Next, his nails were torn from his fingers with pincers; and as he still adhered to his religion, he was then tied by the feet to the tail of a mule, and so dragged through the streets of Luzerna. Seeing him now at the point of death, his executioners tied a cord so tight round his head that the eyes and the brain were forced out; and the mangled carcass was then thrown into the river.

From the bell-tower of the catholic church of St. Germain l'Aúxerrois issued the signal of the massacre of St. Bartholomew! From the cathedral of Palermo was announced the Sicilian vespers! From the tower of St. Mary, in the castle of La Torre, glared the fire that lit up the Piedmontese Easter. Oh, Mary! mother of the Saviour! if any sword pierce thy breast, it is that of the church which pretends to honour thee the most; the church which, calling thee queen of the angels, represents thee to the world as queen of the demons!

So monstrous were the cruelties with which the work of extermination was accompanied, that several, even of the officers who had been appointed to execute it, were struck with horror, and resigned their commands, rather than fulfil their orders. In consequence of the general indignation expressed by the protestant states of Europe, upon receiving intelligence of the massacre, the duke of Savoy thought it expedient to publish a statement of the transaction. This narrative, printed in Italian, French, and Latin, under the title of *The Factum of the Court of Savoy*, though it endeavoured to make out a favourable case for the duke's government, and charged the Waldenses with bringing all the mischief upon themselves, yet acknowledged quite enough to show that the atrocities complained of had really been perpetrated.

Chapter Nineteenth.

GIANAVEL.

We have mentioned that the Waldenses of Angrogna and the fugitives from the plain of Piedmont had, for the most part, retired to the valley of Perosa. Those of San Martin, forewarned by a benevolent catholic of the approach of the marquis Galeazzo, with orders to put everything to fire and sword, had hastened to the valley of Pragela, while such of the inhabitants of Bobbi as had escaped the massacre had made their way to Queyras, over the rocks and snows, all these places of refuge being then under the rule of the king of France.

In the hope of excluding the Waldenses from this hospitable country, the duchess of Savoy, who seems to have taken a far more active share than her son in these calamitous events, wrote to the court of France in order that the Waldenses might be restricted within their own valleys and there massacred; but Mazarin replied that humanity prescribed to him the duty of affording an asylum to the fugitives.

This concession enabled the latter to rally, to arm, and to organize themselves, with every prospect of returning to their native country more numerous than they had left it, for in these retreats many of their co-religionists from Queyras and Pragela joined them. Meantime, an ener-

SCENE IN THE VALLEY OF ISERE, NEAR TIGNES.

getic and able man, sustained, doubtless, by the hand of God (in whom none had ever a more absolute and unquestioning confidence than had this intrepid warrior), Captain Joshua Gianavel, who alone had foreseen the contemplated treachery, kept the hostile army in check, and by degrees drove it from the valleys.

It will be remembered that the 24th of April was the day fixed for the general massacre of the Waldenses; troops had accordingly been quartered in all the larger villages and towns, excepting Rora, which, however, it was by no means designed to spare. On the morning of the day of extermination, the marquis of Saint-Damian had despatched from Villar, to surprise Rora, a battalion of five or six hundred soldiers, under the command of count Christopher of Luzerna, who was called count of Rora, that village being his appanage. These soldiers had crossed the river, and were ascending the little hill of Rumer, when Gianavel, who lived at the foot of an extension of the mountain towards Luzerna, saw the soldiers approaching the menaced village. He at once hastened to ascend the hill by a different route, and collecting on his way six men, determined as himself, and excellent marksmen, posted them advantageously, and long before the troops expected, if at all, to be received by an armed force, and even before they deemed it requisite to form in any regular order, they were received by a fire of musketry from front, and right and left, so surely directed that seven soldiers fell dead; their comrades retrograded, and those in the rear, imagining there was a numerous ambush at hand, turned round, so that the vanguard were separated from the main body. The Waldenses concealed amid the rocks, which rendered it impracticable for the enemy to ascertain their real number, fired discharge after discharge, until the vanguard, in utter confusion, and with half their number slain, also turned and hastened up the hill they had just turned. The rear, which had scarcely attained the summit, seeing the van returning, themselves hastened back at utmost speed, without even waiting to see the assailants, and all fled together towards Villar; on their way, they had to traverse a wood, which lies between the mountains and the Pelice. Gianavel and his men pursued, but in such a manner as still to keep out of sight; and, concealed, as they advanced, by the trees and shrubs, poured a murderous fire upon the fugitives.

On his return to Rora, Gianavel informed the inhabitants of the peril which had menaced them. Ignorant of the massacres which, during the same day, had been perpetrated in the valley of Luzerna, the Rorans went to the marquis di Pianeza to complain of the aggression which had been essayed against them. He affected to disclaim the whole proceeding. "If any attempted to attack you," said he, "it was not by my orders; the troops under my command would never commit such an outrage. It must have been some party of brigands or Piedmontese vagabonds, and I only wish you had cut them all in pieces. However, I will take care that no such thing shall occur again."

Non servanda fides hæreticis! On the very next morning, five hundred soldiers were despatched to accomplish what the other detachment had failed in doing. Gianavel was again on foot; he had at this time sixteen men with him, a small force, numerically, but, under his command, and in such a cause, equivalent to an army. Of these seventeen men, eleven were fully armed, the rest had only slings. Gianavel disposed them in three parties, two slingers with each; the post he had selected was a defile, in which scarcely ten men could manœuvre. No sooner was the van of the popish detachment engaged in this defile, than the Waldenses fired; an officer and ten men fell beneath the discharge, which was immediately followed up by a vigorous volley of stones from the slings; disorder at once arose in the enemy's ranks, and, at the cry, *All is lost! save yourselves!* the entire troop turned round, and commenced a precipitate flight. Gianavel and his men pursued them, leaping from rock to rock like panthers, by their agility, their vigour, and their intrepidity, so multiplying their numbers, that the enemy had no idea but that they were a large force, while their position behind the brushwood and the rocks enabled them to take that deadly aim, which, with the enemy, was quite impracticable; so that no fewer than fifty-two of the soldiers were slain ere they made good their retreat to the plains of Luzerna.

The marquis di Pianeza, thus again frustrated in his projects, sent count Christopher to Rora, to assure the inhabitants of his friendly intentions towards them, and that the advance of the troops against their valley had been the result of a misunderstanding. Certain representations, he said, had been made against them, the falsity of which had been since fully ascertained; and they had now nothing further to fear. He then proceeded to assemble a battalion more numerous than either of the previous, fully resolved at length to accomplish his purpose. It would seem as surprising that the Waldenses should permit themselves to be deceived by such assurances, as that a gentleman should make them, were it not that the former, as protestants, regarded lying a sin, whereas the latter, as a propagandist, deemed it a virtue.

Next day, the 27th of April, a whole regiment made a rapid march upon Rora, occupied the approaches, and then finding the inhabitants fled, plundered and burned the houses, and set out on their return with their booty, driving before them all the herds of the Rorans, who had themselves taken refuge in Monte Friolante. Gianavel, with his men, had seen the advance of the enemy, but their numbers had rendered it futile for him to assail them on their way. When, however, he perceived them returning, laden with booty and encumbered with the herds they were driving before them, he encouraged his sixteen companions, and, after an earnest supplication to Almighty God, hastened to occupy an advantageous position at a place called Damassero. Hence, as the first ranks of the enemy appeared, they were assailed with a fatal discharge. Unknowing what might be the numbers of the assailing force, and unwilling to abandon their booty, the soldiers, upon witnessing the fall of their comrades, turned about, and drew off towards Villar. The Waldenses, better acquainted with the locality than were the foreigners, took a bye-path, which led them past the enemy, to a place called Pian-Pra, a commanding post near the summit of the mountain that separates Rora from Villar. Presently the hostile army made its appearance, advancing slowly with its booty, and in complete disorder, for its adversaries had disappeared, and it fancied that it would meet with no further obstruction.

Suddenly, a discharge, point blank, prostrated fourteen or fifteen of its numbers. The soldiers, instead of seeking to defend themselves, hurried on their march with their booty. They were now on the slope of the mountain, and, availing themselves of this circumstance, Gianavel's party rolled down an avalanche of great stones upon them. As they were hurrying aside to avoid this storm, the Waldenses with fierce shouts dashed down upon them; this completed their confusion, and, leaving their booty behind them, they fled, each man for himself. The great bulk of the regiment reached Villar, but many remained behind, slain on the ascent, or hurled from the precipices. On regaining the Pian-Pra, Gianavel called upon his men to halt. "Let us," he said, "return thanks." The whole party knelt. "O Lord God," exclaimed their intrepid leader, "we bless thee for having preserved us! Protect our people in these calamities, and increase in us thy faith!" This brief address was followed by the Lord's Prayer, and the Apostle's Creed, and the Waldenses then rising, sought their families in their mountain retreat.

The marquis di Pianeza, frantic with rage and shame at hearing of this new check, commanded that a simultaneous attack should be made upon the Waldenses by all the royal forces from Bagnolo, Cavour, Barges, Bubiana, and Villar. All these were to assemble on a given day and hour at Luzerna; but the ardent slaughterer of Bobbi, Mario di Bagnolo, resolved to appropriate the entire glory of destroying the "miserable handful of adventurers," as the heroic mountaineers who so valiantly defended their faith and their families were designated, marched to the attack two hours in advance of the other troops. He had with him three companies of regulars, one of Piedmontese volunteeers, and a brigade of Irish, who, banished by Cromwell from their own country for the cruelties exercised by them on their protestant countrymen, had been welcomed as brothers by the massacrers of the Waldenses. These worthies, to encourage their zeal, had been promised the gratuitous cession of the lands depopulated of the Waldenses whom they should kill, so that fanaticism and self-interest, the two most potent incentives to courage, urged them on.

Bagnolo arranged his troops in two squadrons, one of which took the right side, the other the left, of the valley of Rora. He reached, without resistance, the rocks of Rumer, signalized, four days previously, by the first victory of Gianavel, and in which that chieftain had again entrenched himself, his little troop being now augmented to the number of thirty or forty men. But the right wing of the count di Bagnolo, having advanced along the heights, were above the rocks of Rumer, and, suddenly showing themselves, menaced the Waldenses with an attack in the rear, while the other wing of the enemy assailed them in the van. Gianavel, with that promptitude of decision and that energy of action which characterize military genius, at once saw what course to adopt, and at once adopted it. *To the summit!* he cried; and, turning about, he left the troops below to pursue their slow and toilsome ascent, while himself and his men, taking steady aim at the troops above, who were just turning the point of the hill, and had not yet had time to form, fired a deadly volley, and then instantly throwing themselves flat on their faces, avoided the discharge which the enemy returned. Amid the smoke of that discharge, the Waldenses then turned suddenly to the right, and, sword in hand, cut their way through the left wing of the assailants, weakened in number by the concentration which the fire of the Waldenses had just attracted in the opposite direction. In a few moments, they were on the summit which Gianavel had indicated to them, and there, posting themselves amongst the rocks, and, strong in the triple energy of a just cause, confidence in their God, and recent success, they intrepidly faced the foe. It was to no purpose that the two detachments, now combined, advanced to assail them: they could not get beyond a certain point; for there the semicircle which they formed, with each surging movement onward, found its first ranks prostrated by the unerring fire of the practised marksmen above themselves, protected from harm by their position. As the snow melts away from the hill-side under the fire of the sun, so did these troops melt away under the fire of the Waldenses, till at length, their heads growing confused at this so unexpected result, a panic seized them, they turned, and fled, leaving sixty-five of their number dead on the spot, besides the wounded and the dead whom they carried off with them.

The Waldenses wished to pursue them along the valley, but Gianavel, with sounder judgment, hastening along the heights, passed the fugitives below, and awaited them, with his invincible fusileers, at a narrow pass called Pierro Capillo. By and bye, the soldiers came slowly on, taking breath after their flight, and observing no order, in the supposition that their foes had departed. All at once, a fresh discharge of fatal musketry assailed them; heavy rocks rolled down upon them; and then, with vehement shouts, a body of men, whose numbers, amid the rocks and brushwood, they could not count, precipitated themselves, sword and pistol in hand, upon them. Resistance was not even attempted: a panic terror, or rather the fear of the God of Jacob, seized upon these utterly amazed troops, so that, instead of fleeing, as best they might, along the road before them, they threw themselves over the rocks and precipices, or essayed to let themselves down by ropes and roots, so that most of their number perished, either drowned in the torrent below, or dashed against the rocks, or slain by the lead and the steel of their adversaries. Their leader himself, with difficulty extricated from a deep pool, was conveyed, wounded, bruised, and half naked, to Luzerna, where he died a few days afterwards.

So great was the exasperation of the marquis di Pianeza, that he assembled all the disposable troops under his command, and actually marched ten thousand men against the little commune of Rora, defended with such perseverance by a handful of mountaineers. This was in the commencement of May, 1655. Three thousand soldiers advanced from Bagnolo, three thousand from Villar, and six thousand from Luzerna, to assail, with a combined effort, a little village of fifty houses, already half burned down.

The battalion coming from Villar arrived first. Gianavel attacked it from the heights; but meanwhile the other troops occupied the lower portion of the valley, pillaged the village, burned the buildings, committed the most monstrous outrages, and carried off as prisoners such of the wretched inhabitants as had not perished in the attack. The position had become untenable; Gianavel had nothing now to defend; Rora was destroyed, its inhabitants killed or captives. He retired with his heroic cohort to the valley of Luzerna.

The next day he received from the marquis di Pianeza, a letter in the following terms: "To captain Gianavel. Your wife and daughters are in my hands, having been made prisoners at Rora. I exhort you, for the last time, to abjure your heresy, as the only means of securing from his royal highness pardon for your rebellion, and of saving your wife and daughters, who will be burned alive if you do not surrender. As to yourself, if you persist in your obstinacy, I shall not trouble myself to send any more troops after you, but simply put such a price upon your head as, had you the devil himself in you, would ensure your being taken, dead or alive; and if you fall alive into my hands, be sure there are no torments so cruel but that you shall undergo them. This letter is for your guidance: I advise you to profit by it." This was Gianavel's reply: "There is no torment so cruel that I should not prefer it to the abjuration of my faith; and your menaces instead of deterring me from, fortify me still more firmly in, that faith. As to my wife and children, they well know how dear they are to me; but God alone is master of their lives, and if you make their bodies perish, he will save their souls. May he receive them into his grace; them and me, if it befal me to come into your hands."

A price was immediately set upon the head of the heroic mountaineer.

A son was left to him, a young boy, who had been entrusted to the charge of a relative at Villar. Fearing that he too might be made a prisoner, the intrepid father conveyed the child across the Alps into Dauphiny, where he left him in the care of a friend. Then, after giving a few days' rest to his devoted band, and recruiting its numbers from among the Waldenses of Dauphiny, he returned to the valleys, and, stronger, more formidable, and more feared than ever, resumed hostilities against the enemies of his faith and of his people.

Meanwhile the moderator of the Waldensian churches, Leger, had repaired to Paris, where he had printed a manifesto, addressed to all the protestant powers of Europe, in reply to which, expressions of the most vivid sympathy and the most active interest came from all directions. No foreign power took so energetic and spirited a part in behalf of the Waldenses at this fatal crisis, as England. Cromwell, as soon as he was informed of what was going on in the valleys, addressed a Latin letter, the composition of Milton,* and of which the following is a translation, to the duke of Savoy:—

"Most serene Prince,

"We are informed by letters received from several places in the vicinity of your dominions, that the subjects of your royal highness, professing the reformed religion, have been commanded by an edict, published by your authority, to quit their habitations and lands, within three days after the promulgation of the said edict, under pain of death, and the confiscation of their property, unless they shall enter into an engagement to abjure their own, and to embrace the Roman catholic faith, before the end of twenty days. We have learnt also, that, regardless of their humble petitions to your highness, praying that you would be pleased to revoke the said edict, and to grant the same privileges which were anciently conceded by your serene ancestors, your army fell upon them, cruelly slaughtered great numbers, imprisoned others, and drove the rest to fly for refuge to desolate places, and to mountains covered with snow, where hundreds of families are reduced to such extremity, that, it is to be feared, they will all shortly perish with cold and hunger. Upon receiving intelligence of the melancholy condition of this most oppressed people, it was impossible not to feel the greatest commiseration and grief; for we not only consider ourselves united to them by common ties of humanity, but by those of the same religion. Feeling, therefore, that we are invoked by the sacred voice of brotherly love, we declare that we should fail in our duty to ourselves, to God, to our brethren, and to the religion we profess, if we were not deeply

* The original, in the handwriting of the poet's second daughter Mary, is preserved in the State Paper Office.

moved by a sense of their calamities, and if we did not employ every means in our power to obtain an alleviation of their unparalleled sufferings. It is on this account that we most earnestly entreat, and conjure your highness, in the first place, to call to mind the enactments of your serene ancestors, and the concessions which they made and confirmed from time to time in favour of the Waldenses: which concessions were granted, no doubt, in obedience to the will of God, who desires that liberty of conscience should be the inviolable right of every man, and in consideration of the merits of these their subjects, who have ever been found valiant and faithful in war and obedient in time of peace. And as your serene highness has graciously and nobly trodden in the steps of your predecessors in all other things, we again and again beseech you, that you will not depart from them in this instance, but that you will revoke this edict, and any other that is oppressive to your subjects, in consequence of their professing the reformed religion; that you will restore them to their paternal habitations and property; that you will confirm their ancient rights and privileges; that you will cause reparation to be made for their injuries; and order an end to be put to all vexatious proceedings against them. If your highness will comply with this request, you will do what is most acceptable to God; you will comfort and support the minds of those unhappy sufferers, and you will be conferring a favour upon the neighbouring protestant states, and especially upon us, who will ever consider such clemency as the effect of our intercession; which will constrain us to do every kind office in return, and will be the means not only of strengthening, but of renewing and increasing the relations and friendship which have subsisted between this commonwealth and your dominions. Promising ourselves much from your justice and moderation, we heartily pray God to direct your minds and thoughts, and so to grant you and your people the blessings of peace and truth, and to prosper all your undertakings.

"Given at our court at Westminster, the 25th day of May, 1655.

"OLIVER, PROTECTOR."

On the other hand, the court of Savoy, or rather the duchess, under the influence of the propaganda and of the pontificial nuncio, pursued with vigour the great aim of the papists, the expulsion or extermination of the evangelical worshippers of the valleys. From Mazarin, who had refused to deny the Waldenses a refuge in France, a promise was obtained, that, at all events, no Frenchmen should aid the Waldenses in their valleys.

The captain of the Swiss guards of the duke of Savoy, a native of Glaris, in which canton there were a number of catholic families dissatisfied with living in a protestant country, proposed to Charles Emanuel to exchange these families for an equal number of protestant families from the valleys. Cromwell, on his part, offered to settle the Waldenses in Ireland, in place of the natives whom he had found it expedient to expel. But the reply of the moderator was more conformable with the interests of his own country. He supplicated the Protector rather to send a plenipotentiary to Turin, to negotiate the re-establishment of the Waldenses in their valleys, than to remove them. The plenipotentiary sent in accordance with this request was Sir Samuel Morland, who performed a leading part in the pacification of this unhappy country, and who afterwards wrote a remarkable history of the events which had occurred there.

Most of the protestant powers added their representations to those of England in favour of the Waldenses, and celebrated fasts and made pecuniary collections in their interest, Cromwell taking the lead also in this matter. He had a narrative printed and dispersed through Britain, setting forth the distress of the Waldensian church, and recommending a general subscription. He himself set the example of liberality, by contributing two thousand pounds from the privy purse; and a sum was shortly raised amounting to not less than thirty-eight thousand two hundred and forty-one pounds, of which, however, only about twenty-two thousand reached the Waldenses. Charles II. at the Restoration, to his everlasting disgrace, appropriated the rest of this sum to the gratification of his mistresses, saying, when interrogated about it, that he was under no obligation to pay the debts of a usurper!*

Another measure of the Protector was to address letters of urgent recommendation to the protestant sovereigns and

* The subsequent history of this matter is curious. The sixteen thousand three hundred and thirty-three pounds, which Charles so infamously squandered, had been reserved by the Protector as a permanent fund for the assistance of the Waldenses in time to come. In the reign of William III., the queen consort, Mary, desirous of effacing the national disgrace, gave to the Waldenses, during her life, an annual pension of four hundred and twenty-five pounds. This ceased with her death. It was afterwards renewed by queen Anne, and the sum increased to five hundred pounds. This sum continued to be issued from the royal exchequer, until the year 1797, under the name of royal bounty. The valleys coming for a time under the dominion of France, the pension was then discontinued, and the subject was soon lost sight of by those in power. At length, Dr. Gilly and other British Christians succeeded, in 1827, in calling the attention of the government to the subject, and in having the annuity restored. It was, however, reduced to two hundred and seventy-seven pounds.

states, that they should come forward in support of the protestant interest. To the king of Sweden he represented the noble conduct which his royal progenitors had pursued, when the reformed religion was menaced in Germany. In a strain of equal eloquence he explained to the king of Denmark the motives of policy which should induce all protestant princes to make a common cause with those who were defending such as were persecuted for the reformed faith. "We proclaim," said he, in a tone which was likely to fix the resolution of the wavering, "that we are prepared, in conjunction with your majesty, and our other allies of the reformed religion, to use every means in our power to relieve the wants, and secure the safety and liberty of the unhappy sufferers."

In a letter to the States General, he reminded their High Mightinesses of the effectual struggles which they themselves had happily made in the adverse times of the protestant church in their own country, and declared his readiness to take any measures, in conjunction with them, for the preservation of the same faith in the valleys of Piedmont. The Protector's negotiation with the king of France was still more honourable to his character, because he had the difficult undertaking of persuading one Roman catholic prince to act against another. His first letter to his Most Christian Majesty boldly touched upon a very delicate topic, and intimated that the troops of France had been concerned in the cruelties in Piedmont.

"Most Serene King,

"The groans of those wretched men, the protestant inhabitants of Luzerna and Angrogna, and other Alpine valleys, within the dominions of the duke of Savoy, who were lately most cruelly murdered, and the lamentable tidings of the despoliation and the banishment of the survivors of this massacre, which have reached our ears, have constrained us to write this letter to your majesty: more particularly as it has been reported to us (with what truth has not yet been ascertained), that this carnage has been committed by some of your own troops, conjointly with those of the duke of Savoy. It is scarcely possible to believe that such proceedings have been resorted to, for they are neither consistent with the principles of good government, nor with those of your majesty's wise ancestors, who judged that they were best consulting their own interests, and the peace not only of their own kingdom, but of all christendom, by permitting their subjects of the reformed religion to live securely and quietly under their protecting sceptre: in return for which indulgence, those grateful men did often perform the most eminent services for their sovereigns, both in peace and war. The dukes of Savoy, in like manner, were wont to treat their subjects of the Alpine valleys with the same benignity; who, on their side, also displayed the most devoted loyalty, and never spared either their lives or their fortunes in the service of their princes. We feel confident, that your majesty's influence and authority with the duke of Savoy are such, that if you would only employ your mediation, and express your good wishes, you would obtain indemnity for these poor people, and their restoration to their country and former privileges. Such an act would not only be worthy of your majesty, and of the wise example of your ancestors, but would re-assure your own subjects, who would then feel that they need entertain no fears on their own account; and it would conciliate your protestant confederates and allies, and bind them to your majesty by the strongest ties of respect and affection. With regard to ourselves, whatever indulgence shall be conceded to your own subjects of the reformed religion, or obtained by your intercession for the subjects of others, will be received not only with the same, but even with greater gratitude than we could express for any personal favour that we hope to derive from your majesty's friendship.

"Given at our court at Westminster, the 25th of May, 1655.

"OLIVER, PROTECTOR."

In a second letter, Cromwell gave the king of France to understand, that he expected him, not only to employ his mediation with the duke of Savoy, in behalf of the Waldenses, but to afford shelter and protection to such as should fly for refuge into the French dominions.

"Most Serene and most Potent King,

"I am happy to understand, from your majesty's letter in answer to mine of the 25th of May last, that I was not wrong in the opinion, that those most cruel murders, and barbarous massacres, committed by certain troops of yours upon the professors of the reformed religion in Savoy, had neither your command nor authority. I am also extremely rejoiced to find that your majesty has signified your strong disapprobation to your military commanders, who took upon themselves to perpetrate such atrocities without your orders; and that you have remonstrated with the duke of Savoy upon the subject of such monstrous cruelty, and have interposed your influence and good offices with so much humanity and earnestness, for the restoration of those unhappy exiles. I did hope that that prince would have conceded something to the intercession of your majesty; but since neither your mediation, nor that of the other sovereigns and states, has been of any avail in their favour, I have thought it my imperative duty to send an ambassador extraordinary to the duke, to give a full explanation of my sentiments, in regard to his excessive cruelty towards the professors of the same religion with ourselves, on no other account but their religion. And in order to promote the success of this mission, I trust your majesty will be pleased to renew your remonstrances, and to give them greater weight than before: and as your majesty has already declared yourself responsible for the fidelity of these poor people to their prince, so you will now take upon yourself to guarantee their security and protection, that repetition of such inhuman cruelty may not be inflicted upon them again. We cannot but expect this from your majesty, as being nothing but a just and royal proceeding, and perfectly consistent with the benignity and clemency with which you have watched over the safety and welfare of so many of your subjects who profess the same religion. By such an act you will conciliate the affections of all the protestants throughout your kingdom, who have given you so many proofs of their loyalty and attachment; and you will satisfy those of foreign nations, that you are not implicated in this iniquity, however much your ministers of state and commanders may be: more especially if your majesty will punish those ministers and commanders who have presumed, upon their own authority and out of their own malignity, to commit such monstrous atrocities. In the mean time, since your majesty disavows this most inhuman and detestable policy, I am confident you will give shelter and protection to such of the distressed refugees as shall fly into your dominions for an asylum, and will not suffer any of your own subjects to assist the duke of Savoy against them. It remains for me to assure your majesty of the value I set upon your friendship, and of my readiness, at all times to give proof of the sincerity of my respect.

"Given at our court at Westminster, July, 31, 1655."

In pursuance of this interposition, Louis XIV. ordered Lesdiguières to give a favourable reception to all fugitive Waldenses, and to assure them of his royal protection. In the valleys of Queyras and Pragela, belonging to France, men took up arms in support of their persecuted brethren. Many men deserted from the regular army for the same purpose; and at about this time Gianavel returned to the valleys with his reinvigorated and reinforced troop.

Captain Giaheri, a native of Pramol, had retired to the valley of Perosa, in the confines of France, with the inhabitants of Bubiana and Angrogna, fugitives under the decree of 22d April. A month afterwards, he returned at the head of these exiles, supported by their co-religionists of Pragela, and re-established them in the valleys of Angrogna and Pramol. He then wrote to Gianavel to join him. The latter had, at first, taken a position on a lofty mountain, called la Pelaya di Geymeto, whence he had essayed an attack upon Luzernella, a catholic village, half a league from Luzerna. Repulsed by numbers, he had effected a masterly retreat, in the course of which he received in the leg a bullet, which was never extracted. The wound, however, did not prevent him from pursuing his expeditions; and this attempt upon Luzernella, though in itself frustrated, had important results, for it gave a new aspect to that war of extermination in which, hitherto, the Waldenses had only acted on the defensive. Inexpressible terror now began to agitate the Piedmontese towns that lay nearest to the mountains; and each insisted upon having its entrenchments and its garrison. Some Irish troops, for example, were garrisoned at Bubiana, but they committed such excesses there, that the inhabitants were necessitated to expel them; and thus the persecutors began to destroy one another.

Giaheri effected his junction with Gianavel on the 27th May on the banks of the Angrogna, and by this combination the two warriors became infinitely more formidable than ever. The first enterprise which they essayed in common was directed against Garsigliano, which they attempted to surprise that same evening; but troops hastening, at the sound of the tocsin, from all the adjacent villages, they were obliged to retire, carrying off with them only some cattle, and six yoke of oxen. Next morning, at day-break, having strengthened themselves by prayer, and feeling the urgency of some energetic demonstration, in order to save their country, they attacked the town of San Segonzo, and took it. To protect themselves, in the assault, from the fire of the enemy, the Waldenses rolled before them great bags full of hay, in which the bullets showered upon them from the walls buried themselves, without touching one of the besiegers. On reaching the foot of the entrenchments, they set fire to the hay, the smoke of which hid them from the townspeople while they were battering in the gates: these once thrown down, they rushed in impetuously, and, after effecting great slaughter, retired with considerable booty. An entire Irish regiment, numbering from seven to eight hundred men, was cut to pieces, with six hundred and fifty Piedmontese troops: all such of the inhabitants as presented themselves unarmed were spared, and only a portion of them taken away prisoners. The town was then burned.

It was a terrible execution; but terrible as it was, it was

expedient, in the essential necessity which the Waldensians felt, of making their strength appreciated by foes who had hitherto acted towards them as towards, sheep, who were to permit themselves to be slaughtered unresistingly. Besides, the Waldensian valleys had been so cruelly devasted, the blood that had been shed cried out so loud, the irritation had become so profound, that, without attributing such reprisals to the mere spirit of vengeance, one may fairly regard them as a consequence—a necessity. They were useful, moreover, as forcibly impressing on the persecutors the fact that the persecuted were a people not altogether so despicable as had been supposed. Men heed, it is said, only those they love, or those they fear; the Waldenses, sure of not being loved, were fain to make themselves feared. They effectually attained this object.

Already the taking of San Segonzo was worth the gain of a battle to them. They had made fourteen hundred enemies bite the dust, while the loss on their own side had been but seven men; a fact which, incredible as it may seem, was not only a fact, but became immediately known as such, and diffused a panic terror of Gianavel and Giaheri through all the surrounding towns, which thereupon formed a league for their common defence, and arranged telegraphic signals, which, from the bell-towers, were to give warning of the approach, in any direction, of the Waldenses, and to indicate their position.

The population, who suffered at once from the interruption of trade, the maintenance of the troops, and the incursions of the Waldenses, were loud in their demands for peace.

The marquis de Pianeza endeavoured to get rid of his antagonists by setting a price upon the heads of their leaders; but their numbers, so far from diminishing were augmented daily by new recruits from Queyras and Pragela. By the 2d June, they consisted of four companies, commanded respectively by Gianavel, Giaheri, Laurens, and Benet. In a council of war, these four captains resolved to attack Bricherasio. In order to execute this design, the four companies were to take different routes, so as not only to surprise the town, but also to check any succours that might advance towards it. Accordingly, Gianavel occupied the slopes of San Giovanni and La Tayarea, in order to oppose the troops from La Torre and Luzerna; Laurens posted himself near Rocappiatta, to cut off the succours from San Segonzo, which had been partially rebuilt; while Giaheri, descending into the plains of Bricherasio, proceeded to devastate it on his way to the town itself: but the tocsin sounding, the garrisons of the adjacent towns hastened out in such numbers, as to cover Bricherasio, and to compel Giaheri to retrograde to the hills of San Giovanni, where Gianavel had kept in check the troops who had advanced in that direction, and who were now attacked with such impetuosity by the combined Waldensian forces, that they fled after a short resistance, leaving one hundred and fifty of their number dead on the field, while the Waldenses had but one man slain.

Gianavel next repaired to the mountain Palaya di Geymeto. Opposite this hill was the town of Villar, which had hitherto escaped destruction at the hands of the enemy, by reason of the number of its inhabitants who had catholicized. Gianavel sent word to these men of Villar, that they must forthwith, by joining him, augment the number of the defenders of their common country, or, on refusal, be treated as apostates, traitors, and enemies. Upon this energetic appeal, the Villarons, from fear or from patriotism, joined the rough warrior who had addressed it to them; and who, his forces thus increased to more than six hundred men, now resolved upon recovering the protestant capital of the valleys—the town of La Torre. The attempt was made, and failed; but more than three hundred of the enemy's troops fell in the defence of the place.

Gianavel and Giaheri having established their head quarters on one of the heights of Angrogna, called Le Verné, found it necessary to take energetic measures for the support of their troops, and, accordingly, the inhabitants of Crussol, a village situated in the valley of the Po, having inflicted much injury on the Waldenses during the recent massacres, Giaheri resolved to put them under contribution. He accordingly departed in the night, at the head of four hundred fifty men, and next morning, at daybreak, before the Crusolians could adopt any defensive measures, their village was taken possession of; they themselves fled unimpeded to a large cavern in the vicinity, and the Waldenses drove off more than four hundred cattle and six hundred sheep, which were transported to the mountain Lionza, and there portioned among the victors.

Meanwhile, the catholics of San Segonzo and the neighbouring villages had marched to attack the one hundred and fifty men left at Angrogna; but were vigorously repulsed by Laurens and Benet. In their retreat they came upon an unhappy Waldensian, Pietro Reggio, solitary and unarmed, whom they seized, and put to a cruel death.

Two day afterwards, 15th of June, 1655, the marquis di Pianeza, having set on foot all the troops under his command, sustained by a regiment which had just arrived under the orders of M. de Marolles, advanced to attack Gianavel in Angrogna. The troops, who were in four divisions, were to strike all at once; but this simultaneity of operations could not be effected, by reason of the different routes which the army had followed, and the points, remote from each other, which it had occupied. The detachment arriving by Roccapiatta, gave the signal for attack prematurely, so that Gianavel, who had with him only three hundred men, had obtained an advantage over the first assailants, before he was assailed, in his rear, by the troops arriving from Pramol.

In order to keep them separate, he at once made his way to the heights of Roccamanante; but there he found himself fronted by the troops arriving from San Giovanni, and at the same moment he perceived the detachment from La Torre advancing.

In this critical position, assailed from every direction, and having only half of his men with him, the hero of Rora, quick of eye and prompt in execution, retrograded before the battalion from Roccapiatta had time to form, dashed through the centre of that from Pramol, and then, as he had so successfully done at Rora, took up a position on the brow of a hill, the formation of which, on the other side, was a succession of gentle slopes, but, on the other, a sharp and precipitous descent. The four hostile battalions were drawn up at the foot of the slope. Thus hemmed in between a rugged precipice, and an army ten times more numerous than his own force, Gianavel maintained unbroken a defensive attitude for nearly five hours: then, perceiving some indications of lassitude and hesitation in the opposing ranks, Gianavel, having first raised his hands to heaven, and exclaimed, "Oh God! it is in thy cause! aid and preserve us!" gave the word to his men, "Forward!" and, like an avalanche of pikes, swords, and bullets, the Waldenses dashed down the slopes with all the impetuosity of long pent-up valour. Without awaiting their shock, the enemy fell back, for the purpose of deploying in the plain. By this manœuvre they weakened their line: the impetus of the Waldenses broke it. Utter disorder ensued, and those three thousand men fled in panic fear, pursued by the Waldenses, who killed more than five hundred of their number, themselves having but one man killed and two wounded.

But, unhappily, the work did not end here. Having cleared the basin of Angrogna from these invaders, Gianavel returned to his entrenchments, at the same moment that Giaheri arrived from Pragela. The troops of both leaders were fatigued, the one with fighting, the other with marching; those of Gianavel had eaten nothing since the morning. While they were hastily refreshing themselves, their leader went to reconnoitre the position of the enemy, and found that they were rallying in the plain of San Giovanni, but that the various corps were still dispersed, and evidently without the least idea of another attack. The indefatigable Waldensian general at once called his men together, and having descended unperceived, fell like lightning upon the heedless foe, who were a second time put to the rout, leaving one hundred of their number dead on the field. The triumph, however, threatened to be a calamity far worse than a defeat, for in the rapid engagement, Gianavel, that leader whom the Waldenses could not have replaced, was hit by a ball, which, entering the chest, passed completely through his body. The mouth was at once filled with blood; he fainted, and for a moment his soldiers thought him dead: reviving, he entrusted the command to Giaheri, to whom he gave his instructions, amid the tears and prayers of his loved and loving soldiers.

He was conveyed on a litter to Pinache, where, after six weeks' suffering, his wound healed.

His last direction, on quitting Giaheri, had been to undertake nothing further that day, on account of the fatigued condition of their troops; but an emissary coming with information that the town of Osasco could be easily taken, Giaheri, in whom intrepidity ever got the better of prudence, and who was eager to signalize himself by some effective stroke, took with him a hundred and fifty soldiers, and marched towards Osasco, under the guidance of the emissary. That emissary was a traitor: he led Giaheri into an ambush, where a squadron of cavalry fell furiously upon the Waldenses, and absolutely overpowered them. In this last struggle Giaheri surported himself in valour: seeing he had been betrayed, he first slew the traitor, and then, having invoked the aid of God, threw himself with his men, sword in hand, upon the Savoy cavalry, and made terrible slaughter of them; and it was not until he was absolutely covered with wounds, that he fell. His son died by his side, and of all his men, but one survived, who, having concealed himself for some hours in a marsh, swam the Clusone at night, and conveyed the intelligence of their deplorable loss to his countrymen.

Giaheri was a man zealous alike in the service of God, and in the cause of his country; brave as a lion, humble as a lamb, and ever assigning the praise of his victories to the Lord; a master of the scriptures, and well versed in controversy; a man of great intellect, and whose only fault was the incapacity to moderate his valour.

Chapter Twentieth.

NEGOTIATIONS AND CONCESSIONS.

THE death of Giaheri, and the supposed mortal wound of Gianavel, raised the courage of the papists, and persecution seemed to acquire, so far, a new impulse. But, on the other hand, public opinion pronounced itself, more and more energetically, in favour of the Waldenses. The admirers of military skill and soldierly daring were interested by the exploits of the fallen leaders and their heroic followers; the sufferings of the Waldensian martyrs exalted the Waldensian cause in the eyes of the pious. Soldiers from almost all countries came and offered their services to the persecuted folk. In the number, were the French lieutenant-general Descombies, and the Swiss colonel, Andrion; the latter of whom had already distinguished himself in Sweden, France and Germany. The Waldenses themselves possessed leaders of considerable skill. Bertino and Podio, of Bobbi; Albarea, of Villar; Laurens, of San Martin; with Revel and Gortabella, the lieutenants of Gianavel and Giaheri. The moderator Leger himself had arrived in the valleys on the 11th July, 1655, and at once proceeded, accompanied by colonel Andrion, to the valley of Angrogna, where the Waldenses were encamped on La Vachera. In the night, scouts were despatched towards La Torre to reconnoitre the enemy. On reaching

VAL QUEYRAZ, FROM THE ENTRANCE OF THE VALLEY OF ARVIEUX.

the hamlet of San Lorenzo, those messengers discerned a detachment of Piedmontese troops, who were awaiting the daylight in order to advance and attack the Waldenses. The two scouts mingling with these soldiers, conversed with them in their own language, and so learned the designs of their general, M. de Marolles. At daybreak the Waldenses quitted the enemy's camp, and made their way to their own barricades, which they reached just in time to give the alarm. The Piedmontese troops, arranged in four battallions, were occupied from five in the morning till three in the afternoon, in an ineffectual attack upon the Waldensian barricades, though these were defended by only a few hundred men. At length, the lower barricade being taken, the Waldenses retreated to a barricade called the Donjon, higher up, followed by the Piedmontese, who, deeming themselves triumphant, insolently called out: "Advance, wreck of Gianavel!" But down the steep descent the Waldenses rolled stones, or rather rocks, which leaping with thundering roar upon the enemy's ranks dispersed, broke, and crushed them, as though it had been a massive discharge of grape-shot.

"Advance, wreck of San Segonza!" cried the Waldenses in their turn, as, sword in hand, they poured down their serried ranks upon the amazed and discomfitted foe. The result was almost instantaneous; after a brief show of resistance, the Piedmontese troops, their ranks broken by the avalanche of rocks, and driven in by the avalanche of pikes and swords, turned and fled, leaving two hundred dead behind them, and carrying off with them twice that number of wounded.

Some days afterwards, the garrison of La Torre made another incursion into the valley of Angrogna, for the purpose of burning the remnant of the crops, but they were repulsed by captain Bellino, who pursued them to the very gates of the town.

The Waldenses themselves, under the command of Descombies, and aided by a small body of cavalry under another French refugee, Charles Feautrier, made, in their turn, an attempt upon La Torre; their numbers had now reached eighteen hundred armed men, and Gianavel, restored to health, was once more with them. The combined forces marched during the night to Monte Chiabasso, distant scarcely a mile from La Torre, and the Waldenses were eager instantly to assault the town; but the fatal prudence of Descombies interposed. This officer had never yet seen the Waldenses fight, and was ignorant of the locality, so that when some of his French followers, whom he had sent to reconnoitre the citadel of La Torre, reported that it was impregnable, he sounded a retreat, being desirous, as he said, of not compromising, in his first engagement, the men who had been entrusted to his command. The march of the Waldenses, however, had, meantime, become known, and M. de Marolles at once hastened from Luzerna, towards La Torre, at the head of his regiment, to attack them. The van of the Waldensian army, following Descombies, had already withdrawn towards La Vachera, but two of the Waldensian leaders, Bellino and Peronello, resolved to attack the town, and precipitated themselves towards it, with the other moiety of the Waldensian forces, Gianavel himself, as yet not strong enough to take part in the actual engagement, remaining on an eminence which commanded a view of the town, in order to sound a retreat, should circumstances so dictate. The Waldenses, well acquainted with the locality, made their way into the town, took and burned the Capuchin monastery, occupied all the leading streets, and then advanced to assault the citadel. The garrison, after a brief resistance, were about to surrender, when the regiment of M. de Marolles appeared in sight, and Gianavel at once sounded a retreat, which the Waldenses effected, avoiding the superior force of the enemy by their closer knowledge of the locality.

Meanwhile the remonstrances of protestant Europe were assuming a still more and more emphatic form. Cromwell, especially, displayed in favour of the Waldenses extraordinary zeal and activity. In reply to his letter of the 25th of May, already given, Louis XIV. had said: "To show you that I entirely disapprove of the employment of my troops for such a purpose as attacking the Waldenses, I have already sent several messages to the duke of Savoy, to prevent the further pursuit of that people, and I have ordered the duke de Lesdiguières, governor of Dauphiny, to receive, foster, and protect them. I will assuredly continue my good offices with the duke in their behalf." The French ambassador in Piedmont also received orders to act in the sense of this letter; similar instructions were given by Holland and Switzerland to their representatives at Turin; and the Protector of England sent Sir Samuel Morland upon a special mission to the court of Turin, to present letters of strong remonstrance to the duke of Savoy himself, and to demand an audience, for the purpose of making a public declaration of the indignation which the proceedings against the Waldenses had excited in England. Cromwell could not have chosen a man better qualified to discharge the duties of such an embassy than Morland. Young, ardent, full of courage, and conscious of the dignity of the character which he had to sustain, as the representative of the commonwealth of England, he procured an audience at Rivoli, where the royal family of Savoy were then residing, and in the presence of Madame Royale, and the whole court, he addressed the duke in a Latin oration, which, after a few customary expressions of courtesy, contained truths that none but a stern republican could think of sounding in royal ears. It was the pride, and perhaps the policy, of Cromwell, to transact all his negotiations with foreign powers in the language of ancient Rome. He would not condescend to hold intercourse in any but his own, or a learned tongue, and he considered that by this means neither himself nor his ministers could be made the dupes of equivocal and ambiguous phrases. Milton was the secretary whom he employed to put his own expressions into a correct and classical form.

The oration, as given by Morland himself, in his quaint translation, ran thus:—

"May it please your Most Serene and Royal Highness,

"I am sent by the most serene prince Oliver, lord Protector of the commonwealth of England, Scotland, and Ireland, unto your royal highness, whom he heartily saluteth, and with a very high and singular affection of mind towards the person of your serene highness, wishing you life, a long reign, and prosperous success in all your affairs, together with the love and affections of your people. And this respect doubtless is due to your merit, whether a man consider the most noble inclination, and royal extraction of your highness, together with the high expectation which the world hath from so many eminent virtues, or whether, from perusing the monuments of time past, he call to mind the ancient alliance of our kings with the royal family of Savoy. As for myself, though I be a young man, I confess, and have not much experience in affairs, yet it pleased my most serene and most gracious master, to send me, being one that is much devoted to your royal highness, and a great lover of all the people of Italy, to negotiate matters of great importance, for so those affairs are to be called, wherein the safety of many poor distressed people and all their hope is comprehended, which indeed consisteth wholly in this, if so be that by all their loyalty, obedience, and most humble petitions, they may be able to mollify and appease the mind of your royal highness, which hath been provoked against them.

"In behalf of these poor people whose cause truly even commiseration itself may seem to make the more excusable, the most serene Protector of England is also become an intercessor; and he most earnestly entreateth and beseecheth your royal highness, that you would be pleased to extend your mercy to these your very poor subjects, and most disconsolate outcasts; I mean those, who inhabiting beneath the Alps, and certain valleys under your dominion, are professors of the protestant religion. For he hath been informed, (which no man can say was done by the will of your royal highness,) that part of these most miserable people have been cruelly massacred by your forces, part driven out by violence, and forced to leave their native habitations; and so, without house or shelter, poor and destitute of all relief, do wander up and down, with their wives and children, in craggy and uninhabited places, and mountains covered with snow. Oh! the fired houses which are yet smoking, the torn limbs, and ground defiled with blood!*

* * * * *

* Fumantia passim tecta, et laceri artus, et cruenta humus. Virgines post stupra, differto lapillis ac ruderibus utero, miserè efflarunt animas.

"Some men, an hundred years old, decrepit with age and bed-rid, have been burnt in their beds. Some infants have been dashed against the rocks, others have had their throats cut, whose brains have, with more than Cyclopean cruelty, been boiled and eaten by the murderers! What need I mention more, although I could reckon up very many cruelties of the same kind, if I were not astonished at the very thought of them. If all the tyrants of all times and ages were alive again, (which I would speak without any offence to your highness, seeing we believe none of these things were done through any default of yours,) certainly they would be ashamed when they should find that they had contrived nothing, in comparison with these things, that might be reputed barbarous and inhuman.

"In the meantime, the angels are surprised with horror; men are amazed; heaven itself seems to be astonished with the cries of dying men; and the very earth to blush, being discoloured with the gore blood of so many innocent persons! Do not thou, O thou most high God, do not thou take that revenge, which is due to so great wickedness, and horrible villanies! Let thy blood, O Christ, wash away this blood!*

"But it is not my business to make a narrative of these things, in order as they were done, or to insist any longer upon them; and that which my most serene master desireth of your royal highness, you will better understand by his own letters, which letters I am commanded, with all observance and due respect, to deliver unto your royal highness; to which, if your royal highness shall, as we very much hope, be pleased to vouchsafe a speedy answer, you will thereby very highly oblige my lord Pro-

* It was in reference to these same atrocities that Milton wrote his memorable sonnet, which we have prefixed to the present volume.

tector, who hath laid this thing deeply to heart, and the whole commonwealth of England. You will also, by an act of compassion, most worthy of your royal highness, restore life, safety, and spirit, country and estates, to many thousands of afflicted people, who depend upon your pleasure; and me you will dismiss back to my native country with exceeding joy, and with a report of your eminent virtues, the most happy proclaimer of your princely clemency, and one for ever most obliged to your royal highness."

This oration, stamped with the energetic unction of the puritan, pronounced with the manly confidence of youth and courage, produced a deep sensation. Charles Emanuel made no reply; but the duchess, instructed beforehand by her Jesuit advisers, said: "We are deeply sensible of the interest your master takes in our subjects, but surprised that he should listen to such inaccurate statements as those upon which he has evidently acted. Were he better informed of the facts, he would know that what have been represented to him as barbarities, were nothing more than mild and paternal chastisement, inflicted on rebellious subjects, whose revolt no sovereign could overlook. Nevertheless, in manifestation of our desire to be agreeable to his serene highness, we will not only pardon them, but restore them to our favour, and to the privileges which their ill-conduct has forfeited."

Morland thrown off his guard by this promise, quitted Turin, on the 19th of July, promising to return and take part, on behalf of the Waldenses, in the negotiations which were to take place respecting them. But care was taken to precipitate those negotiations in his absence, in order that less might be granted; and accordingly, on the 18th of August, 1655, in presence of the Swiss envoys, who had arrived after the departure of Morland, and under the influence of the French ambassador, Servient, was concluded, at Pignerol, the treaty of peace, designated the Patent of Grace, which left the poor Waldenses more completely than ever at the mercy of their oppressors, under the mask of establishing their security. This shameful treaty, by which the protestant states were duped, and the Waldensian churches left in the unprotected situation as ever, was very appositely compared to a leper, arrayed in rich clothing and gay attire; and to Ezekiel's roll, "written within and without, in the mouth as honey for sweetness, but within there were written lamentations, and mourning and woe."

The Swiss plenipotentiaries had endeavoured to secure more solid guarantees for the security of the Waldenses, such, for example, as the demolition of the fortress of La Torre; but these were all either refused or eluded.

Chapter Twenty-first.

INFRACTIONS OF THE TREATY OF PIGNEROL.

THE baneful effects of this Jesuitical affair were soon felt by the deluded Waldenses, who, in their pathetic appeals for redress, used some of the most affecting expressions in Scripture to signify their distress. "We have no grapes in the vineyard," they said; "no cattle in the fields; no herds in the stalls; no corn in the garners; no meal in the barrel; no oil in the cruse. The tongue of the suckling cleaves to the roof of his mouth, and the young children ask bread, and no man gives it to them." In the translation of a letter, written by the ministers and elders of the valleys to their brethren of Geneva, dated Pinaches, 14th February, 1657, and preserved, among many other Waldensian records, in the State Paper Office at London, there occur these touching passages:—

"Our people are in extreme necessities, the greatest part of our families being destitute of houses, moveables, cattel, or any thing else whereby to subsist.—If you did but know, sirs, the greatness of our miseries, you would certainly have compassion on us, and pitie our sad condition. God is now in good earnest chastizing us for our sins and iniquities, to which wee most willingllie submitt, kissing the rod, and confessing that hee is still just and righteous."

To the French king, whom they justly considered the main author of their grievances, since it was he who had patched up the perfidious treaty, they addressed an humble petition, imploring his interposition, and urging to see justice done to them. But their only answers were some angry letters, written by the French ambassador (Servient), who had himself assisted in framing the treaty; and who had sharply rebuked them for their presumption and discontent. One of these letters even reproached them for accepting supplies and moneys from foreigners. These moneys were the contributions received from England. "Alas! said the poor sufferers, "was it ever known before that miserable men, after losing the whole of their estates, after having had their houses burnt, and their goods plundered, should have it objected to them, that they received the charity of those who had pity on them, to prevent their perishing of hunger!"

One of the Swiss ambassadors was so dissatisfied with the terms of the treaty, in the first instance, even before it was concluded, that he strongly remonstrated with his colleagues, and urged them not to consent to it; and afterwards subscribed to a protest, the original attestation of which is among the manuscripts in the university library at Cambridge.

Cromwell was furious upon finding how completely the protestant states had been overreached, in their negotiation with the duke of Savoy, and in the faith they placed in the mediation of the king of France. He wrote to Louis XIV. in a high tone of indignant remonstrance:

"Most Serene and Potent King,

"Your majesty may remember, that at the time when the negotiation began between us, for the renewal of the alliance, which has proved so beneficial to the two nations, and so detrimental to our common enemies, the cruel massacre of the Waldenses took place; and that we earnestly and pathetically commended the cause of that unhappy people, who appeared to be oppressed and abandoned by all, to your pity and protection. We cannot believe that your majesty neglected to make use of your authority and influence with the duke of Savoy, when it was so incumbent upon you to exert yourself in the pious and humane character of a mediator; as for ourselves, and many other princes and states, we interposed all that we could, by embassies, letters, and entreaties. The result was, that after a most barbarous slaughter of persons of both sexes, and of all ages, a treaty of peace was concluded, or rather secret acts of hostility were committed, the more securely under the name of a pacification. The conditions of the treaty were determined in your town of Pignerol; hard conditions enough, but such as these poor people would gladly have agreed to, after the horrible outrages to which they had been exposed, provided that they had been faithfully observed. But they were not observed: the meaning of the treaty is evaded and violated, by putting a false interpretation upon some of the articles, and by straining others: many of the complainants have been deprived of their patrimonies; and many have been forbidden the exercise of their religion: new payments have been exacted; and a new fort has been built, to keep them in check; from whence a disorderly soldiery make frequent sallies, and plunder or murder all they meet. In addition to these things, fresh levies of troops are clandestinely preparing to march against them; and those among them who profess the Roman catholic religion have been advised to retire in time; so that everything threatens the speedy destruction of such as escaped the former massacre. I do therefore beseech and conjure your majesty not to suffer such enormities, and not to permit (I will not say any prince, for surely such barbarity never could enter into the heart of a prince, much less one of the duke's tender age, or into the mind of his mother) those accursed murderers to indulge in such savage ferocity, who, while they profess to be the servants and followers of Christ, who came into the world to save sinners, do blaspheme his name, and transgress his mild precepts, by the slaughter of innocent men. Oh that your majesty, who has the power, and who ought to be inclined to use it, may deliver so many supplicants from the hands of murderers, who are already drunk with blood, and thirst for it again, and who take pleasure in throwing the odium of their cruelty upon princes. I implore your majesty not to suffer the borders of your kingdom to be polluted by such monstrous wickedness. Remember that this very race of people threw themselves upon the protection of your grandfather, king Henry IV., who was most friendly disposed towards the protestants, when the duke of Lesdiguières passed victoriously through their country, as affording the most commodious passage into Italy, at the time he pursued the duke of Savoy in his retreat across the Alps. The act or instrument of that submission is still extant among the public records of your kingdom, in which it is provided that the Waldenses shall not be transferred to any other government, but upon the same condition that they were received under the protection of your invincible grandfather. As supplicants of his grandson, they now implore the fulfillment of this compact: they would rather be your subjects than the duke's, and hope that it may be effected by some mode of exchange, if possible, and if not, that at least they may be taken under your patronage and protection. There are other reasons of state which might induce your majesty not to neglect the Waldenses; but I would not wish so great a king to be influenced by anything but his regard to the faith pledged by his ancestors, and by his own piety, and royal benevolence and magnanimity. Thus the honour and praise of so glorious an act will be entirely your own, and your majesty will propitiate the grace and favour of the Father of Mercies, and our Lord Jesus Christ, whose name and doctrine you will vindicate against such nefarious and inhuman proceedings.

"Given at our court at Westminster, this 26th of May, 1658."

Cromwell also despatched a letter to the Swiss cantons, plainly signifying his own readiness to go all lengths, in conjunction with them, for the benefit of the Waldenses, and warning them that they were bound, by every consideration of interest, as well as feeling, to see that the most ancient stock of the reformed religion be not destroyed, in the remains of its old faithful professors, lest the next blow should fall upon themselves.

It had been, during the negotiation of the treaty, agreed, on the part of Savoy, that, though the duke could not "so far humiliate himself before his subjects" as to have a clause inserted formally decreeing the demolition of the fortress of La Torre, an object very material with the Waldenses, by reason of past sufferings and future fears, yet that, so soon as the treaty should be signed, his highness, "requiring no other fortress than the hearts of his grateful people," would have the castle of La Torre rased. The treaty was signed; and then, in the space between the text and the signatures, the ducal counsellors interpolated this paragraph: "His royal highness grants to the Waldenses the right of addressing to him supplications that the citadel of La Torre may be demolished absolutely, or removed elsewhere." This implication of the right to reject such supplications, rendered that an open question which had been distinctly settled and conceded: this was pointed out by the Waldenses; the answer was, that the interpolation had been made from some negligence of the copyist. The Waldenses, omitting to insist upon the point, addressed the supplication which the forged clause derisively suggested. The duke replied, with an affectation of extreme amenity, that he was happy to grant them a fresh proof of his benevolence, and that he would, accord ingly, destroy all that portion of the fortress of La Torre "which was not necessary for the defence of his states."

He did, in fact, pull down a small detached tower, in the plain of La Torre; but, at the same time, he added largely both to the size and to the strength of the citadel, and, upon the completion of these new works, increased the number of the garrison.

The French authorities, however, became uneasy at this augmented strength of a fortress so near their own frontiers; and both Lesdiguières, the governor of Dauphiny, and La Bretonnière commandant of Pignerol, loudly declaring their dissatisfaction, Louis XIV. himself volunteered to guarantee the full execution of the treaty which had been concluded under his auspices. A synod was held at La Torre to deliberate upon this offer, and the Waldenses thence forwarded to the monarch a memorial, in which they set forth the various respects in which the *patents of grace* had been altogther violated: the Waldensian prisoners, they said, were not restored to them; their children were still forced or stolen from them; and the soldiers of the Piedmontese garrison perpetrated, with utter impunity, the gravest outrages upon their persons and properties. Pillage and assassination, violence and violation, continued, then, to be the catholic *work of faith;* the propaganda proceeded with its "holy mission."

One labour of this mission was to sow division among the Waldenses, by the medium of Jesuits, who, under the guise of protestant refugees from Languedoc, introduced themselves into the valleys, and applied all their talents to the perfidious task. Among other vile insinuations, they spread rumours of malversation against those pastors who had been entrusted with the distribution of the collections made abroad for the use of the Waldenses; and misery being ever mistrustful, these calumnies served, for a while, the treacherous purpose of those who propagated them. New trials, however, soon united all against a common danger.

The auditor Gastaldo, who, still a member of the propaganda, had become governor of the valleys, issued, 15th June, 1657, a decree prohibiting the Waldenses from publicly celebrating their worship at San Giovanni, under a a penalty of one thousand crowns of gold against the presiding minister, and of two hundred against each person present. New papist missions were established in the valleys; the Jesuits got a footing in every direction; exemptions from taxes, and other privileges were granted to all catholic converts, while the protestants were treated with systematic rigour; the Dauphinese pastors who had come to minister sympathy and consolation, religious and fraternal, to the Waldenses of the valleys, were expelled, on the pretext of their being foreigners.

The persecuted people complained of the oppressions to which they were subjected, in a memorial to the Swiss ambassadors who had negotiated the treaty of Pignerol, and the latter, in their turn, addressed a memorial to the

Piedmontese government, complaining of the infraction of the treaty to which they were parties. The president, Truchsi, in his reply, threw the whole blame upon the Waldenses, who, he absurdly said, were the real infractors of the treaty. The synod of the Waldensian valleys then drew up a detailed statement of their grievances, which was printed at Haarlem, in 1662, and again in 1663; but the Piedmontese authorities, so far from remedying the evil, seemed more and more bent upon aggravating it.

The treaty of Pignerol had exempted the protestants from the payment of the arrears of the public charges for the deplorable year 1655, on the distinct ground of their total inability, by reason of their losses and privations, to pay them. Despite the deep misery from which foreign subscriptions had but partially relieved them, the Waldenses were now imperatively required to discharge these very arrears; and, to render the exaction more oppressive and more insulting, the catholics of the valley of San Martin were, at the same time, exempted from the payment of these charges, "as a compensation for the damage done to them by the protestants."

It was, however, less these money-wounds, than the wounds which affect the spiritual life, that aroused the Waldenses to renewed exertions. The prohibition to perform their worship in the commune of San Giovanni, was not only a grievous evil in itself, but a menace to all their churches. The edict of Cavour had guaranteed the free exercise of their worship in all places where it was then already established, and San Giovanni was one of these places. The treaty of Pignerol had in no way restricted this guarantee. If one of their parishes were effectually assailed, the rest would soon succumb beneath similar strokes. Public preaching had, indeed, been forbidden to the Waldenses at San Giovanni, so long back as 1620, but the other functions of the protestant ministry had been maintained.

A general synod was assembled in March, 1658, to discuss this grave question. It was resolved that a memorial should be addressed to the sovereign in person, and that, meanwhile, the pastor of San Giovanni (Leger, the historian) should continue to exercise his ministry there, until the question, so submitted to the duke himself, had been definitely decided.

This determination on the part of the synod created great indignation at the court of Turin. "The first duty of subjects," it was insisted, "is to obey their prince. In resisting his orders, the Waldenses have rendered themselves guilty of revolt, and must be treated as rebels, as traitors;" and the protestant powers whom the synod had entreated to intercede in the matter, were met with the haughty declaration, that the persons in whom they interested themselves, without understanding the real state of the question, were rebels, who must be treated accordingly.

The object of especial irritation, on the part of the propaganda and the popish clergy, was Leger, that courageous pastor, who remained at his post, despite menaces and peril.

Already twice condemned to death, he now braved it for the third, and, as his enemies hoped, last time. He was cited to appear at Turin; the citation set forth no cause, and Leger did not obey it. A second citation was equally ineffectual. The count of Saluzzo, who took a deep interest in the Waldenses—an interest which appears hereditary in the family—then went to the minister, and, in a friendly manner, remonstrated with him upon the practical inexpediency of his resistance to authority; but the pastor persisted, and, on the 3d of May, 1658, he received another citation, ordering him to appear, under pain of banishment, and of the confiscation of his property. The pastor hereupon assembled his colleagues at Pinache, then a French town, in order to consult with them what course he should take; and the result of their deliberations was, that a solicitation should be addressed to the authorities to maintain Leger in his church. This proceeding, which should have been resorted to in the first instance, came too late. The request was rejected by the court; and after three years of sterile negotiations, Leger was, on the 12th January, 1661, condemned, by the senate of Turin, to death, and his co-accused, the deacons and elders of the church of San Giovanni, to ten years labour in the galleys. Leger, thus compelled to withdraw from his native land, retired first to England, then to Geneva, and lastly to Leyden, where he published his *General History of the Waldensian Churches*, and where he died, about 1684.

Chapter Twenty-second.

THE WAR OF THE EXILES

SAN GIOVANNI'S pastor, Leger, and Gianavel, had been condemned to death, twenty other persons to the galleys, and many more were still under prosecution, for having resisted the orders of their sovereign in exercising the protestant worship at that town. The condemned men having fled, a price was put upon their heads, and meanwhile troops were sent to demolish their houses and devastate their little farms. The command of the fortress of La Torre was confided to the count di Bagnolo, one of the massacrers of 1655, the zealous servant of the propaganda. His soldiers, with corresponding zeal, committed all sorts of excesses—pillage, conflagration, murder, violation. Many of the poor villagers fleeing from their cottages to escape these outrages, di Bagnolo issued a proclamation forbidding any person to receive these unhappy creatures, under penalty of having his own property destroyed. Every conceivable and inconceivable mode of injuring and irritating the Waldenses was had recourse to. Di Bagnolo, who afterwards died on the scaffold, convicted of one hundred and twenty odious murders, was ably aided in this work by the commandant of the fortress of Miraboco, himself a man who, having been prosecuted for more than sixty murders committed prior to the marriage of the duke of Savoy, had, on that occasion, received a pardon for his crimes.

The only mortal help of the Waldenses, under these cruel persecutions, was Gianavel, whose troop of exiles was daily augmented by Waldenses expelled from their homes. Daily, also, did some daring exploit signalize the valour of Gianavel and his *banditi*, as the patriots were designated, who, deprived of their own legitimate means of subsistence, were necessitated to levy contributions for the support of themselves and the distressed mountaineers, on the catholic towns and villages. Not a day passed in which some action, more or less effective, did not take place between the Waldenses and their adversaries; the 25th May, 1663, and the following 17th June, were especially marked by triumphs on the part of the protestants.

On the 25th of the latter month, the duke of Savoy issued an edict, which, under the pretext of pacifying the Waldenses, commanded them all to take arms against the *banditi*, who were coolly described as persons assembled together for mere purposes of pillage, having no sort of connexion with the real question at issue. Two hundred and sixty men, drafted from the different communes, were to collect at Chiabasso, over against La Torre, and there await the orders of the commandant of Bricherasio. Each commune was to give a hostage for its fidelity; and, on his part, the duke promised to institute an inquiry at Turin into the conduct of the count di Bagnolo, and, to crown these wondrous benefits, to pardon all the fugitive protestants, on condition of their returning home—that is to say, of their placing themselves within his power—in the space of fifteen days. By the same beneficent and friendly edict, Gianavel, was condemned to be torn with pincers, to be quartered, and then to have his head cut off and stuck at the end of a pike on some elevated point. The condemnation of Leger to death was reiterated, and Artus, Bastia, Rivorio, the brothers Muston, Revel, and others, in all thirty-five persons, the prominent leaders of the little Waldensian army, were condemned to death, and the confiscation of their property. Six other persons were condemned to the galleys, and four to ten years' imprisonment. Such was the *clemency* of the propaganda! What its *rigours* were, may be readily imagined.

The governor of La Torre and the ducal treasurer-general urgently solicited the Waldenses to accept these conditions; but the Waldenses left the duke's *ultimatum* without reply. The commune of Prarustin alone declined to undergo the responsibility of refusal, with the valley of Luzerna; and the neighbouring seigneurs at once essayed their utmost efforts to augment this dissension. Unable to effect their object, they insisted that, at least, the inhabitants of the valley of Luzerna should give a proof of their peaceful spirit, and of their fidelity, by escorting a convoy of provisions and ammunition to the fortress of Miraboco.

This fortress commanded the narrowest part of the valley of Luzerna, and closed the passage into Dauphiny, whither, as has been seen, the Waldenses had frequently withdrawn in times of persecution. It was not, then, without much distrust that, in conveying war munitions to this fortress, the protestants contributed to close this retreat, in case of need, against themselves. But the governor of La Torre and the treasurer-general solemnly assured them, that, in acknowledgment of this act of submission, the most complete peace would be accorded them; and they and their families might return home without the smallest fears for the future.

The Waldenses were conforming to these counsels, when they heard that troops, secretly despatched from Turin, were marching against them. Six regiments of the royal guard had, in fact, quitted the capital on the 29th June, under the command of the marquis de Fleury, eleven days before the expiration of the delay which had been granted to the Waldenses, within which they might return home, and four days before the expiration of that within which they were to give their answer on the conditions proposed to them. Indeed, as was afterwards ascertained, fresh troops had been secretly directed towards La Torre and Luzerna, even before those conditions were propounded. It is, therefore, futile to excuse the aggression of which the Waldenses were now the object, on the plea that they had not obeyed the edict of 25th June, since the aggression commenced, not merely before they had replied to the conditions of that edict, but even before the edict was communicated to them.

The marquis de Fleury marched directly towards Angrogna, by the San Giovanni road. The marquis d'Angrogna, at the head of the cavalry of San Segonzo, proceeded towards the same point by the heights of Roccapiatta, while the infantry advanced thither by the ascents of Bricherasio. These various corps formed, at daybreak of 6th July, a junction on the higher plateau, where all these roads met, their object being to occupy La Vachera. which, rising above that plateau, commands, as from a central point, the divergence of the three valleys.

But already a Waldensian corps of observation defended this important post.

The main body of the Waldensian army, commanded by

Gianavel in person, had taken up a position lower down, on the slopes of San Giovanni; but when the chief witnessed the junction, in his front, of the corps of De Fleury and of Di Bagnolo, he despatched a body of sixty picked men to occupy *Le Porte d'Angrogna*, a defile opening upon the plateau, and covering at once La Vachera and Roccamanante, and himself, by the mountain paths so intimately known to him, led the rest of his little army, now numbering not more than six hundred men, to the heights of Roccamanante, natural escarpments, almost inaccessible by the enemy. "Here," cried he to his men, "here is our Tabor! Let us pray to the Almighty for aid and encouragement."

The Waldenses had scarcely risen from their devotion, when the enemy were heard approaching. Instantly the besieged spread themselves amongst the rocks, occupying every access, and from every opening pouring down a destructive fire upon the assailants. Di Bagnolo, directing a halt, examined the position as closely as he could, and then essayed to carry it by assault; but he was signally repulsed. After taking breath, the soldiers attempted another assult, but they were again repulsed. The count had already lost three hundred men: he ordered his soldiers to scale the rocks; but they had no sooner reached the summit than they were hurled back, one upon the other. Hereupon, a superstitious terror came over them; they called to mind all the tales that had been forged by the priests, of the Waldenses having made a compact with the devil, in order to secure invulnerability; of their receiving in their shirts the bullets that, with ordinary men, would have riddled their bodies; they hesitated and drew back; the quick eye of Gianavel perceived the advantage thus afforded him: "Let us sweep these cowards from the hill!"

he cried to his men; and those hardy warriors rushed from their entrenchments upon the wavering foe, who, confirmed in their panic by this daring and impetuous movement turned, and, carrying the count di Bagnolo with them in their flight, precipitated themselves tumultuously down the ascent, nor stayed until they had got far into the plain, after losing, on their way, a considerable number of their body.

Gianavel, rallying his heroic army, returned to the plateau, and thence, after a thanksgiving to God for the victory thus vouchsafed, proceeded to rejoin the sixty warriors whom he had sent the Porte d'Angrogna to protect his rear. As he had foreseen, these sixty men so placed had sufficed to keep in check, hitherto, the entire force of the marquis de Fleury. But the latter, having gradually advanced from rock to rock, were about to hem the Waldenses in, when Gianavel, coming up with his six hundred victors, took the enemy in flank; and the sixty besieged, becoming immediately assailants, and dashing from their defile upon the advanced ranks of the foe, the latter, who, on seeing Gianavel's army approach, at once understood that Di Bagnolo had been defeated, also gave way, and, after a short struggle, turned and fled, hotly pursued by the Waldenses. Not fewer than six hundred of the enemy fell dead in this engagement, and several hundreds more died afterwards of their wounds, while the Waldenses, favoured by their position, and their knowledge of the ground, lost in all not more than six men.

Various minor skirmishes took place in the course of the following days; by each of these the numbers of the enemy were more or less diminished, while those of the Waldenses, so far from lessening, were augmented by fresh accessions, not only of Waldenses, but of French protestants, who came to aid their persecuted brethren.

The court of Savoy, incredulous that "a handful of rebels" could thus defeat so powerful an army, under competent command, imputed the blame to the marquis de Fleury, and accordingly superseded him, appointing the count di San Damiano in his place. The latter resolved to signalize himself, marched, the day after his arrival, from Luzerna, at the head of one thousand five hundred troops, to attack the village of Rora, defended by fifteen Waldenses and eight Frenchmen. These heroic men did their utmost against the overwhelming force that assailed them, but, as a matter of course, were defeated, and cut in pieces, one of them excepted, who was taken prisoner.

Intoxicated with this glorious victory, the marquis, next day, made an irruption into the valley of Luzerna, and had reached and set fire to the village of Santa Margarita, when the Waldenses, two hundred in number, descending by the defile of Copiere, attacked them on the sudden, dispersed them, put them to flight, and killed several hundred of them.

Charles Emanuel, finding that unskillfulness in his generals was not the only cause of the disastrous turn for him which this intestine war was assuming, resolved to try the effect of one comprehensive stroke of intimidation, and accordingly published, 10th of August, 1663, a decree by which all the inhabitants of all the valleys were declared guilty of high treason, and, as such, condemned to death, and the confiscation of their goods. The decree, as a matter of course, produced no effect whatever ; and the Waldenses, suffering as they were from bitter privations, still kept the field, and still defeated the ducal troops, wherever these presented themselves. Next peace was offered to the persecuted folk, on condition that they would lay down their arms, that they would not raise the question of religion, and that each commune of the valleys having any representation to make should make it separately. In other words, the Waldenses were to place themselves defenceless in the hands of their relentless foes, were to surrender the very point for which they were contending, and were to dissolve the very union which constituted their strength. The offer was at once rejected. Next, the propaganda published a declaration, purporting to be a repudiation, on the part of the Waldenses of Prarustin, of the proceedings of their co-religionists; an appeal to the clemency of the duke; an entire submission to his will; and a full acceptance of the edict of 10th August. It was ascertained, upon investigation, first, that this declaration was that of only six persons, five of whom could not even sign their names; and, secondly, that even these six persons had only contemplated a solicitation for a truce of a few weeks in order that they might gather in the vintage, then ripe. Such was the pitiable policy of the propaganda!

At length, upon the mediation of Holland, Germany, and the protestant Swiss cantons, the duke, wearied and, disgusted with a contest in itself revolting to his naturally good sense and good heart, consented to a conference. Ambassadors from the mediating powers reached Turin, in November, 1663, and, an insidious attempt on the part of the priests to compromise the Waldenses in the eyes of their foreign allies having failed, eight deputies from the valleys soon afterwards joined them there, and the conferences commenced.

ST. GERMAIN—(IN THE VALLEY OF THE CLUSONE.)

Chapter Twenty-third.

CONFERENCES AT TURIN.—ARBITRATION OF LOUIS XIV.

On the 17th of December, 1663, the conference between the representatives of the six protestant cantons of Switzerland and the representatives of Charles Emanuel, on the subject of the complaints of the Waldenses against the governor of La Torre, opened at the Hôtel-de-Ville of Turin. The ducal representatives commenced the proceedings by narrating their view of the events which had led to the war, and which, according to them, resolved themselves into repeated rebellions of the Waldenses. The deputies of the latter replied that the real cause of the conflicts they so much deplored, was the aggressions and violence of the governor of La Torre. They cited, in proof of their allegations, infinite murders, robberies, tortures, and other violences that had been committed by the count. The count replied that the murders of which he was accused had not been committed by him, but had been the result of private vengeance; that the only persons who had been killed by his orders were outlaws, who were in rebellion against the state, or their friends and relatives. He admitted that private houses might have been broken into; but this, he said, had only been for the purpose of domiciliary visits, necessary for the discovery of persons denounced by the law. He added that, after the 25th of June, he could not be responsible for any excesses which might have been committed, because troops had then come into the valleys over whom he had no effectual control. He distinctly denied the insults and menaces which had been imputed to him; but he admitted that he had retained a band of devastators, in order to oppose the men of the valleys. The memorial which set forth this defence concluded with the assurance "that the sieur di Bagnolo had endeavoured, with every sort of mildness and especial care, to keep the valleys in peace, and to separate them from all intercourse with the bandits, who had precipitated them into so inexcusable a rebellion." The Waldenses were then formally charged with a series of contraventions of the obedience due to their sovereign. And it was said that if they had to complain of violence, they should have appealed to the laws. The answer was, that they had appealed to the laws, and had obtained no redress. With regard to public worship, the Waldenses contended that the right to celebrate their religion had been granted to them by repeated edicts. Upon this point, as upon the preceding, there was a long discussion between the representatives on both sides, originating in the most futile objections on the part of the popish councillors. The heaviest charge against the Waldenses was, that they had given aid and asylum to the exiles. The simple answer to this was, that the exiles in question were the brothers, fathers, or other near relatives of those who had given them assistance, and that to make the assistance so rendered matter of criminality, even against the individuals, was altogether unreasonable and inhuman; still more unreasonable was it to make the whole people responsible.

These first conferences terminated on the 31st of December; and, as their result, the ducal commissioners decided that the Waldenses had no cause of complaint; and that their taking up arms had been merely for the purpose of exciting sympathy in their favour abroad, with a view to the obtaining pecuniary assistance. The allegation was simply ridiculous. The collateral conduct of the propaganda was odious: *Nulla fides servanda hæreticis.* While these conferences were proceeding, while the poor mountaineers, hoping a favourable issue, observed on their part the suspension of hostilities, the natural pendant of the state of negotiation, the propaganda were plotting their complete extermination by an act of treachery. The second sitting of the commissioners was on the 21st of December; on the 20th of December an order was drawn up, regulating "the distribution of the troops for four attacks on the rebels of the valleys of Luzerna and St. Martin, to be made to-morrow." On the morrow accordingly, 21st of December, 1663, the count di San Damiano marched upon Prarustin, by San Segonzo, at the head of sixteen hundred and fifty-five foot and fifty horse; the marquis de Parelli advanced towards Angrogna by La Garsinera, with fifteen hundred and seventy-six foot and fifty horse, and the count Genegli towards the same point, but by Le Porte and San German, with a battalion of seven hundred and eighty-six men. Captain Cagnolo occupied the plain of San Giovanni with one hundred horse, ready to proceed wherever circumstances should call him; while the governor of La Torre, the same count di Bagnolo who was so solicitous for the peace of the Waldenses, was to march against the protestants, at the head of eleven hundred and eighteen men, by Le Copiere and Santa Margarita. It was in this latter direction that the attack began. The Waldenses were driven from Santa

Margarita upon Le Copiere, and from Le Copiere upon Tagliarette. Here, however, they made a stand, entrenched among the rocks, until they saw a troop of their brethren marching up from Angrogna. Thus enforced, from assailed they became assailants, and while making an impetuous sortie upon the front of the enemy, while the Angrognese attacked them in the flank, the superstitious terror which the Waldenses had so often before excited in the minds of their adversaries again manifested itself. The papist troops, once vacillating, were speedily put to the rout by the combined Waldenses, who drove them down into the plain of La Torre. At Angrogna itself, defended by captain Prionello, the marquis de Parelli was especially unsuccessful. At San Germano, on the other hand, the count de Genegli completely defeated the Waldenses, devastated their fields and their vineyards, and burned their houses. At Roccapiatta, a poor woman, nearly a hundred years old, and bed-ridden, was burned alive; at San Germano, a young woman, after being monstrously outraged, had the flesh cut from her bones in long shreds, and was then left to die in their torture. Several men, in the same place, were mutilated in a manner that cannot be described. Such are the tender mercies of popery! But the Waldenses, though themselves vanquished, made the victory very bitter to their enemies: more than a hundred of the popish soldiery were slain, and there fell, besides, the count de la Trinité, a descendant of him who so cruelly persecuted the Waldenses in the preceding century; the young count de Saint-Frons, a descendant of the old persecutors of the Waldenses in the valley of Praviglelmo; captain Biala, and M. de Grand-Maison.

When the Swiss ambassadors were made acquainted with these aggressions, they loudly complained to the duke's ministers of so outrageous a violation of the armistice. It was replied, that the troops of his royal highness, being in want of provisions, had merely taken measures for extending their quarters. "But how do you account for these burnings, these massacres, that have taken place!"—"The Waldenses resisted the movements of our troops, and some slight collisions occurred, in which a few men were killed, and a few houses burned, *by inadvertence!*

Was the distribution of the troops, on the 20th of December, "for the four attacks on the rebels," an inadvertence?

The Swiss deputies, fain to be content with these manifest falsehoods, resumed the negotiations; and at last it was agreed that the basis of an arrangement should be preserved to the Waldenses, under the title of *patents of grace;* for the duke of Savoy could not consent, from the height of his sovereign dignity, to treat these "miserable heretics" on equal terms. Whatever was granted therefore was to be granted as wholly matter of grace: and, being so accepted by the Waldenses, necessarily involved an acknowledgment that there had been rebellion on their part, which neither they nor the Swiss ambassadors at all admitted. The Waldenses, accordingly, hesitated whether they should accept the propositions on such terms; but their Swiss protectors urging them not to compromise the question by insisting upon mere points of language, they assented, and it was agreed that a general amnesty should be granted to the Waldenses with the exception of such as had been condemned by the edict of the 25th of June, 1663; and, secondly, that Charles Emanuel, should ratify the patents of grace granted at Pignerol, the 18th of August, 1655; reserving to himself power to require from the Waldenses guarantees for the future, and fitting satisfaction for recent occurrences, under the arbitration of the king of France.

This arbitration, as a matter of course, became the source of a thousand difficulties. The next clause of the *patents of grace* of 1664 related to religious exercises at San Giovanni. Public worship was forbidden there to the protestants. A pastor might repair thither, twice a year, to visit the faithful, but he was not to reside there, nor even to pass a night there, except in case of absolute necessity. He might visit the sick, but he was not to hold any religious meeting, nor even instruct any catechumens within the limits of the parish.

This clause, also, became the source of infinite vexations to the Waldenses, of charges easily made, but with difficulty refuted. A narration of the annoyances and oppressions which the Waldenses endured under this clause would alone occupy a volume.

Article sixth enacted that the pastors of the Waldensian churches must thenceforward be natives of the valleys. This condition was beneficial to them, in fortifying their evangelical individuality, which was in danger of becoming enfeebled under the too protracted direction of foreign pastors.

Article seventh declared that the catholic churches and chapels which had been destroyed in the last war should be rebuilt at the cost of the Waldenses.

Article eighth provided that the prisoners on both sides should be released.

An agreement to disarm was respectively adopted upon the promulgation of this document, and the duke of Savoy wrote to the Swiss cantons, by their delegates, that he would in every respect adhere to the terms of the settlement.

After their infinite troubles, the Waldenses now began to hope that they should enjoy some repose; when all at once they received orders to send to Turin delegates empowered, in the name of the entire people, to recognise the guarantees and indemnities required by Charles Emanuel in virtue of Article second of the treaty.

On assembling at the appointed place and time, the duke of Savoy informed the Waldenses that they must pay him five hundred and eighty-one thousand francs, as the expense of the war, and a further sum of three hundred and thirty thousand three hundred and sixty-seven francs to indemnify the catholic towns for damages undergone during the war; fifty thousand francs for rebuilding the walls of Luzerna; forty thousand for customs' duties omitted; twenty-five thousand for other taxes omitted; the sum necessary for repairing the fortifications of La Torre and Miraboco; &c. &c. In other words, the persecuted were required to sacrifice the last wreck of their fortune, and to indebt themselves for the future, in order to defray the expenses occasioned by the barbarities of their persecutors. Such were the indemnities demanded by Charles Emanuel; the guarantees he required were, that at the entrance of each valley, the Waldenses should, at their own cost, erect a fortress, to be garrisoned by ducal troops, who were to be maintained at the expense of the Waldenses; that they should hold no synod without the presence of one of his officers; that the Waldensian communes should not thenceforward hold any political union, but each manage its own affairs, without consulting the others; in other words, that they should hand themselves over to the enemy, to be destroyed in detail. The Waldenses rejecting these preposterous terms, Louis XIV. was appealed to, by common consent, as an arbitrator.

The award of his most Christian majesty was far more moderate than might have been expected. He decided that the Waldenses should contribute fifty thousand francs towards the expenses of the war, and cede to the duke the vineyards of Luzerna, in compensation for the losses he had incurred by "the rebellion" of the protestants. Various intercessions for more favourable terms, on the part of different foreign powers, protracted the settlement of the matter, from month to month, from year to year, and at last, in 1670, the duke modifying his demands and granting new privileges, he and his Waldensian subjects came to a good understanding; and the latter, both at the siege of Genoa and at the revolt of Mondovi, did such good service to their sovereign, as to merit, on both occasions, the emphatic thanks proclaimed in the manifest form of orders of the day. On the former occasion, the duke wrote to the apostolic nuncio: "Were I to heed only the dictates of sound policy, I should wish the Waldenses to multiply instead of diminishing, for they are faithful, laborious, well-disposed, useful to the country," &c.

Victor Amadeus, with whom the ducal was destined to become a regal crown, succeeded his father in 1675; and being at that time only nine years of age, the affairs of the state were administered under the regency of his mother, who, in his name, fully ratified all the rights and privileges which had been granted to the Waldenses. The independence and repose of this people seemed now established on a permanent basis; but the ways of God are not our ways, and the poor churches of the valleys, already so sorely tried, were now, in reality, more than ever in danger of annihilation.

Chapter Twenty-fourth.

COMMENCEMENT OF THE FOURTH PERSECUTION.

GIANAVEL, excepted from the amnesty, and fain to seek refuge in a foreign land, had retired to Geneva, where, in his privacy, he never ceased to apply his energetic mind to the affairs of his oppressed faith and his oppressed country.

France was, at this time, of all the states of Europe, that which weighed heaviest in the scale of their respective destinies; but the monarch of France, potent as he was in many respects, was quite as weak in others. Resolute towards terrestrial powers, he bowed beneath the power of superstition, and submitted himself, in the credulous terror of ignorance, to the iron sway of the ministers of superstition. His dissolute life, varied with fits of devotion, his haughty soul, his utter selfishness, could only be swayed by the accommodating and ambitious power of popery, which, in its turn, used him as a means of crushing liberty. The greatest enemy of superstition being the Bible, and all who appealed to the authority of that book incurring the pertinacious hostility of catholicism, the confessors of the most Christian king persuaded this monarch that the most effectual mode by which he could secure at once his renown and his salvation, was the extermination of the protestants. The first proceeding of this respectable champion of popery was to set about the purchase of conversions; and a regular account current of expenditure and receipts—the former in money, the latter in conversions—was opened, and submitted to the king. Whole troops of vagrants turned this plan to their own account: calling themselves protestants, they would abjure by scores, in one town; having received the price of their *conversion*, they would proceed to some other town, abjure again, and receive a fresh reward; and so, from one end of France to the other, the scandalous farce proceeded, until the money available for such venal apostacy had become exhausted. Before long, however, the royal spouse of Maria Theresa having committed another crying sin against his marriage vow, the popish counsellors about him took advantage of the circumstance to excite a reaction of spiritual fervour in him, of which the protestant worship soon suffered the cruel effects. Twenty-one of their churches were demolished, in the Vivarais, in the single year 1680; proscriptions multiplied, the exercise of public functions was prohibited to the reformers; nay, by the ordinance of the 2d of December, 1681, they were absolutely forbidden to practice as physicians, notaries, printers, &c., that is to say, were forbidden to make their living by the honest industry to which they had been trained.

The *dragonades* came next. Louvois, already laden with the crimes and calamities inflicted upon the Palatinate under his command, wrote to Louis XIV., with reference to the Vivarais: "We must make such desolation in that district that it may ever after operate as an example." This was not enough: in order to strike a comprehensive blow at protestantism, the edict of Nantes was revoked, 18th October, 1685. The effect of this revocation was instantaneous and terrible. A great number of French protestants transferred to foreign lands their intelligence, their information, their virtues, and their fortunes, acquired or to be acquired. This single act did more to enfeeble France than all the victories of Louis XIV. had done to strengthen her.

Hitherto, while men had interdicted the reformed worship, belief had not been interdicted. This improvement was now adopted; civil death was pronounced upon all protestants, and, of consequence, all their acts were declared null and void; their marriages were set aside, and their children born, or to be born, declared illegitimate. Whoever, having therefore abjured, or appeared to abjure, protestantism, refused, on his or her sick bed, the sacraments of the popish church, was drawn out on a hurdle and thrown on the wayside, if he died, or condemned to the galleys if he recovered; and whether dead or alive, his whole property became confiscated to the king.

Proceeding from bad to worse, this same king, prostrate and drivelling at the feet of his imperious confessor, Letellier, next signed an edict, by which, all protestants being, in the first clause, declared converts to catholicism, all such of these converts as refused to conform to the practice of the communion to which they were so annexed, were to be treated as *relapsed* persons; that is to say, were to be drawn out on a hurdle and thrown on the wayside, dead, or condemned to the galleys, living, their property being, in either case, confiscated to the use of his most Christian majesty.

Never had such revolting iniquities sullied even the cruel persecutions of the dukes of Savoy. Victor Amadeus himself emphatically expressed his disapprobation. Many distinguished catholics, such as the cardinal de Noailles, Flechier, Fenelon, protested against the injury thus inflicted on the interests of France. Vauban, the great engineer, drew up a memorial, representing this involuntary exile of a hundred thousand Frenchmen as a grave political and social calamity for France; showing that the revocation of the edict of Nantes, and its attendant measures, would most materially damage commerce and trade, disorganize society, and strengthen hostile fleets with nine thousand sailors, and hostile armies with six hundred officers and twelve thousand soldiers, among the best then in France. Hereupon "the great king" issued an *ordonnance* that whosoever should expatriate himself should be condemned to death and confiscation of goods; that is, he said to his protestant subjects: "You shall be massacred and despoiled if you stay in my kingdom, you shall be exterminated and despoiled if you quit it!"

On the 12th of October, 1685, Louis wrote to the marquis d'Arcy, his ambassador at Turin, informing him that he had ordered d'Harleville, governor of the French valleys of Perosa and Pragela, Cesana, Usseaux, Meano, Exili, Traversa, Salabertrans, and Bardonneche, to *ccnvert* the valleys within his jurisdiction, "by lodging his troops,"* and desiring him to exhort the duke of Savoy, "whose ancestors had ever ill endured the exercise of the protestant religion," to adopt similar means, in his own valleys, to the same end. On the 27th of October, the marquis informed his sovereign that he had duly impressed upon the duke the extraordinarily favourable opportunity afforded by the vicinity of the French troops, for bringing the followers of the pseudo-reformed religion to reason; the duke

* All protestants, "obstinate in their heresy," were compelled to lodge, board, and pay for the soldiers, who, on their part, were directed to injure, insult, and annoy, in every conceivable and inconceivable way, those upon whom they were billeted.

he said, had requested time to consider the matter, for that the enterprise thus counselled had been attempted repeatedly by his ancestors, not merely without success, but with great detriment to the state. To this, the marquis reported, that he had replied that those ancestors had never had facilities so great as were now proffered by the most Christian king, but that, of course, his royal highness "would do as he pleased in the matter; it was his interest alone that his most Christian majesty thought of."

On the 10th of November, Louis XIV. again wrote to the marquis, complaining that the duke of Savoy "manifested no firm resolution to labour efficaciously at this great affair, which yet can never be brought to a successful issue by such slight attempts as those proposed by his royal highness;" urging that the duke must be made to understand that his glory was concerned in bringing his subjects, at whatever cost, to the feet of the church, and promising to aid him with any troops he might require 'for the execution of so pious a design." In his reply, on the 24th of November, the marquis states that "he had renewed to the duke the offers of his most Christian majesty in aid of the conversion of the Waldenses, but that his royal highness—a prince of extreme reserve and of a very independent turn—had merely repeated his thanks for the interest taken by the most Christian king in his affairs." The ambassador adds: "It seems very doubtful whether the duke will adopt the measures proposed by your majesty, for when the ministers, the marquis di San Tommaso and the president de Truchsis, who both entirely concur with your majesty, have spoken to him on the subject, he has scarcely given them an answer at all." The popish counsellors of his most Christian majesty were not to be thus frustrated, and, on the 7th of December, Louis again wrote to his ambassador at Turin: "So long as the duke shall suffer Huguenots to subsist on the frontiers of my state, his authority will not suffice to prevent desertion on the part of my Calvinist subjects; this, he must be clearly sensible, I shall not endure; and the insolence of these heretics exciting my irrepressible indignation, the result might be that I should no longer entertain towards him those sentiments of friendship which I have hitherto manifested. I feel assured he will seriously reflect hereupon."

The duke, apparently, did reflect seriously upon this very emphatic intimation, for, on the 31st of January, 1686, appeared the fatal edict which caused such infinite misery to the valleys, and seemed, for awhile, to have effected the complete annihilation of the Waldensian church. "Heresy," the edict set forth, "has extended from the centre of the valley of Luzerna to the heart of Piedmont. Our ancestors have often undertaken to extirpate it, but, by means of the succours which the religionists have received from foreign countries, the holy work of their return to the Romish church has not been accomplished; and since, at present, the principal reason that existed for tolerating them has been removed, by the zeal and piety of the glorious monarch of France, who has brought to the true faith the heretics contiguous to the Waldensian valleys, we deem that his most Christian majesty might accuse us of ingratitude for his signal favour, which we still enjoy, were we to let pass the opportunity of executing this important design, pursuant to the intention ever entertained by our glorious predecessors.

"Upon which grounds, and for other pressing reasons, we have, of our full authority, certain knowledge, good pleasure, and absolute power, decreed as follows:—

"I. The Waldenses shall henceforth and forever cease and discontinue all the exercises of their religion.

"II. They are forbidden to have religious meetings, under pain of death and penalty of confiscation of all their goods.

"III. All their ancient privileges are abolished.

"IV. All the churches, prayer-houses, and other edifices, consecrated to their worship, shall be rased to the ground.

"V. All the pastors and schoolmasters of the valleys are required either to embrace catholicism or to quit the country within fifteen days, under pain of death and confiscation of goods.

"VI. All the children born, or to be born, of protestant parents, shall be compulsorily trained up as Roman catholics. Every such child, yet unborn, shall, within a week after its birth, be brought to the curé of its parish, and admitted of the catholic church, under pain, on the part of the mother, of being publicly whipped with rods, and on the part of the father, of labouring five years in the galleys.

"VII. The Waldensian pastors, who shall abjure the doctrine they have hitherto preached, shall receive a salary greater by one-third than that which they previously enjoyed; and one-half thereof shall go in reversion to their widows.

"VIII. All protestant foreigners settled in Piedmont are ordered either to catholicise or to quit the country within fifteen days.

"IX. By a special act of his great and paternal clemency, the sovereign will permit all such persons to sell, in this interval, the property they may have acquired in

Piedmont, provided the sale be made to catholic purchasers."

It is impossible adequately to describe the consternation, the affliction, the indignation, created throughout the valleys by the promulgation of this monstrous edict. All the parishes immediately appointed delegates, who assembled at Angrogna, to deliberate upon the defence of the common interests. Their first proceeding was to draw up an earnest but respectful supplication to the duke, for the revocation of the edict; but all they could obtain was a brief delay in its execution. The next course was to seek the intervention of the protestant cantons of Switzerland. That generous nation, at once responding to the appeal, addressed earnest letters to the court of Turin, in favour of the Waldenses. The letters remained unanswered. Next, by an extraordinary assembly, held at Baden, 26th of February, 1686, it was resolved that special envoys should be despatched into Piedmont, for the purpose, if possible, of rescuing the Israel of the Alps from the destruction that menaced it. The ambassadors selected, Gaspard and Bernard de Murat, both councillors of state, reached Turin in the beginning of March, and solicited an audience of Victor Amadeus: it was refused.

Meanwhile, the delay which had been granted to the Waldenses was on the point of expiration, and the urgency of the French ambassador, of the papal nuncio, and of the propaganda, grew daily more pressing upon Victor Amadeus. Already, in their persecuting ardour, several bands of popish volunteers had commenced hostilities upon the inhabitants of the valleys, and the impatience of the French troops cantoned at Pignerol could hardly be restrained.

The mountaineers, who numbered three thousand fighting

men, and whose strength was daily increased by the accession of foreign brethren, though they prayed for peace, were quite ready to resist the foe with vigour. In the few casual skirmishes to which reference has just been made, they were victorious; and they daily occupied themselves in the organization of plans for the campaign, which were as regularly communicated to the commandant of La Torre, by a French spy, named Desmoulin, who had got among them in the character of a Dauphinese refugee. The chiefs and the pastors adopted at the same time, a series of regulations which had been drawn up for that purpose by Gianavel, ever watchful and earnest in his retreat, and of which the first clause presents a not uninteresting illustration:—

"Since the war that is raised up against us is an effect of the hatred against our religion, and that our sins are the cause of that hatred, it behooves every one of us to repent and to amend his life; to which end, it is expedient that the officers shall have good books to read to the men in the guardhouses, and have prayers celebrated every morning and evening."

Meantime, the Swiss envoys, having failed to effect an audience of the duke, drew up a memorial, in which, after reciting the edicts by which liberty of conscience and other rights had been guaranteed to the Waldenses, they represented that fidelity to treaties constitutes the stability of states, and their repose; that if the word of princes were not held sacred, protestant powers might treat their catholic subjects as he proposed to treat his protestant subjects; and that his own glory, his own character, his humanity, justice, the prosperity of Piedmont, were all interested in his not becoming the executioner of a faithful people, of whom he was the natural protector, and whom he had promised to treat as a father.

The marquis di San Tommaso, who was entrusted with the charge of replying to this memorial, sought to throw the whole blame upon the Waldenses, as having taken up arms against their lawful sovereign. The ambassador pointed out that it was the duke who had taken up arms against the Waldenses, not only without cause on their part, but avowedly for the purpose of suppressing their religion. "Potent engagements with France," rejoined the minister, incautiously, "have dictated our conduct."—"If that be so," at once returned the envoys, "you cannot say the Waldenses are to blame, and should cease to persecute them."—"Matters have gone too far, said the marquis; "but if the Waldenses, to save appearances, will outwardly conform to the edict of the 31st January, things may, perhaps, be arranged."

This proposition was altogether too vague to be accepted, and the envoys accordingly rejected it. They offered, however, to go the valleys, and see what could be done, and a safe conduct was accordingly given to them; their interposition being all the more heeded, that at this juncture, Brandenburg, Holland, and England, had also addressed fresh representations to Victor Amadeus, in favour of his protestant subjects.

The Swiss envoys reached the valleys on 22d March, and immediately invited the attendance of deputies from all the Waldensian communes, to consult with them. The meeting took place at Chiasso, on 23d March. The Swiss envoys having stated what they had done since their arrival at Turin, and being requested by the Waldenses to counsel them in this emergency, suggested that the best course would be to obtain leave to sell all they had, and quit, in a body, a country whose sovereign had manifestly resolved that they should not dwell there in peace and in liberty of conscience. "Your valleys," said the envoys, "are hemmed in by the states of your enemies; al. the paths to it are guarded; there is no nation in a position to wage war with France, solely in your behalf; no succours can reach you; and you yourselves have at the most, three thousand fighting men; you have more than twelve thousand mouths to feed; your supplies are cut off, and your every step is watched; an overpowering force awaits but the signal to massacre you. How can you resist? Rather, we implore you, transport elsewhere the torch of the gospel, of which you are the depositories, than to keep it here to be extinguished in blood."

The Waldenses, who had expected other counsels, who were prepared for strife, and hoped for victory, replied that they could not consent, on behalf of their countrymen, to expatriate themselves without a struggle; and that, at all events, so grave a position must be decided by the whole population.

The Swiss deputies, unable to wait for this decision, returned to Turin, whence they despatched their secretary to receive the reply of the aggregate Waldenses. On the arrival of this functionary in the valleys (28th March), he found the population in a state of the greatest agitation. Even those who were willing to emigrate were fearful that the proposal to give them free egress from the valleys was merely a snare, so that while journeying forth, in isolated groups, they might be assailed and slain by the enemy. Most of the pastors were, from the outset, in favour of submission; the mass of the people, were, at first, for resistance; but, after awhile, the communes of Perosa, San Martin, Prarustin, Roccapiatta, Rora, Villar, and La

Torre, consented to submit; the communes of Bobbi, San Giovanni, and Angrogna, with a portion of La Torre, adhering to resistance. In the hope of turning this division to advantage, the enemies of the Waldenses induced Victor Amadeus to sign (9th April) an edict, which treated the emigration of the Waldenses as an affair quite settled and agreed upon. When this edict, however, was published (11th April) in the valleys, it agumented the excitement which already prevailed there; and three days afterwards, at a meeting of delegates from all the communes, at Roccapiatta, it was resolved, that, the conditions imposed by this edict being wholly inadmissible, all idea of submission should be abandoned, and that the Waldenses, acting as one man, should resist to the last gasp, and, relying upon the aid of Providence, defend their hearths and altars, as their fathers had done before them.

Thus the measure which had been designed to separate them had the effect of uniting them more compactly than ever.

On the 17th April, being Good Friday, the solemn covenant was confirmed by another meeting of delegates at Roccapiatta; and on Easter Sunday the holy communion was received by all the sons of the valleys, heroic disciples of the gospel, and resolute to defend it and themselves against vile oppressors.

It was the last communion they were to partake of before the terrible castastrophe we are about to narrate, and which for awhile effected the total dispersion of this people.

Chapter Twenty-fifth.

MASSACRES AND EXPATRIATION.

THE generous Swiss ambassadors, finding that their mediation between the two parties was useless, resolved to leave Piedmont. But foreseeing the inevitable and approaching destruction of that Waldensian church, which was so dear to them, they wrote to Frederic William, grand elector of Brandenberg, to beg him to receive into any vacant territory within his states, a colony of Waldenses, if they should be expelled from their native country. The elector graciously replied that he would give them an asylum at all risks.

Already the combined forces of France and Piedmont were approaching the Waldensian valleys. Victor Amadeus II. reviewed his troops in the plain of San Segonzo. His army consisted of two thousand five hundred and eighty-six men of the regiments of Mondovi, Barges, and Bagnolo; a corps of Piedmontese infantry, and a regiment of horse; while the French auxiliaries were several regiments of dragoons and other calvary; seven or eight battalions of infantry from Dauphiny; and a portion of the garrisons of Pignerol and Cassale. The signal of carnage was to be given on Easter Monday, 22d April, by three cannon-shots, fired at dawn of day, from the hill of Bricherasio, when a general attack on the two valleys was forthwith to tak: place; the duke of Savoy assailing that of Luzerna, and Catinat, general-in-chief of the French auxiliaries, that of St. Martin. The latter general quitted Pignerol in the night of Easter Sunday, and, after marching two hours by torch-light, reached the village of St. German as day was dawning. Catinat immediately sent forward a detachment of infantry under the command of lieutenant-colonel Villevielle, who took possession of the town, and drove the Waldenses from their first entrenchments; but presently the Waldenses, turning about, repulsed the aggressors. Catinat hereupon sent a detachment of horse to sustain his infantry; the fighting extended along the whole line, and lasted for ten consecutive hours. The French infantry grew weary, and the calvary could not operate with any effect on slopes covered with brushwood, and so pertinaciously defended by the mountaineers; and at length the latter, finding the fire of the enemy slacken, made, all at once, a *sortie* so impetuous, that the French surprised and driven in, turned, fled and were chased out of the territory to the left bank of the Clusone. More than five hundred of the enemy were killed or wounded in this engagement, while the Waldenses lost only two men. Villevielle himself, with thirty men, made his way to the protestant church St. German, where he gallantly defended himself till the evening, against a series of energetic attacks, directed by Henry Arnaud, who, at first a Dauphinese pastor, had emigrated to the valleys from the tyranny of Louis XIV., and was, at this juncture, at once a pastor and a captain of the Waldenses. At night, a detachment of troops from Pignerol rescued the gallant French officer from his perilous position.

Meanwhile, Catinat had marched to Perosa. There he

distributed his forces into two divisions; the first of which, under the command of Melac, penetrating the valley of Pragela, by Salvage, turned the heights of Pomaret, while the second, led by Catinat himself, was directed towards Les Clots. The next day, 23d of April, this general attacked Rioclaret, opposite the position he had thus taken.

All the inhabitants of the valley of St. Martin had declared, four days before, that they were willing to avail themselves of the edict of the 9th of April, and to lay down their arms. But Victor Amadeus was not made acquainted with their resolution till the evening before the battle; he then refused to accept it, declaring it came too late. His troops were already in possession of the approaches to the valleys; the envoy sent by that of St. Martin could not return thither. The inhabitants of this district were ignorant of the duke's answer; they trusted to the articles of the edict, and, not expecting an attack. they had made no preparations for defending themselves. The army of Catinat surprised them, thus unprepared, cut them to pieces, and spread themselves over the valley, killing, burning, pillaging. Six families, who were made prisoners, and were sent to Perosa, were basely massacred on their arrival there. Two young girls of Villa-Secca were slain in their resistance to the outrages of the soldiers: the latter glutted on their dead bodies the brutality of which they had not been able to render them the victims while living.

Giovanni Ribeto, of Macel, had his limbs burned off in succession, as he successively refused the injunctions to abjure which were made to him in the intervals of his tortures.

At the hamlet of Fontane, near Rodoret, four women were seized as they were fleeing with their infants; the hapiess babes were dashed ruthlessly to the ground, and the still more hapless mothers outraged till they died on the dead bodies of their children.

In all directions the horrors of 1655 were renewed, with even aggravated atrocities. Husbandmen were fastened to the end of the ploughshare, and dug into the earth they were tilling. Others were hurled from precipices upon the rugged points below; others torn in pieces by horses; others tortured to death by mutilations too monstrous to be described.

After having thus devastated the valley of St. Martin, Catinat left a few troops there, and marched on to Pramol.

Melac, who joined him there, had perpetrated at Pomaret horrors of the same atrocious character; and on his way he had absolutely, at the pike's point, compelled the outraged Waldensian women and girls, whom he had taken prisoners, to march naked, at the head of his troops, in order to guide them on their way.

The combined forces of Melac and Catinat encamped on the basin of Pramol, at the hamlet of La Rua, over-against that of Pemiano. The latter was occupied by fifteen hundred Waldenses, the inhabitants of the locality, augmented by the men of St. German, who had so valiantly resisted the first attack of the enemy; so that the protestants were in a condition once more to resist, and, perhaps, once more effectually. Seeing this, the enemy recurred to treachery, a weapon at which the papists are peculiarly expert; and Catinat sent word to the Waldenses that the inhabitants of the valley of Luzerna had laid down their arms, had waited on Victor Amadeus, and had been received by him into his full grace, which he was equally ready to accord to all his Waldensian subjects who would take the same course. The Waldenses, hereupon, sent two envoys to the French general, to receive from his own mouth the confirmation of this news and of this promise. Soldierly honour revolted not in the breast of this soldier against a deliberate lie: "Lay down your arms," he said, "and all is pardoned."

The Waldenses, true themselves, believed in the truth of others: they laid down their arms, and received the French regiment, who the next morning entered Pemiano, without distrust. The officer in command of the regiment, captain St. Pierre, then assembled the men of the place, informed them that the duke had been informed of their submission, and was waiting to receive them graciously. They at once departed, under escort, to receive from their sovereign the promised grace, and, the defenders thus removed, and none of the Waldenses being left in the place but women, children, and aged people, the soldiers of Catinat rushed like wild beasts upon this inoffensive multitude, massacreing some, torturing others, despoiling all; and as to the women and young girls, subjecting them to atrocities so brutal, that the pen refuses to describe them. The children were taken away, and distributed among the monasteries and convents of Piedmont, or with popish families. Their fathers, who had gone to the camp of Victor Amadeus to make their submission, were cast into the dungeons of Luzerna, Cavour, and Villafranca, where many of them died of privation, grief and sickness.

But popery was triumphant: treason had served it; half the population of the valleys was massacred or imprisoned; carnage had done its work; and what remained of the Israel of the Alps was destined to be of short duration. The Te Deums of St. Bartholomew were soon to be heard once again.

Victor Amadeus had remained in the plain which forms the entrance to the valley of Luzerna, towards La Torre and Rora. It was there, at a later period, after the wonderful return of the Waldenses to their country, that this prince, vanquished and a fugitive in his turn, came to seek an asylum among the same mountaineers whom now he was using his utmost efforts to destroy or exile.

His uncle, Gabriel of Savoy, advanced towards the heights of Angrogna. His line of operations extended from Bricherasio to San Giovanni, while the Waldenses occupied, on the summit of the hills of Le Cotière, a series of posts above and parallel with them. On the 22d of April, Don Gabriel made a simultaneous attack on these posts, from all sides. The Waldenses fought the whole day. On the approach of night, the bivouac fires were lighted on both sides. This girdle of fire environed the mountain at about a third of its height. Serres and Castelluzzo belonged to the enemy, Roccamanante and Le Porte d'Angrogna were in the hands of the Waldenses.

On the 23d of April the battle was resumed. The Waldenses retired towards the crest of the mountain, in good order, and fighting incessantly the whole day. Towards the evening they encamped all together, at the foot of La Vachera, and fortified their position with entrenchments of rocks and earth. Next morning, Gabriel of Savoy was informed of the surrender of the Waldenses of Pramol, who had trusted themselves into the hands of their foes, and whose defenceless families had been massacred.

He immediately resolved to employ the same means against his opponents, and sent word to them that their co-religionists of the valley of St. Martin having laid down their arms and obtained grace, he advised them to follow this example, to avoid greater evils; for if they did not surrender, the French troops, who were in possession of the valley of St. Martin, and that of Pramol, would ake them in the rear, and they would be inevitably crushed.

The Waldenses of the valley of Luzerna, entrenched at the foot of La Vachera, were amazed at this intelligence, and, in their turn, sent envoys to Gabriel of Savoy, who confirmed the news, and sent them back a despatch, signed by himself, which ran thus:—"Do not hesitate to lay down your arms; be assured that, in submitting yourselves to the clemency of his royal highness, he will receive you favourably, and that he will not injure your persons, nor those of your wives and children."

A promise so formal, and signed by a royal hand, it seemed unreasonable to doubt; but the Waldenses should have borne in mind that the hand so signing was also a popish hand, taught to trace, without a shudder, whatever atrocities a priest might dictate.

The Waldenses, however, put faith in Don Gabriel, and, that very evening, opening their entrenchments to him, placed themselves, without arms and without distrust, amidst his troops. The latter immediately, under pretext of friendly conversation, got around them, then seized them, and, binding them like criminals, dragged them to Luzerna, where they were thrown into the dungeons, already half filled with betrayed Waldenses.

Thus, almost without striking a blow, the enemy gained possession of these formidable valleys, where the Waldenses had posts so advantageous, and entrenchments so strong, that, as a popish writer of the time admits, they might have maintained themselves there for ten years. But treachery had immured the male defenders of this sanctuary and of the gospel in the dungeons of popedom, and imprisoned their children in its monasteries and its nunneries; their outraged wives and daughters, their helpless parents, were massacred; their houses were despoiled and burned, their fields devastated.

In the valley of Luzerna, Victor Amadeus himself attacked two posts of Waldenses, who were covering the entrance to Pra-del-Tor and the road to Villar. The fight continuing till evening, without any result, the same stratagem was resorted to by the papists which had succeeded so well at La Vachera and Pemiano: upon the solemn assurance of the Piedmontese chiefs that the duke, who was at hand, would receive them into favour, on their laying down their arms, "as he had already received into favour their brethren of Angrogna and La Vachera," many of the Waldenses surrendered, and were at once sent to join their brethren in the dungeons of the duke; while those who would not surrender, finding their numbers so fearfully reduced by stratagem or surprise, abandoned their posts, and withdrew to Bobbi, the last village of any importance in the valley that remained to the protestants. Here, after repulsing several separate attacks, they were surrounded, on the 13th of May, by the entire army of Victor Amadeus and his French allies, and, finding themselves unable to withstand this immense force, they cut their way through the enemy's lines, and dispersed amid the depths of La Sarcena and Garino. The popish troopers then proceeded to the work, in which they were so skilled, of massacre, outrage, spoliation, and incendiarism. Two sisters, Anna and Madalena Vittoria, after undergoing indescribable brutalities, were burned alive in the shed which had been the scene of their dishonour. Daniel Pellenc was flayed alive, and then, a huge stone being laid upon his prostrate and palpitating body, was left to die in agony. One poor woman, who had taken refuge in a cavern, where a goat supplied her with the nourishment which she, in her turn, communicated to her baby, was surprised by the soldiers; the infant was thrown down the abyss, on the rocks below; the mother was dragged before the marquis de Benil, colonel of the regiment of Savoy, and interrogated as to the place where her co-religionists had retired. She would give no answer. To make her speak, the soldiers crushed her fingers between iron bars; this producing no effect, the heroic defenders of the Roman catholic faith broke her legs, and, having violently tied her heels to her neck, rolled her down into the gulf where they had just before cast her infant. Daniel Mondon, one of the elders of Rora, was compelled to witness the decapitation of his two sons, the eventeration of his daughter-in-law, and the massacre of her four children; he was then driven at the pike's point, his sons' heads and the bleeding remains of his daughter-in-law being suspended round his neck, to Luzerna, where he was hanged.

"All the valleys are wasted, all the inhabitants killed, hanged, or massacred." So wrote, on the 26th of May, 1686, a French officer in the army of Catinat; and the destruction of the Waldensian churches seemed, indeed, at length accomplished. More than one thousand persons had been massacred, more than six thousand lay in prison, and two thousand children, torn from their parents, were immured in various popish establishments. All the Waldenses, dead or alive, had been declared guilty of high treason, and their property, of whatever description, confiscated to the state. Nothing seemed to remain for the valleys but the silence of death and desolation.

It was from this very desperation of circumstances that the remnant of the Waldenses derived fresh courage. No sooner had their most formidable enemies—the French troops and the militia of Mondovi—withdrawn altogether, and the Piedmontese army partially, than, from the depths of the woods and ravines, and from the heights of the craggiest rocks, there crept forth men worn with fatigue and privation, but resolute in their faith and in their patriotism, who, by degrees collecting together on Mont Beces, numbered in all eighty men, with whom were a few women and some children. We know not the names, nor the leader, of this small band, destined, by their heroic valour, to emancipate from prison their betrayed countrymen, to recover their confiscated property, and to obtain for them and for themselves, an honourable retreat, with baggage and arms, to a foreign land.

Animated with the spirit of Gianavel, and aided by the hand of God, these last defenders of the valleys fell like a thunderbolt on the persecutors, who supposed them all exterminated, defeated successively the garrisons of Villar, La Torre, Luzerna, and San Segonzo, seized a large convoy of ammunition and provisions on its way to Pignerol, and then, returning to the mountains, multiplied their numbers by their activity, their strength by their valour, their power by the fear they inspired, and their chances of safety by the incessant losses to which they subjected the enemy.

Unforeseen in attack, unattainable in retreat, they would fall suddenly on some heedless post, some sleeping cantonment, fire the buildings or the tents, slay numbers of the enemy, and then retreat, ere the survivors had time even to look at their assailants; or, in the middle of the night, they would assail some village in the plain, set fire to the outskirts, and menace the entire conflagration of the place, unless a heavy ransom was paid. The marquis de Parelles and Gabriel of Savoy marched against these desperate guerrillas, but to no purpose, and, after having undergone two defeats, the Piedmontese generals offered to the Waldenses free egress to any foreign country they might select, if they would consent to retire. The offer was accepted; but only on condition that all the Waldenses who were detained in prison should be released, and included in the concession. Further, these hardy mountaineers stipulated that, in their retreat to a foreign land, each division of exiles should be accompanied by an officer of the royal guard, by way of hostage; and, moreover, that, to the frontiers of Savoy, the cost of journey should be defrayed by Victor Amadeus. After some hesitation these terms were accorded: it was agreed that the prisoners should be released, and have free egress from the country, and it was further conceded that all the Waldenses should be at liberty to dispose of their goods. But as to these goods, the far greater portion had been a prey to pillage and incendiarism; and as to the prisoners, so many of them had died under their sufferings in the popish dungeons, that, altogether, of the fifteen thousand Waldenses who constituted the protestant population of the valleys but a few months before, only two thousand six hundred remained to avail themselves of the liberty of exile now granted to them.

Arrangements having been meanwhile made with the Swiss protestant cantons for the reception of the exiles within their territory, the first two detachments, consisting of the men whose valour had procured from the court of Savoy the concession upon which they were acting, arrived at Geneva, on the 25th of November, 1686, in number eighty persons, men, women and children. On the 3d of December, the Waldensian prisoners at Turin were released, and despatched on their way to Switzerland; and on the 3d of January, 1687, they were followed by the remainder of their countrymen.

The numerous Waldenses whom persecution in their dungeons had induced to catholicize, were not permitted to return to their valleys, but detained in prison for some days after the departure of their countrymen, that they might not join them in their exile. They were then deported to the marshy plains of Vercelli, where they were ordered to remain, under penalty of ten years' labor in the galleys, and where great numbers of them speedily died of typhus fever. Any of them who should presume to set foot in the valleys was to be punished with death.

The total number of Waldenses, men, women, and children, who reached Geneva—for hundreds died of the effects of their ill-treatment in prison, of cold and hunger, on their way—was two thousand six hundred and fifty-six. Their reception was most generous; one-half of the population of Geneva, headed by the patriot Gianavel, came to meet them at the Arve, the confine-river of their sublime territory, and there competed with each other who should receive, within his hospitable dwelling, the greatest number of the exiles. Of the third band of Waldenses, one party, in especial, aroused the interest, the enthusiasm of the Genevese—a patriarchal barba, ninety-six years old, who, heading a tribe of seventy-two children and grandchildren, revived the imposing image of those biblical migrations, which the constant study of the Bible had rendered so familiar to protestants.

The numbers thus arriving at Geneva could not, of course, be all entertained in that city; some were distributed among the other protestant communities of Switzerland, some were conveyed to Brandenberg, some to Holland, and thence to America; but all who had the choice remained in Geneva, to be near those beloved valleys, which all cherished the hope and expectation one day to recover.

CASTLE OF IVOIRE.—(LAKE OF GENEVA.)

Chapter Twenty-sixth.

THE GLORIOUS RETURN OF THE WALDENSES UNDER ARNAUD.

THE Waldenses, such of them, at least, as were not still retained in prison, among whom were all the ministers, having quitted the valleys, it became a question how these valleys should be re-peopled. It was at first proposed to settle on them the Irish exiles, who were leading a vagrant life in Montferrat, but there was more than one objection to this plan; first, the idleness of these islanders, by whose neglect these districts, once so flourishing, would soon become barren and waste; secondly, the superior advantage of selling the lands. It was determined, therefore, that they should be put up to auction, and that what remained unsold should be let. The richest properties were added to the private domain of Victor Amadeus; and others given to his officers. Many catholicized Waldenses were permitted to remain for a few months on their lands; but ultimately the sale of the confiscated property began on the 15th July, 1689. Some were purchased by individuals, but most by companies formed for the speculation at Susa, Chambery, Saluzzo, and other places. The whole territory of Angrogna was sold in one lot; that of Bobbi was bought by bidders from Susa, for forty-four thousand francs; that of Villar, by a company of ten persons at Saluzzo. Generally speaking, the preference was given to Savoyards, who, coming from a mountainous and over-peopled country, presented, in both circumstances, greater probabilities of their introducing competent labourers, and plenty of them, into the country. But the expectation was by no means realized; so that when the Waldenses themselves returned home, they found their valleys in almost the same depopulated and devastated condition that they had left them in.

These Waldenses themselves, meanwhile, repulsed from Wurtemberg by the policy of its rulers, willing to favour the protestants, yet still more anxious to avoid a collision with their persecutors—repulsed from the palatinate by the dragoons of Louvois—repulsed from Brandenberg by the ill-will of the population—wandering about on the banks of the Rhine and in the mountains of Switzerland, an unwilling burden upon their co-religionists there,—had resolved to attempt the recovery of their valleys, not simply as a means of subsistence, or as satisfaction of patriotism, but as a duty of conscience. It seemed, indeed, under the circumstances, utterly improbable that this scattered remnant should rally under a leader of their own, and march, sword in hand, for the recovery of their possessions; but Henri Arnaud thought otherwise. Patriotic, ardent, and enthusiastic, his love for his native valleys would not suffer him to be happy in a foreign land, his courage would hear of no obstacles, and his warm imagination represented the arm of God as lifted up to succour the holy undertaking. *Lux lucet in tenebris*, "the light shineth in darkness," was the motto of his community, and the words which were ever in his mouth. He thought he saw the cloud which was to go before him by day, and the pillar of fire which was to give him light by night, and he was incessant in his importunities, until he had communicated his own martial spirit to a few faithful friends, and had girt on what he called the sword of the Lord and of Gideon, which he solemnly swore never to resign, until the images should be torn down from the altars of the thirteen sanctuaries, which, until this fatal epoch, had never been so idolatrously decorated. In a short time his little troop was increased to upwards of eight hundred daring adventurers, whom he had persuaded to join his standard, from different parts of Germany and Switzerland.

They were obliged to meet in secret, and their nocturnal assemblies were held in the dark retreats of a forest, which then spread over a long tract of country between Nion and Rolle, and extended down to the edge of the lake of Geneva.

On the night of Friday, the 16th August, 1689, Arnaud had completed all his preparations; and, putting himself at the head of his men, he seized some boats on the coast, and crossed the lake. Yvoire, in Savoy, was their place of landing, and they would have had to encounter an enemy at the first village through which they passed, if they had not wisely taken two persons of some distinction, as hostages for their safe conduct through this part of the country. The route, for the first two or three days, was by passes to which they were perfect strangers, but their hostages were answerable for the fidelity of the guides. On the second day, however, they were nearly betrayed, in spite of all their precautions. The inhabitants of Cluses, on the Arve, at first refused to give them a passage through the town, and afterwards despatched a messenger to Sallanches, with instructions for the people of that city to attack the Waldenses in the narrow defile of Maglan, while they themselves would assail them in the rear. Most providentially the treacherous scheme was discovered in time, and no other vengeance was taken than to carry off two more hostages from Cluses. The tremendous pass of Maglan, where a few peasants, armed with stones, might stop the progress of a whole army, was cleared before the troops of Sallanches had notice of this extraordinary march; and though it rained torrents the whole day, the eight hundred reached Cablau before they halted for the night.

It took them two days only to surmount the difficulties of the Montagne de Haut Luce, and that of the Bon Homme. The latter is a chain of the Allée Blanche, and forms part of the Graian Alps. After descending from these snow covered heights, they followed the course of the mountain torrent called Reclus, and penetrated, through a woody ravine, into the plain of Scez, where they encamped on the fourth evening. It was on this day's march that they passed by the large rock of Gypsum, which stands at the entrance of the defile that leads to Scez, and is well known as La Roche Blanche, which is supposed to be the celebrated white rock on which Hannibal spent the night, after the furious attack which was made upon him by the barbarians.

On the 21st August, the protestant heroes traversed the valley of the Isere; and though they expected to find this one of the most perilous of their journeys, yet they arrived at Laval in safety. Nothing can be more fertile, or better cultivated, than this lovely valley, which presents some of the finest Alpine scenery to the eye that is to be met with in Savoy: it was not, therefore, from the difficulty of the passes, or the scarcity of provisions, that Arnaud's troops apprehended interruption; but from the hostility of the inhabitants. The population is numerous on each side of the river; and it was never satisfactorily explained, why the eight hundred were permitted, not only to traverse the valley of the Isere, but also to cross Mont Iseran, and the still more formidable Mont Cenis, without any well-ordered attempt to stop their progress; for by this time the object of their march was well known at Turin. A few skirmishes was all they had to encounter; and it was not before the eighth day of their enterprise that they first came in conflict with any large body of regular troops.

To avoid the garrison of Susa, it was determined to proceed along the banks of the Dora, at the foot of the Col d'Albin, which closes in upon the river, and leaves a pass, which is barely practicable at places even for troops who have no enemy in front. The narrowest part of the defile is near Salabertrand, where a bridge is thrown over the Dora. At this point the Waldenses found their passage disputed by twenty-five hundred French, who summoned them to surrender at discretion. The superiority of numbers against them was fearfully great; the garrison at Susa were prepared to act against them, if they retreated; and hemmed in by the rocks on one side, and the river on the other, the little band had no alternative but to advance.

Having first reconnoitred, to discover if there was any ambuscade, the Waldenses advanced towards the bridge. Some of the enemy, who were entrenched on the other side, called out, *Qui vive?* to which the Waldenses replied, very sincerely, *Amis;* intending to remain so, if they had been suffered to pass without interruption. But the French did not desire to be friends upon these terms; and shouted "Kill them." A firing then commenced, which lasted a quarter of an hour, during which more than two thousand shots were discharged; but Arnaud having ordered his men to lie flat upon their faces, there was but one of them wounded. A Savoyard gentleman, one of the hostages, declared that he had never seen so terrible a firing take so little effect: and, what was more remarkable, Arnaud, Captain Mondon, of Bobbi, and two other refugees, were not only obliged to expose themselves to it, but held in check two companies, who attempted to charge the Waldenses in the rear. The Waldenses finding themselves thus placed between two fires, saw that no time was to be lost, and that every thing would depend upon the promptitude of the moment. At this critical juncture, a voice exclaimed, "Courage, the bridge is gained!" In an instant, the men rose up, and rushed forward, some sword in hand, and others with bayonets fixed. The bridge was carried; and with such impetuosity did the assailants advance to force the entrenchments, that they were at the very muzzles of the guns, and cut many of the enemy down, before they could fire at them. Never was so violent a shock. The sabres of the Waldenses shivered the swords of the French to pieces.

The victory was so glorious and decisive, that the marquis de Larrey, who commanded and was dangerously wounded in the arm, cried out, blaspheming in the usual French style, "Is it possible that I have lost the battle, and my own honour!" Seeing that there was no remedy, he added, *Sauve qui peut*, and then fled, with several wounded officers, to Briançon; but not considering himself safe even there, he was conveyed in a litter, to Embrun.

The conflict lasted two hours; and the enemy were so completely routed, that many of them, finding themselves intermixed pell-mell among the Waldenses, hoped to escape by being mistaken for them; but they were all put to the sword. The field of battle was covered with the dead. Several companies were reduced to seven or eight men, without any officers. All the baggage and ammunition fell into the hands of the Waldenses; and when the moon rose that evening, not an enemy was to be seen.

The exiles might have re-established themselves at once among the fastnesses of the valley of St. Martin, but these brave men were not satisfied with a secure retreat; they resolved to dispossess the Roman catholics, and to restore their brethren to their lands and habitations, or to perish in the attempt. The valley of Luzerna was occupied in great force by French and Piedmontese troops, a detachment of whom was ordered to seize the passes of the Col Julien, and to prevent Arnaud's approach on that side of the valley. But nothing could check his impetuous attack. The heights were carried with scarcely any loss on the part of the Waldenses; and the enemy were pursued from one summit to another, till they retreated into the vale of Bobbi, and took shelter in that village. Bobbi was, at this time, in the hands of the papists, to whom the confiscated property of the protestants had been assigned. It was taken by storm, and pillaged by the exasperated exiles, who, upon this occasion, lost sight of the moderation, by which they had hitherto been governed.

After these successes, the gallant patriots took an oath of fidelity to each other, and celebrated divine service in one of their own churches, for the first time since their banishment. The enthusiasm of the moment was irrepressible; they chanted the 74th Psalm to the clash of arms; and Henri Arnaud, mounting the pulpit with a sword in one hand and a Bible in the other, preached from the 129th Psalm; and once more declared, in the face of heaven, that he would never resume his pastoral office in patience and peace, until he should witness the restoration of his brethren to their ancient and rightful settlements.

Encouraged by their success at Bobbi, the Waldenses marched against Villar, where there was a strong garrison, and pressed the enemy so hard, as to force them to retire within the walls of a convent; but while they were investing the convent, a strong reinforcement arrived from Pignerol, relieved the blockade, and obliged the protestants to abandon the valley of Luzerna, and to retire among the strongholds of the valley of St. Martin. This was on the twenty-second day after their landing at Yvoire; and the detachments, both of French and Piedmontese, who were sent in pursuit, carried such devastation with them, that, for a time, all supplies of provisions were cut off; and for several days, they had nothing to subsist upon but fruit and vegetables. The warfare now assumed a more extraordinary turn than ever. The eight hundred had to maintain their ground against brigades sent against them, by the French king on one side, and the duke of Savoy on the other; it was no longer a detached force, but a well-appointed army with which they had now to contend. The rocky and barren district of St. Martin afforded them no resources; the defiles that led into the more fertile valleys were in the hands of the enemy: famine, fire, and sword menaced them in every direction, yet they refused to surrender. Even the fastnesses which, in former persecutions protected their fathers, were untenable for any length of time, from want of provisions. Scarcely had they taken up a position before they were obliged to abandon it, in search of supplies; and it is an extraordinary fact, that for several weeks they had neither food nor ammunition, but what they took from the enemy.

Under these circumstances, it was impossible that the

little band should concentrate its force, or remain together. It was obliged to separate, and to act in detached parties. Engagements were therefore taking place, almost every day, in different quarters of the valley; the enemy never knew where they would be attacked next, and at length were so intimidated, that a whole company would fly at the sound of a single Waldensian fusil. The Waldenses have always been good marksmen, and upon this occasion they exercised their skill most successfully. From the summit of a mountain, from the top of a crag, or from behind a rock or tree, a marksman would frequently take his stand, and deliberately fire several shots before he could be dislodged; or, knowing every pass and defile, a few of them would make a detour, and pour in a volley upon a bivouacing party of their adversaries, which never failed of causing dreadful slaughter and consternation.

One great thing in favour of this intrepid force was, that they had no women nor children to encumber them, for these were still in Switzerland; there was nothing to check the most perfect freedom of their movements, no strong places to attack or defend—for what were strong places to them? They could fall upon their enemy as they pleased and when they pleased; and if too hardly pressed, they had a secure retreat in their mountains, from which they could sally forth at a more favourable opportunity. They were neither to be beaten by force, nor baffled by cunning. The enemy would, as they thought, surround them. Every possible means of escape seemed cut off; but their intimate knowledge of the mountains, and fearless habits, would enable them to march off by paths which were either unsuspected by the enemy, or considered as utterly impracticable.

As the winter set in, the hardships and deprivations of

these poor men increased; without any shelter for several nights together, worn down by constant fatigue, and half famished for want of food, it is wonderful how they supported their courage. We find them one day at Prali, on the second taking Perrero by storm, and the day afterwards surprising Pomaret. We read of them as being at the last-mentioned place on the 26th day of the month, and on the 29th attacking and defeating five hundred of the Piedmontese at Angrogna.

There was one fortress which was was deemed quite impregnable, and this the Waldenses succeeded in supplying with provisions. It was that of Balsille, situated in front of one of the defiles that lead into the valley of St. Martin, and near the source of a mountain stream which flows into the Germanesca. Just at the point where the craggy sides of the Guignivert, the highest ridge of this chain of Alps, slope down towards the foot of the Col del Pis (a lofty mountain, which prevents all access from the side of Pragela), a rampart of rock stands at the entrance of the pass, and forms of itself a barrier, which requires but little art to render it secure against any force that can be brought against it. The highest part of this rock rises as steep as a wall, and has three stages or terraces, surmounted by a sort of natural platform. Upon this platform stood a tower, and in the sides of the rock which rose above each terrace, caverns were hollowed out to serve for barracks. Three fountains supplied the fortress with water, and there was no approaching it with any probability of success, but from the side where the stream gushes from the mountain. Numberless assaults were made by the enemy upon this position, but nothing could dislodge the little garrison to whose charge it was confided. When they were most pressed, a messenger from the fort

THE BALSILLE DURING THE ATTACK.

was despatched to Prali, and a detachment from their comrades made an unexpected attack upon the French in the rear, while they themselves sallied from their bulwarks, and caused an incredible slaughter.

One more attack, made by Catinat with all his forces, was repelled; and the general, resolved not to lose his chance of the *baton* of marshal, from being again defeated by a handful of mountaineers, delegated the further siege of Balsille to the marquis de Feuguiéres, who, on the 14th May, 1690, succeeded in battering down the bastions of the fortress. The French army then mounted to the assault, assured of taking the besieged prisoners; but a thick fog, which arose at this juncture, enabled the Waldenses to make their escape, under the guidance of captain Poulat, a native of the place, along the edge of precipices never before trodden by the foot of men, and along which they were compelled to creep on their hands and knees: the path was so perilous, that men accustomed to climb the most frightful rocks shuddered when they returned to the spot afterwards, and saw the danger they had escaped. "He who has not seen such paths as these," says Arnaud, in his narrative of this nocturnal retreat, "cannot conceive the danger of them, and will be inclined to consider my account of the march a mere fiction. But it is strictly true; and, I must add, the place is so frightful, that even some of the Waldenses themselves were terror-struck, when they saw by daylight, the nature of the spot which they had passed in the dark."

From precipice to precipice, the Waldenses attained the valley of Angrogna, and it was there that they learned the strange vicissitude which had occurred to crown their hopes.

A rupture had taken place between Louis XIV. and

Victor Amadeus: each was anxious to conciliate the Waldenses, and to secure the services of the gallant band who had maintained their ground so manfully in the valley of St. Martin, and great offers were made by both parties. Always loyal, the protestants turned a deaf ear to every proposal but that which came from their own sovereign. A treaty was effected, a general amnesty was proclaimed, the exiles and their families were invited to return home, and an order published, that their lands and houses should be immediately restored, and their churches re-opened for protestant worship.

The quaint style in which Boyer's* translator relates the termination of the war, and his reflections upon the subject will not be considered uninteresting. "The duke of Savoy being forced to break with France, by reason of the hardships that were imposed upon him, this rupture was the cause of the liberty and deliverance of the Waldenses; for having understood that the king of France did solicit them to embrace his part, with offers of re-establishing them in the valleys, and giving them liberty of conscience, with free and public exercise of their religion, which would have been very prejudicial to his interest; for, instead of one enemy, he would have had two upon his back, and would have been deprived of the succours that the protestant princes promised the Waldenses, and of the considerable service that they might do him, in keeping the passes, and in hindering the communication of the troops that were in the Delphinate, with the army commanded by monsieur Catinat; this prince resolved to draw them to his own party. And, to this effect, he set at liberty all the Waldenses that were in prison, as well ministers

* Boyer's and Arnaud's accounts were published soon after the events took place, and were never contradicted.

as others. He sent an act of oblivion to all those that were in arms in the valleys; and gave to those that were in foreign countries leave to come home, with necessary passports, with orders to all to turn their arms against the French, whom they must look upon as their true persecutors, and the cause of all their miseries.

"He made be brought before him all those that were prisoners at Turin, and told them that he was touched with a deep sense of their miseries; and commanded them, in his presence, to be clothed, and to be furnished with all things necessary. He excused himself that he had handled them so roughly; and cast all upon the king of France, as the true author of all that had befallen them; and because the number of the Waldenses was so much diminished that there were scarce two thousand left, after the last persecution, the duke of Savoy made proclamation, that all those protestants that were fled out of France, that would come and dwell in the valleys, and join themselves with the Waldenses, might do it, and be safe under his protection, and have necessary passports. He ordered, likewise, that at their entrance into Savoy, both the Waldenses and the French should be furnished with arms, and all things necessary for to pass into the valleys; which was punctually put into execution.

"The return of the Waldenses into their country, their entrance into their valleys, and their subsisting there for eight months, are so many wonders and miracles. Is it not a miracle that eight or nine hundred men should undertake to cross an enemy's country of fourteen or fifteen days' journey, where they must climb up high mountains, force divers strait passes, where an hundred might not only stop, but beat three thousand? And that which is most astonishing is, that these passes were guarded with great numbers, and more expert soldiers than the Waldenses; they, notwithstanding, forced all those passes with their swords in their hands, and routed them that guarded them, killing a great number in gaining them, with very little loss on their side.

"It is likewise another miracle, that they got into the valleys the entrances being so difficult, being peopled with Roman catholics, who might have hindered their entrance, being more in number than they; or at least they might have possessed themselves of the most advantageous posts which were in the mountains, and defend themselves easily, till the succours from France and Savoy, which were in readiness, could come and second them; but a dreadful fright from God fell upon them, so that they had no courage nor conduct to defend themselves, against Waldenses, who, without any trouble or resistance chased them out of the valleys.

"Is it not likewise a great miracle that a handful of people, without any commanders experienced in warlike affairs, should subsist eight months in the valleys, and fight nine or ten battles against the army of France and Savoy, who were sometimes twenty, but oftener thirty, against one, without being able to drive them out of their fastnesses, having killed more than two thousand of their enemies? So many happy successes make it clear that the God of battles inspired them with the generous courage of returning into their own country, to kindle again the candle of his word, that the emissaries of Satan had extinguished there; that he marched before them, and fought for them, without which it would have been impossible to have forced so many difficult passes, and gained such signal victories.

"The conduct of God in the re-establishment of the Waldenses is admirable, and make it evident that his divine providence has judgment and ways incomprehensible, surpassing all human understanding."

All the Waldenses who arrived from their foreign asylums were incorporated in the Waldensian regiment which William III. of England, the ally of Victor Amadeus, raised at his own expense, and placed at the disposal of the duke in the common interest of the allies. Throughout the remainder of the year, it was the Waldenses of this regiment, and their co-religionists, who were mainly instrumental in saving the duke of Savoy from being utterly overwhelmed by the forces of France; and even after the arrival of prince Eugene to the succour of the duke, the Waldenses still continued to be the most effectual strength of their sovereign. In June, 1692, accordingly, the duke issued a decree by which he granted to the Waldenses full amnesty for all their past offences, of whatsoever kind, the complete restoration of all their rights and privileges, and of all their lands and goods, and unconditional license to exercise their religion, and for such as had catholicized on compulsion to revert to their former faith. This edict was renewed in March, 1694, after another campaign, in which the Waldenses had taken a distinguished share, had been operated.

On the 4th of July, 1696, the duke of Savoy detached himself from the league which had been acting against France, and made an alliance with that power, under the terms of which all the fortresses that had been taken from him were restored, and his eldest daughter, Marie Adelaide, was married to the duke of Burgundy, being the fifteenth direct alliance that the house of Savoy had contracted with that of France. On the 5th of November, 1696, Victor Amadeus, who, a few weeks before, had been generalissimo of the coalition against France, was nominated generalissimo of the French army opposed to the coalition.

Chapter Twenty-seventh.

FRESH EDICT OF EXPULSION.

THE edict of rehabilitation which the duke of Savoy had issued in 1694, in favour of his faithful subjects of the Waldensian valleys," had excited great indignation at the court of Rome; and it was said that the pope's nuncio at Turin had been ordered to protest against the concession, and then to return home, while, on his part, the duke's envoy at Rome had been requested to. withdraw from the Eternal City. France, on her part, anxious to create the largest possible amount of antagonism against Victor Amadeus, had augmented to her utmost power the irritation of the court of Rome. At length, Innocent XIII., the same pontiff who had not long before granted liberty of conscience to the inhabitants of Civita Vecchia, in order to attract commerce to that port, denounced the edict of restoration to the Holy Office, to be examined, or, in other words, condemned. The tribunal of the Inquisition assembled in the presence of the pope, and, after an appearance of deliberation, issued an edict, by which the ducal decree was "annulled, quashed, and reprobated, with all that it contained, as enormous, impious, and detestable," and "all archbishops, bishops, inquisitors, &c., were enjoined to act as theretofore against the heretics, without regard to the act."

The duke of Savoy was for an instant stupified, as it were, by this edict; but, recalling his dignity as a crowned sovereign, and well knowing that Rome would crush whomsoever showed fear of her, he ordered the senate of Turin to examine the edict. The attorney-general, Rocca, moved, in the senate, that the edict should be declared null, and that the decree for the re-establishment of the Waldenses should be maintained, still more as an act of justice than as an act of grace. The solicitor-general, Frechignone, supported this motion, and the senate, by a decree of 11th September, 1694, quashed the edict of the Inquisition, prohibited its publication in the states of Savoy, under pain of death, and confirmed in all its integrity the edict in favour of the Waldenses. Victor Amadeus communicated this decree to the pope, with the distinct intimation that no sovereign of Europe would thenceforth permit, on the part of the holy see, any such abuse of power. Spain and Austria communicated similar protests, and the pope, thereupon, alleging that he had been misinformed, ordered his nuncio at Turin to withdraw the edict which had met with such emphatic resistance.

The Waldenses meanwhile applied themselves to re-establish their old organization. Nearly all the Waldensian families, proscribed or catholicized, had returned to the bosom of their church and of their country. The Waldensian militia had taken a prominent rank in the regular troops of Victor Amadeus. The fields were once more cultivated, the houses rebuilt, the altars raised up, and the ecclesiastical directors of this little people endeavoured to have their numbers augmented.

In the year 1692 there were twelve churches in the valleys; but the people could not support as many pastors. The Queen of England, as related on a previous page, having been informed of their misery, instituted twelve pensions of a hundred crowns each, for each pastor, and of fifty crowns for each schoolmaster. These payments, not having appeared on the civil list of William III., were suspended for some years after his death; but a deputation of Waldenses to London then obtained its restoration. There were but nine pastors in the valleys in the earlier part of 1692, but the number was increased by several others in June. In the same year was established the Waldensian Table, or board for managing the affairs of the church; and its officers immediately wrote to the various protestant states in Europe which had interested themselves in behalf of the Israel of the Alps, acquainting them with their new position, thanking them for their past benefits, and earnestly soliciting a continuance of that tutelary benevolence by which alone they could raise themselves up from the domestic ruin accumulated by six years of calamity. The appeal was liberally responded to by Holland, Switzerland, and England, whose bounty established several schools, and alleviated the more pressing distresses of the Waldenses.

A series of synods occupied themselves with the organization of the church, the confirmation of discipline, the strengthening of morals, relaxed by so many years of agitation, the release of brethren from the galleys, the institution of a system of arbitration, and other reforms and improvements: and matters seemed settling upon a basis of permanent security and repose, when the peace made between Victor Amadeus and France, placed the Waldenses once more at the mercy of their ancient foes. Children were once more forcibly taken from their protestant parents, and no redress afforded. The Waldenses were called upon for extraordinary imposts to repay the cost of troops; and were peremptorily required, moreover, to pay all the taxes that had accrued in respect of the lands they now occupied, during the time of their exile, and while the lands had been utterly uncultivated. The population, already immersed in poverty, thus found themselves laden with a demand amounting to 300,000 francs, of which, in default of the principal, they were to pay the interest yearly. It became manifestly impossible that they should satisfy this extortion, together with the other imposts that were required from them; and many of them prepared once more to leave that native land which they had recovered so arduously, and the right to the tranquil enjoyment of which they had earned by such signal aid to their sovereign in his difficulties.

In the spring of 1698, a Jesuit, accompanied by several monks, made a detailed inspection of the valleys; and upon the report which he made to the pope of his inspection, the marquis di Spada immediately proceeded from Rome to Turin, where he had a long conference with the apostolic nuncio. Louis XIV. was at this time persecuting the Protestants of Dauphiny with the most cruel rigour, and the protestants of the valleys divined that this conference between their deadly enemies had for its object their own extirpation. Their alarm was but too well founded. In the treaty of peace of 18th August, 1696, between France and Piedmont, there was a secret article (the seventh,) which ran thus: "His royal highness shall prohibit, under pain of corporal punishment, the inhabitants of the valley of Luzerna, known under the name of Waldenses, from having any religious communication with the subjects of his most Christian majesty; nor shall his royal highness permit henceforth the subjects of the king of France to establish themselves in any manner in the said

26

valleys, nor allow any preacher, subject to him, to set foot on the French territory, nor permit the worship calling itself reformed, in the territories which have been ceded to him." These territories were precisely the valleys of Perosa and Pragela. Pursuant to this treaty, the duke of Savoy, on the 1st of July, 1698, issued an edict by which he ordered that all French protestants established in his states, even the ministers, should, without reference to any permission theretofore obtained to the contrary, quit his states in the space of two months, under the penalty of *death.* Such of them as had become proprietors in the country, and had not sold their properties within that period, were to receive the market price of the same from the intendant at Pignerol. Further, the Waldensian pastors were forbidden to enter the states of the king of France under pain of ten years' labor in the galleys. Moreover, "in order to satisfy the signified desires of his majesty," the inhabitants of the Waldensian valleys were ordered to have no communication with the subjects of his most Christian majesty in matters of religion, under pain of a public whipping for each transgression.

The agitation and misery occasioned in all the families affected by this edict may be readily imagined. Most of the foreign refugees had formed alliances with the Waldenses, by marriage or otherwise; yet all had now to seek another asylum, and more than three thousand emigrants were thus compelled to journey forth into foreign lands. Thither, in the succeeding chapters, we shall follow them.

Chapter Twenty-eighth.

THE WALDENSES IN WURTEMBERG.

Of the thirteen pastors who, in 1698, served the Waldensian church, seven were foreigners, and were obliged accordingly to expatriate themselves under the edict of the 1st of July. Two of these immediately repaired to Switzerland and Germany, to prepare there an asylum for their fugitive flocks. A certain number of families had already quitted Pragela, in order to avoid the vexatious proceedings of Louis XIV.; and towards the close of 1697, a portion of the inhabitants of the valley of Perosa joined these first exiles, in consequence of the refusal of Victor Amadeus to recognize, in the reformers of the territory yielded by France, the same rights as those enjoyed by the reformers of the other Waldensian valleys.

These families, having traversed Switzerland without being able to find a settlement there, addressed themselves, in the commencement of 1698, to the duke of Wurtemberg, with the view of obtaining lands in his territory. This prince, though well disposed in their favour, found his benevolence impeded by the faculty of theology, at Tubingen, who considered the Waldenses as stained with Calvinism, and who were energetically supported in their opposition by the ducal council. A prince of secondary rank, however, the count de Nieustadt, a man of ability and of excellent heart, did not permit himself to be influenced by these prejudices. He rightly considered that the active energies of the Waldenses might benefit his district, in which they proposed to establish certain manufactures; and he assigned to the emigrants portions of land in the neighbourhood of Gochseim, with fifteen acres of arable, two of pasture land, and one of vineyard, for the especial use of their future pastor. The privy council, however, operated upon by the enemies of the unfortunate colonists, presented to the count a report, in which they declared that the opinions of the Waldenses were neither conformable with the old Waldensian confession, nor with that of the Moravian brethren, but were altogether tainted with Calvinism, and that therefore the emigrants ought to be refused an asylum in Wurtemberg, unless they consented to adopt the confession of Augsburg.

The count de Nieustadt, nevertheless, persisted in his project of colonization, as generous towards the exiles as beneficial towards his own territories; and if at a later period the Waldenses obtained a footing in Wurtemberg, it was owing to the independent spirit and far-seeing intelligence of this nobleman.

Meanwhile was issued the decree of the duke of Savoy, which ordered all foreign protestants to quit his states; and two thousand exiles made to the gospel the sacrifice of their adopted country, of the beautiful valleys which they had inhabited for ten or twelve years, and in which they had, by official edicts, received authorization to dwell. These two thousand exiles were joined by many Waldenses allied with them by family and other ties, and by all the protestants who had remained in the valley of Perosa, and who were precluded, by a special clause of the treaty between Louis XIV. and the duke, from exercising in that valley the reformed worship; so that the total number of emigrants was upwards of three thousand. These put themselves in movement, towards the close of 1698, in seven bands, each led by a pastor. The duke of Savoy had consented to defray their travelling expenses; but on the third day the minister of finance withdrew this concession, in the hope that want of means might perforce keep the Waldenses in the country, and that there they might be impelled by want and persecution to become Roman catholics.

But the spirit of unity and of Christian enthusiasm which animated them all, did not permit one of them to wander from the straight path; the richer among them paid for the very poor, and all arrived together at Geneva, that hospitable station of all our great migrations, sustained by their confidence in God, the welcome of their brethren, and the succours cordially transmitted from Holland and England. The evangelical cantons of Switzerland consented to entertain them during the winter, on condition, considering the over-population of Switzerland and the bad harvest of 1698, that they would migrate further in the spring of 1699.

Meantime, Henri Arnaud, and other Waldensian delegates, had been taking steps in Wurtemberg to obtain for their co-religionists a fixed establishment in that country. Arnaud, as chief spokesman, showed to the ducal commissioners that the Waldensian church admitted the confession of faith of the Bohemian brethren, as well as that of St. Cyril; and declared that the Waldenses, if received into Wurtemberg, would be faithful to the government of the country, in peace as in war.

Pressing solicitations in favour of the Waldenses were

made at the same time to the duke of Wurtemberg, by the courts of Holland and England, from both of which countries large pecuniary aid was also transmitted to facilitate the establishment of the exiles in the duchy; and eventually, despite much opposition, the duke permitted them to take up their abode in his states, on very favourable terms, negotiated chiefly by the Dutch envoy, Walknaer. They were to have full and free exercise of their religion; to have in each of their churches a consistory, formed of the pastor, deacons, and elders; to hold synods when occasion required, at which deputies from all the Waldensian colonies around might attend, a government commissioner being present; one half of the property of those who should die, intestate, during the first twenty years of their residence in Wurtemberg, was to be distributed among the poor brethren of the commune; they were to be exempt from certain imposts for ten years after their establishment; all the lands in the bailiwicks of Maulbronn and Leonberg, that had remained waste since the Thirty Years' War, were assigned to them in full gift, and all the villages they should build were to enjoy the same privileges with the other towns of the duchy; for the exercise of justice and municipal administration among themselves, they were to establish, in each community, a secular council, consisting of a mayor, sheriff, and such other persons as they might judge fittest for the purpose, and which was to have jurisdiction in all civil matters, up to the value of twenty florins; no foreigner might settle in the colonies they should establish without their consent, and that of the duke; they were permitted to trade throughout the duchy, and to export and import all sorts of merchandise, on payment of the regular dues; and they might establish such fairs and markets as they deemed necessary.

These privileges were, for the most part, the same with those which the Landgrave of Hesse Darmstadt had just granted to the Waldenses, at the solicitation of Walkuaer, and they served as the model of all similar concessions which were granted to the faithful in the contiguous states.

To aid in the support of the Waldensian pastors in these foreign settlements, Arnaud, during his residence in London, obtained the consent of the British government that the sum of 555*l.*, which was assigned from the civil list to the pastors of the valleys, should be divided, in fair proportions, between them and the pastors of the colonies.

With respect to the Waldensian colonies in Wurtemberg, six months before the completion of the patent authorizing their establishment in that country, most of their number had arrived (April, 1699) at Maulbronn, where they were lodged, temporarily, in the stockades which had been constructed at the time of the invasion of Louvois, in 1688. The establishment here of the unhappy exiles was materially aided by pecuniary succours, to the extent of ten thousand crowns, furnished by the States-general of Holland; and already, in August, 1699, the bailiff of Maulbronn reports, that in the commune of Pinache, the Waldensian, men, women and children, had made an excellent beginning; had brought into cultivation lands which had been waste for more than half a century; and that the happiest results to the land of their adoption were to be expected from their skill and industry in agriculture, and from their admirable conduct.

The autumn and winter of the first year were, however, a sore trial for the poor colonists. Most of them were without adequate shelter against the inclemency of the weather, and they had neither corn, nor cattle, nor many other articles of first necessity. Thanks, however, to the kindness of the Dutch ambassador and of the Wurtemberg government, their wants were gradually remedied, and there arose among them the following villages, all bearing names derived from the Waldensian valleys.

First, in the bailiwick of Leonberg, where, near Heimsheim, there had been nearly a thousand acres of waste land, was established the colony of Pinache, in a modest hamlet, whose cottages were each surrounded with a little garden and orchard. The church was built on the hill of Halberg, overlooking on the one side rising ground covered with forest, on the other the verdant and undulating plain of Eltingen. Next, in the bailiwick of Mermsheim, rose Pinache, composed, in the first instance, of one hundred and seventeen families, divided into three groups; one near Durmentz, another near Grossen-Glappach, and the third near Iptingen. This was one of the most energetic, and consequently one of the most flourishing, of the colonies, and its houses were altogether of a superior construction.

South of this, in the bailiwick of Dietlingen, was the colony of Luzerna, in German, Wurmberg; between which and Pinache was the hamlet of Serres, the wretched huts of which were scattered over a gentle eminence.

Beyond Pinache, towards the valley of Eintz, from which it is separated by a magnificent forest, is the bailiwick of Durmentz. Here a hundred and fifteen Waldensian families, who were subsequently joined by ninety-six other persons, established themselves on the two banks of the Eintz; the one colony about the imposing ruins of the castle of Lœffelstelz, or Mugensturn, the other towards Lommersheim and Ortisheim; the village built by the former receiving the name of Chorres, that by the latter, of Sengach. The artisans among them were permitted to take up their abode in Durmentz itself, where they occupied a street still called after them *Welchstrass* (French street.) On the opposite bank of the Eintz is Mulacre, where some of the Waldenses settled, Arnaud being one, the house built by whom still stands there, the last but one in the village, on the left, as you leave towards Durlach. Several of the companions of Arnaud took up their abode at Schönberg, further on towards the mountains of Maulbron. Arnaud himself lived at Schönberg, as pastor, for twenty years, and, dying in 1721, aged eighty, his remains rest in its humble church, which so often re-echoed his evangelical voice. His place of sepulture is marked by a flat, plain stone, in front of the pulpit, under the communion table.

Between Schönberg and Maulbronn is the bailiwick of Knittlingen, wherein the Waldenses, on their way to Maulbronn, took possession of the soil, by depositing therein the remains of one of their pastors, M. Dumas, who had died immediately after reaching the land of refuge. The district of Maulbronn received more than three hundred families, who distributed themselves into three groups; the first of which, towards Dertingen, built the villages of Little Villar and Pausselot; the second, towards the lake of Breitheim; the third, towards Knittlingen, founded the town of Great Villar, which became the largest of these colonies, numbering, after a while, more than a thousand inhabitants. A suburb of Great Villar forms the hamlet of Diefenbach, where, at present, there remains only one family of Waldensian origin.

Two years after their expulsion, and when the expatriated families had founded the colonies of which we have spoken, there still remained a great number of the exiles wandering about without a fixed domicil, which, indeed, many of them had not sought, in the hope of soon returning to their valleys, as after the expulsion in 1686. Some, indeed, had, even retraced their steps, and consented to apostatize, in order to be allowed to remain in the valleys. To check these evils, Walknaer issued a circular, pointing out the impossibility, under the existing circumstance, of a return to the valleys, compatibly with an adherence to the true faith, and calling upon the authorities in each colony to take measures for the maintenance of regular order.

In consequence of this remonstrance, the emigrants who were still wandering about, collected together, and formed a colony in the bailiwick of Calw, in an open space of the Black Forest. The village they built here, at first called Borseto, from a village in the valley of Pragela, is now known as Nieu Engstedt. The Waldenses at first employed themselves upon the manufactures of Calw, but afterwards they established a stocking manufactory of their own, now nearly extinct.

The administration of these little communities was managed by a syndic, a deacon, who was also an elder, and by two other elders, all of whom bore the general designation of justiciaries.

Four years after the foundation of these various colonies, fresh events compelled a thousand persons to quit the valley of Pragela, who were all, in like manner, received in Wurtemberg, and settled in the district of Heilbronn, near Brackenheim, a position far more favourable than that of the other colonies, the vine and the mulberry-tree growing there, and the forests being less near. Money contributions from Holland enabled these exiles to build a church and a school, and aided the erection of their towns, which they variously denominated, after their native seats, Usseaux, Mentola, or Fenestrelles, the district, as being between Nordheim and Hausen, receiving the appellation of Nordhausen. In this settlement, the most purely Waldensian of all—for most of the exiles of 1698 were French refugees—the Waldensian type has remained in its greatest purity, in manners, in costume, and in accent. There, as in the valleys themselves, is observed the custom of giving to each guest at a wedding, a piece of ribband, called *livrée*. The faces of the population still retain the Italian character. One circumstance which contributed to preserve their homogeneity was that, for a long time, they married, for the most part, only among themselves; another was, the practice among them of assembling together, from time to time, and interchanging reminiscences of their native land, its history, its aspect, its manners.

The potato was introduced into Germany by these colonists, who also did much to extend and improve the growth of the mulberry and the grape.

It was, from the first, a great object with the Grand Consistory of Stuttgard to annex the Waldensian exiles to the Lutheran church. Promises and menaces were alternately employed to induce the consistories of the Waldensian colonies to recognize the ecclesiastical jurisdiction of the Lutheran consistory, but with very little success, for so long as Wurtemberg was governed by catholic princes (till 1797), the administration of that country had no interest in favouring the one protestant body over the other.

Under the reign of the first Lutheran prince, Frederick I., the Stuttgard consistory induced some of the French pastors, serving Waldensian cures, to lay a petition before the government that the German language might be substituted for the French, in Waldensian preaching and instruction. The king replied that he would *permit* the introduction of the German language into the colonies, provided that none of the Waldenses objected. This proviso was suppressed by the Lutheran consistory, who, merely announcing the *authorization* to use the German language, issued an order that thenceforth the Waldensian religious service should be celebrated in German. This order, however, was at once protested against by the Waldenses, who waited upon the king, for that purpose, at Ludwigsburg, and his majesty not only quashed it, but expressly directed that no such innovations should be attempted, except upon the proposition of the Waldenses themselves.

On the accession of William I., however, fresh attempts were made to Germanize the Waldensian churches, by favouring mixed alliances between Waldenses and Lutherans, by inviting the school-masters to teach in German as well as in French, and lastly, by promising to undertake the support of both pastors and school masters, on the condition that these should be Germans. In an assembly of the states, held at Stuttgard, in 1821, it was resolved, that a sum of twelve thousand florins per annum should be allotted to such Waldensian churches as should place in the ecclesiastical administration of the country the selection of their pastors and school-masters. At length, in 1822, the last general synod of the Waldensian churches in Wurtemberg took place at Stuttgard. There was much talk of a fusion between the two protestant churches, under the common name of *evangelical*, such as had already been effected in Baden. There was very little discussion on the part of the dissentients, for they were not heard, and, ultimately, the great object with the Lutheran consistory, of substituting German for French pastors and school-masters in the Waldensian colonies was effected. Next the German Bible replaced the French version, but not until, at assiduous conferences of competent men, it had been clearly ascertained by the Waldensian pastors, by the close comparison of line with line, that the contents of the German translation were in conformity with the primitive text. This union of the Waldensian colonies with the national church, though at the time deeply painful to the large proportion of the exiles, put an end to many abuses, to many divisions and intrigues, and introduced greater care and regularity into the selection of pastors and schoolmasters. It had the further advantage of gradually effacing the separation which had previously existed between the Waldenses and the people of the country. So long as the former spoke among themselves a language of their own, they inspired more or less distrust in all who heard but did not understand them. Moreover, the independence of their church had previously excited a certain degree of jealousy on the part of the national church, which was now removed.

Chapter Twenty-ninth.

THE WALDENSIAN COLONIES IN HESSE D'ARMS-TADT, AND ELSEWHERE.

At the period of their first expulsion in 1686, the Waldenses had already applied to the landgrave of Hesse d'Armstadt, for an asylum in his territories, and the faculty of theology at Giessen, having been consulted on the point, had decided that they might be admitted, on condition of their avoiding all polemics, and of their regarding the prince as chief of the church (*Summus Episcopus,*) without, however, their being required to modify, in any manner or degree, their confession of faith.

We have seen these poor exiles returning to their country in 1689, re-established there in 1692, and the influence upon their position of the special peace made by the duke of Savoy with the king of France. In 1698, a body of the unhappy Waldenses, once more expelled from their native homes, sought a refuge in the hospitable territories of Ernest Louis, landgrave of Hesse d'Armstadt, whose concessions, signed 2d May, 1699, served as a model for those afterwards granted to them by Eberhard Louis grand-duke of Wurtemberg. These letters patent open thus: "His Brittannic majesty and their High Mightinesses the States-general of the united provinces of the low countries, having specially recommended to us the Waldenses, who left the valleys of Piedmont, in the month of September last, by the express order of his royal highness the duke of Savoy: several protestant electors and princes of the empire having formally written to us in their favour, and the sieur Peter Walknaer, in his quality of envoy-extraordinary of their High Mightinesses, having urged us to the same purpose:

"We, touched with lively compassion at seeing this people again wandering about, despoiled of everything, and seeking a retreat and an asylum in Germany, have resolved to receive a portion of them into our states, and to establish them there under our protection, so that no one shall molest or annoy them in any way, provided they conscientiously observe our orders, and submit to our laws."

The letters-patent then proceed to set forth a list of thirty-nine privileges conceded to the Waldensian colonists in Hesse d'Armstadt, and which permitted them the free exercise of their religion, in their own language, in their own churches, and by the medium of their own pastors and school-masters, elected by themselves, and who were only to take an oath of fidelity to the landgrave. They were to have their own consistories, their own synods, general and special, their own ecclesiastical government, and their pastors were to have free access to any people of their communion who might be in prison or ill, in any part of the ducal states. In secular affairs, they were permitted to administer justice among themselves, by their own sheriffs, and other officers, and without appeal, up to the sum of fifty florins; even in criminal matters, they were allowed to try and to sentence, execution only being stayed, until the sentence had received the ratification of the duke, who reserved to himself the prerogative of pardon. They were to have authority to wear arms, and to exercise themselves in their use, and, in case of war, were to form a body apart, commanded by their own officers, and not liable to serve beyond the ducal territories. They were declared admissible to all public offices, civil, political, and ecclesiastical, and their children to all the colleges and universities. Their ministers and their secular officers were placed on an equality, in all respects, with the corresponding functionaries of the ducal states. They were to be permitted to dispose of their property as they thought fit; the property of any one dying intestate was to be distributed among his next heirs; if there were no heirs, then it was to be divided between the state and the poor of his commune. The Waldensian colonists were to owe service to no one but the sovereign; and for fifteen years they were to be exempted from the payment of various public taxes. They were to be allowed to trade in any part of the ducal dominions, without license, and to carry on whatever industry they should think fit. Whenever it should please God to visit them with the plague, they were not to be expelled from their villages. They were to be permitted, *in common with the other protestant settlers*, to build a town near Keltersbach, where lands were to be gratuitously assigned to them, to be distributed among themselves, and cultivated as they should think fit. They were, lastly, to be considered as upon an entire equality, in all respects, with the other inhabitants of the country.

The result of all this grand display of generosity and liberality, was a few miserable villages built in wretched localities, the access to which, from Darmstadt, is through a dismal forest, whose few roads, rugged with mud and stones, are almost everywhere impenetrable by conveyances of any sort. There are five Waldensian communities in Hesse Darmstadt: Rohrbach, Wembach, Heim, Waldorf, and Welch Neureth. Rohrbach, the residence of the pastor, Jacob Montoux, was the capital of these Waldensian colonies. Wembach is not far distant, and near this is the hamlet of Heim; Waldorf, like Rohrbach, a pastoral residence, lies amid the woods, on the left banks of the Maine, some leagues from Frankfort.

The exiles in these parishes remained in close union with their brethren who had settled in Wurtemberg, giving each other mutual aid and consolation, holding their synods in common, their pastors participating in the same subsidies, and interchanging, from time to time, their pastoral cares.

The Waldenses in Hesse Darmstadt were, however always poorer than their brethren in Wurtemberg, and their privations became excessively aggravated by the French revolution of 1792, and the consequent wars on the continent. Many of their families have already emigrated to America, and many others only await the means to follow their brethren, artisans, robust labourers, accustomed to hard work, and knowing of the world only its necessities.

In 1801, a colony of sixty-five or seventy families, among whom were four Waldensian families, emigrated to America, under the direction of one Replet, at that time a weaver, afterwards a communist preacher, who is since dead, leaving behind him, it is said, a fortune of £240,000. They purchased lands near Philadelphia, which, after having in seven years, brought them to a high state of cultivation, they sold at a large profit, and purchased, with the proceeds, a vast and fertile tract of land on the Mississippi, on which they have since prospered in a very eminent degree.

Chapter Thirtieth.

HISTORY OF THE WALDENSES OF PRAGELA, AND OF THE ADJACENT VALLEYS.

The history of the Waldenses of Pragela is quite distinct from that of the other valleys, these being often persecuted, while those were tranquil, and *vice versâ;* the reason of this being, that Pragela belonged to the king of France, while the others, up to 1713, belonged to Piedmont.

The valley of Pragela extends along the banks of two parallel rivers, the Clusone and the Dora, between the crest of the Alps to Pignerol, on the one side, and on the other to Bussolino, near Susa. The adjacent valleys that terminate in, or prolong, the basin of the Dora, are those of Mathias and Meano, on the right bank; of Chaumont, Exili, and Bardoneche, on the left bank; and of Thures and Sauzet towards the bottom. The Col de Sestrieres separates this district from the basin of Pragela, where flows the Clusone, on whose banks are the lateral valleys of Traversa, Puy, Pourrieres, and Villaret, the latter communicating with the narrow valley of Meano. Prior to the revocation of the edict of Nantes, the Waldenses of these valleys possessed eleven parishes, eighteen churches, and sixty-four centres of religious assembling, where worship was celebrated, morning and evening, in as many hamlets.

It was at Laus, in Pragela, that was held the famous synod where, two hundred years before the protestant reformation, one hundred and forty protestant pastors assembled; each accompanied by two or three lay deputies; and it was from the valley of Pragela that the Gospel of God made its way into France, prior to the fifteenth century.

Before the dominion of the king of France, the Waldenses of Pragela had been subject to the sway of the Dauphins. In the accounts of the *Chatelain Delphinal*, dated 6th of November, 1315, under the head of the valley of the Clusone, we find the item: "ninety-three livres tournois, three deniers, paid to the inquisitors for the exercise of their functions in the valley; and again, in the accounts for the year 1345, we find the inquisitors of the valley of Pragela in full operation "against the heretics," there being a regular balance-sheet of receipts and expenditure under this head, the expenditure being the money paid to the inquisitors for *pursuing, torturing, and burning* the heretics; the receipts being the amounts realized from the confiscated property of the heretics so burned. In the persecution of the evangelicals which took place in 1556, the Waldensian churches of Larche, Merona, Meano and Suza, were fiercely assailed, and the minister of Meano was cruelly put to death.

Under the reign of Charles IX. the protestants of the valley of Pragela had to undergo all the animosity of the Guise, of the marshal de Retz, and of Mary de Medici, being defended, on the other hand, by the princes de Condé, the admiral Coligny, and the king of Navarre. The chiefs of the Huguenot party in Dauphiny were the intrepid Montbrun and the ferocious Des Adrets, the latter of whom dishonoured the cause by bootless brutalities. He invaded Pragela in the spring of 1562, and committed infinite violence upon the catholics, the only result of which was that, when he withdrew, the catholics made the protestants responsible for outrages with which they had had nothing to do. At Briançon, the Waldenses. who had just taken the town, were themselves hemmed in by fresh troops of the enemy, and pitilessly massacred. Another company of the evangelical soldiers were surrounded in like manner, in a ruined temple, between Rouilleres and Pragela, and all slaughtered.

The wars of religion were for a moment calmed in France by the edict of pacification, which Charles IX. signed at Amboise, 19th of March, 1563, an edict containing provisions more favourable to the reformers than any they had hitherto obtained; but it was modified by a royal ordonnance given at Lyon, 9th of August, 1564.

The haughty and artful Catherine de Medici, however, while affecting a desire to reconcile the two parties, was all the time levying troops wherewith to assail the Huguenots. This was in 1567, and at that juncture the duke of Cleves, traversing Piedmont with a Spanish army, on his way to Flanders, had reached Pignerol. Immediately upon his arrival there, he ordered all the Waldenses, native or foreigners, to register themselves individually with the governor of the province in which they dwelt. The same course was adopted towards the reformers of France, the object being to ascertain the exact strength of the party. Birague, governor of Pignerol, prohibited all persons in his district from receiving protestants into their houses, on pain of death, and from every side and every form, danger menaced the unhappy Waldenses.

Under these circumstances, the Waldensian churches held a synod in the valley of Clusone (May, 1567), and decreed a general fast, in order to avert God's chastisements by humiliation and prayer. The cloud passed on; but it was only for a while. The St. Bartholomew ensanguined France, and fear once more spread itself over the valleys. "The catholics," says Gilles, "rejoiced, and rallied the reformists as *though God had been abolished.*" The protestant worship was forbidden on French ground, and the protestant churches were shut up; the protestants continued to celebrate their religious services in the fields or in private houses; at length, in 1573, the governor of Pignerol ordered the protestants to cease their religion altogether; they refused, and Birague, marching out his troops by night, surprised the town of St. German before daybreak. Five men belonging to the place were seized as they came out to their work, and hanged; but the alarm thus given, the rest of the inhabitants defended themselves valiantly, and captain Frache, hastening from the heights of Angrogna with his band of warriors, chased the assailants back to Pignerol, subjecting them on the way to heavy losses.

Wearied of the fruitless struggle, both parties desired an accommodation, and the Waldenses, in August, 1573, consented to waive, for a month, the public celebration of their worship, and to dismiss their pastor, on the condition that both sides should lay down their arms, that all prisoners should be mutually surrendered, without ransom, and that there should be no prosecutions of individuals by reason of the late events. But in the following year, Charles IX. died a horrible death at Vincennes, and his brother, Henry III., ascending the throne, at once declared against religious liberty; and a great council, held at

Lyon, 6th of September, 1574, decreed the rigorous prosecution of the intestine and cruel war by which it was hoped to destroy the Huguenots. The latter, however, with three princes of the blood at their head, assumed so bold a front, that the papists deemed it expedient to make peace; and by the edict of the 14th of May, 1576, the protestants obtained the free exercise of their religion, admission to the parliaments, and the possession, by their troops, of a certain number of fortresses, to be held as hostages. These guarantees excited intense indignation among the Roman catholics; the more ardent among them leagued together; the crowd followed them, the ambitious placed themselves at their head, the indecision of the king enabled them to acquire strength, and thus arose the League.

To repress the League, the menaced party demanded the assembling of the States-general, which were accordingly opened by the king at Blois, 6th December, 1576. But the Calvinists did not derive thence the advantages they had hoped. The assembly, all the members of which were Roman catholics, revoked their privileges, and decreed a formal authorization of the League, which they compelled the king himself to sign.

Civil war was thus lighted up once more with greater fury than ever; but soon, in the fear lest the reformers might call in foreign troops to their aid, Henry III. granted them (5th of October, 1577) a new *edict of pacification.* It was the sixth, and was as little durable as the rest. The war proceeded, and the agitations which it occasioned throughout France had their echo in the Waldensian valleys belonging to France, where, under the shield of the League, the enemies of the protestants acquired fresh daring. It was said that a coalition had been formed between

Henry III., Philip II., and the duke of Savoy, to annihilate the church of the valleys; and to this cruel menace the Israel of the Alps responded by a public fast (15th, 16th 22d, and 23d May, 1585), consecrated to humiliation and prayer. The duke of Savoy, so far from joining the League, strongly denounced its excesses, and the valleys under his rule were consequently tranquil; but the valleys of the Dora and the Clusone underwent much suffering.

The edict by which, in February, 1602, after the conclusion of peace, Charles Emanuel accorded religious liberty to the Waldensian valleys, restricting the exercise of the protestant worship to the churches comprehended within the precise limits of those valleys, the churches of Saluzzo and Pragela found themselves excluded from its operation. The members of these churches thereupon assembled together by representatives, at Pragela, and drew up a protest against the machinations and violence to which they were subjected. One effect of this spiritual declaration was to augment the ardour of proselytism in the zealous missionaries whom popery had distributed through the valleys, and whose labours were now aided by the archbishop of Turin in person, who, reaching Perosa on the 25th May, 1602, availed himself of the state of well-nigh famine under which the district was suffering, to offer corn, bread, and money to all who would catholicize, and, on the other hand, to withhold from the reapers permission to seek work in the plain of Piedmont, until they had promised to apostatize; but his pious labours found scarcely any success. In 1623, by the exertions of the catholics, an order was obtained from the duke, requiring the Waldenses of the valley of Perosa to demolish six of their churches. The order was disregarded; the ducal troops were ordered into the valley to enforce it, but the Waldenses at once collected in arms, and, aided by the sudden and severe setting-in of winter, expelled the soldiery, and once more amnesty was proclaimed, and the privileges of the Waldenses confirmed.

In 1629 and 1630, Louis XIII. invaded Piedmont by Susa and the valley of Pragela, and his presence amongst the Waldenses had a great influence on their destinies. The last of the wars of religion of which France was the theatre was now at its height. The protestant party, defeated by arms, only raised its head once more by force of discussion. In 1627, the dukes of Rohan and Soubise, the chiefs of the Huguenots, had demanded aid from England, who had thereupon despatched one hundred and fifty ships to Rochelle. The cardinal de Richelieu constructed a celebrated dike to prevent them from throwing any succours into the town; but the siege of the place still lasted from 10th August, 1627, to 28th October, 1628, and it then only surrendered in the last extremity, and after twelve thousand of its inhabitants had died of famine. The fortifications of the town were destroyed, the municipality abolished, and the exercise of catholicism established. Louis XIII., who had entered the town on the 1st of November, received a sort of triumph on his return to Paris, which took place on the 23d December. In the interval, several towns of the second class, had been taken from the protestants in the Vivarais and in Languedoc, but many others still held out.

In the commencement of the year, Charles de Gonzaga, duke de Nevers, had inherited the duchy of Mantua, to which Spain and Savoy disputed his title. The king of France, in his support, marched in person upon Piedmont, the marquis d'Azel commanding his vanguard. In the spring of 1628, he sought to force the Alps, in order to make his way into the valleys of Italy. All the Piedmontese troops were immediately assembled. On his part, colonel Porporato, commander of the Waldensian militia, convoked a meeting of the Waldensian pastors and syndics at Roccapiatta, for the purpose of applying their interest over their people to the setting on foot the greatest possible number of Waldensian soldiers. The Waldenses readily promised their co-operation, on the simple condition they should themselves be left to guard the passes of their mountains, a condition which was at once granted.

The posts so established were inspected by superior officers of the ducal army, and Charles Emanuel himself inspected the entrenchments formed in the valley of Perosa (August 1628). The count de Verrua, one of the duke's most distinguished generals, renewed to the pastors the solicitations for earnest aid made by colonel Porporato, and promised, in his sovereign's name, the most ample religious liberty in return.

On the 16th of January, 1629, Louis XIII. quitted Paris, for the purpose of crossing the Alps at the head of his army. When he had reached Briançon (end of February) the governor of Pignerol ordered all the male inhabitants of the valleys capable of carrying arms to hold themselves in readiness to march. Count Philip of Luzerna placed himself at their head, and led them into the valley of Perosa. Charles Emanuel himself had advanced into the valley of the Dora.

On the 4th of March, Louis XIII. crossed Mont Genevre, and on the 6th, forced, in person, the three barricades of Susa, defended by the duke of Savoy, who was fain to give way before superiority alike in numbers and in courage.

On the 11th of March he concluded peace with the king; and, having just before been the ally of the Spaniards, now undertook to fight against them, and to assist France in compelling them to raise the siege of Casale, in favour of the duke de Nevers.

After the victory he had thus achieved, Louis XIII. received felicitations and addresses of various kinds, among which we may signalize that of the provost of Ouxl.—"Sire," said this functionary, "Providence has blessed your arms, because you have consecrated them to the service of the faith. The numerous triumphs which your majesty has effected in France, over heresy, fill all true catholic hearts with joy; everywhere do they offer up their prayers to Heaven for your majesty's preservation and glory, assured that Heaven, in conducting you to our land, wills to complete its work in augmenting your glory and our consolation, by raising up the catholic worship, which acquires strength wherever your majesty proceeds, and which vehemently needs such succour in these unhappy valleys, where, bitter truth to say, it has been completely prostrated." To this address was annexed a petition signed by several catholics of the neighbourhood, calling upon the king to restore their religion in all the communes of the upper Dora, where, at that moment, not a single curé existed. Accordingly, by a decree of 1st April, 1629, Louis XIII. ordered that the exercise of the Romish religion should be re-established throughout the valleys of Exili, Bardoneche, Cesuna, and Pragela; and that the popish clergy should immediately resume possession of all the property which had theretofore belonged to them, into whose hands soever it might have passed, and whatsoever prescription might be made out in favour of the actual proprietors.

M. de Verthamont, judiciary of the army of Italy, was directed to superintend the execution of these orders, and, accompanied by Henry d'Escoubleau, archbishop of Bordeaux, he the next day proceeded to the scene of his labours. The church of Rome, however, had but very few adherents in the upper valleys; and royal power, though it might give it official access to the villages, could not give it access to men's hearts. Its priests had parishes without parishioners; and their efforts would have probably remained unsuccessful, but for an unexpected circumstance which communicated to them a fresh impulse, and opened to them a wider field of operations.

The duke of Savoy, who had not conformed to the treaty of Susa, was again menaced by France. In the spring of 1630, cardinal de Richelieu marched a considerable army against him. It entered Piedmont by the valley of the Dora, and for a while took the direction of Montferrat, but, suddenly turning to the south, it advanced upon Pignerol, and this city, assailed on the 20th March, 1630, surrendered two days afterwards. The citadel, however, held out till the 29th.

The marshal de Crequi next, on the 21st March, took possession of the valley and castle of Perosa, whence he summoned the valleys of St. Martin and Luzerna to surrender at discretion. They refused, and sent to the duke of Savoy for succours, which he was unable to furnish. The French army advanced, and encamped at Bricherasio. Charles Emanuel, on the contrary, retreated beyond the Po. Seeing that further resistance was impracticable, the Waldenses surrendered, on condition that they should not be required to bear arms against the duke of Savoy, and that the free exercise of the protestant religion should be guarranteed to them. Marshal Schomberg accepted these conditions; and thereupon deputies from each of the Waldensian communes repaired to Pignerol to take the oath of fidelity to the king of France.

Fresh detachments of French troops arrived every day. The country was utterly exhausted; plague, famine, and war desolating it all at once. Louis XIII., who had returned to Lyon in May, passed thence into Savoy, which he rapidly subjected. In July, the duke de Montino readily obtained possession of the marquisate of Saluzzo; nearly the whole of Piedmont then passed under French dominion, and the siege of Casale, the original cause of all these troubles, was raised by the Spaniards on the 26th October, before the victorious arms of France.

Charles Emanuel died of grief on the 26th July, 1630, and his son, Victor Amadeus I., negotiated the peace of Ratisbon in the following October. By this treaty, he recovered all his states, and obtained a few unimportant places in Montferrat. The valleys of the Clusone and of the Upper Dora, and the town of Pignerol, remained in the possession of France.

The Waldensian population of these districts were entitled to avail themselves, for the celebration of their worship, of the edicts regulating the reformed church of France; an edict of April, 1630, indeed, especially authorized them to do so; but the town of Pignerol demanded that the protestant worship should be interdicted throughout its territory, and this prohibition was granted. Meanwhile, the priests who had been established in the valley of Pragela in 1629, and the Capuchin missionaries who had proceeded thither to labour at the conversion of the heretics, had all died, or fled, during the plague of 1630

The prior of Mentola alone remained. Fresh attempts at conversion were made, but without success. The numbers of the Waldenses, so far from diminishing, increased daily. Louis XIII. had granted them the confirmation of their ancient privileges. By their agricultural operations, their various trades, and their acquisitions thence derived, they were occupying greater and greater space in the country. This very progress drew invidious attention upon them. Their enemies made an outcry against their encroachments. The clergy set the magistracy to work, and the attorney-general laid an information before the sovereign council at Pignerol, that many of the protestants of the valley of Perosa were forming establishments beyond the limits within which alone they were permitted to exercise their worship.

In consequence, the council, by a decree of 17th July, 1645, renewed the prohibition to the Waldenses to open schools or churches, to preach, and even to teach, beyond the ancient limits assigned them. It also forbad any foreign protestant to settle in the country, under penalty of the confiscation of his goods, and a fine of one thousand livres upon the commune which had permitted the settlement to take place, without giving notice to the registrar of Pignerol; lastly, the protestants were forbidden to hold any public office, or to purchase or lease any land, beyond their own limits; to work on catholic festivals; to dissuade any persons from catholicizing; to buy or sell any protestant religious book; and to hold any municipal meetings among themselves without the presence of the local judge, under penalty of a fine of two hundred livres from each of the persons present at such meetings. The edict contained *one* prohibition addressed to the catholics: the prohibition, namely, to contribute, in any form or degree, to support of protestant pastors or churches, under penalty of fifty livres fine for each offence. It may be readily imagined that this last prohibition was one of those most exactly observed. Its enactment, however, proves that the manners of the country had been imbued with that spirit of brotherhood which one observes wherever the Waldenses have lived, and of which even the followers of an opposing faith could not help undergoing the influence.

The Waldenses, aggrieved by these numerous restrictions, asserted the rights they had enjoyed under the dukes of Savoy, all whose edicts were preserved by the decree of 17th July; and upon their remonstrance, the sovereign council declared that "it had not intended to make any innovation upon, nor any change in, the rights, state, and condition wherein the petitioners were, under the rule of the dukes of Savoy, in 1630."

But the edict of Nantes had granted to the protestants the free exercise of their worship, and full right to hold any office whatever in judicature or finance. The Waldenses of Pragela now formed a portion of France; they claimed, therefore, that the benefits of the edict should be extended to them, and this demand was granted by decisions of the council, on 10th March, and 19th August, 1648.

Under the influence of this milder legislation, the numbers and the prosperity of the Waldenses of Pragela rapidly increased. The attempts of Louis XIII. to re-establish catholicism in their country, had produced only a momentary effect. The churches which he had founded in 1622 remained empty and closed; the vicarages themselves, in which a solitary shepherd had been placed to tend a non-existent flock, were soon deserted; the plague of 1630 killed or dispersed their useless inhabitants, who were not replaced. In many localities the municipality applied the vacated edifices to other purposes.

At Traversa, the catholic chapel having gone to decay, the Waldenses used its materials in the construction of a church for themselves. This proceeding was denounced by the Romish clergy as a crime, as robbery, sacrilege, rebellion; and there was extreme excitement aroused on the subject. At length Lesdiguières interposed, in his character as governor of Dauphiny, and decided that the Waldenses should contribute, towards the erection of a new popish chapel, the value of the materials which they had taken from the ruins of the old edifice.

The catholics, whose faith old Lesdiguières had adopted, were not peculiarly satisfied with his intervention in this matter, for, a few years afterwards, the town of Pignerol, seeking to keep the Waldenses from its territory, to which rising prosperity was enabling them to approximate, addressed a petition to Louis XIV., in which, after protesting against the religious liberty which the protestants of Perosa and Pragela vindicated for themselves, the petitioners said: "The treaty which gave them this liberty was obtained in January, 1593, by Lesdiguières, sword in hand. True, it was afterwards confirmed, in general terms; but considering that this general professed, at the time, the reformed religion, and the king, Henry IV., had been obliged to bring back his subjects by all possible means; that, moreover, the treaty had been tacitly revoked by the edict of Nantes, which only authorizes the celebration of the protestant worship in those places where it was previously celebrated; and that the Waldenses of Perosa cannot prove that they enjoyed the free exercise of their worship under the dukes of Savoy,—we request your majesty formally to interdict this worship throughout the territory of Pignerol." This petition was dated in April, 1654; on the 24th of the same month, Louis XIV., then scarcely seventeen years old, and who had not yet been crowned, but who had already begun to serve the exclusive pretensions of the Romish church, from that instinct of despotism common to both, granted its prayer; and on the 4th August was published the royal decree, prohibiting to the Waldenses the public exercise of their religion within the territory of Pignerol.

The proselytizing ambition of the monks and Jesuits acquired fresh strength from this sun of tyranny, "unequalled in the world," as the motto of the great king declares. These attempts at conversion, however, were at first rather troublesome than formidable to the Waldenses, and to themselves rather embarrassing than productive. But more active means were in preparation. The propaganda had established itself, and the Piedmontese Easter was at hand.

After that terrible explosion of rampant and pitiless fanaticism, that festival of blood, the massacre of 1655, the fugitives who had escaped sought refuge with their brethren in the valleys of the Clusone and Pragela, who took up arms to defend them. In his capacity of moderator of the Waldensian churches, Leger now convoked a synod at the hamlet of Capella, between the valley of Dora and that of Pragela, where all the surviving pastors and elders of the devastated districts assembled. It was here that, in two days, this zealous defender of the valleys drew up his first manifesto, publishing to the world the inconceivable cruelties with which the Waldenses had been assailed. The world heard the appeal, and Louis XIV. himself dared not withhold combining his entreaties with those of almost all the other potentates of Europe, to induce the duke of Savoy to efface, as effectually as possible, the traces of this atrocious desolation.

The governor of Dauphiny was ordered to receive the exiles with humanity, and to provide for their more pressing wants. But it was most especially from their brethren of Pragela, that they received aid, asylum, and protection. The latter, themselves, were subjected to heavy trials. The council of Pignerol, not content with having procured the prohibition of their worship throughout its territory, sought to impede their industry, and obtained an order (22d November, 1657) that they should never dwell for more than three days together in the town. In April, 1658, a further royal order was published, forbidding all merchants, traders, and innkeepers in Pignerol, from receiving, lodging, or associating with any person of the protestant religion. In the same year the votaries of Pignerol and of all the French possessions beyond the mountains, were forbidden to recognize in any way, any sale or bequest by a catholic in favour of a protestant. In 1659, the syndics of Pignerol ordered all the reformers settled in the town to remove from it, within eight days, and enjoined all catholics who had relations with them, forthwith to discontinue them. A Jesuit mission was established at Fenestrelle, in September, 1659, and the king prohibited, under the severest penalties, the least attempt to interfere with their projects of conversion. The task of the Christians of Pragela thus became more difficult; but they were not wanting to their great cause, and the efforts of their adversaries only served to augment the fervour and union of these persecuted churches.

The valley of Pragela, at the period of the arrival of the Jesuits, was inhabited, from one end to the other, by zealous protestants. "These heretics," wrote their adversaries, "have ten or twelve great churches for Sunday, and more than sixty small ones, where they assemble every other day of the week; whereas the catholics have only one church, and a few chapels, far remote from one another." By such a population the jesuits were naturally very ill-received. They could scarcely procure lodging for themselves, and indeed, as one of them relates, "had it not been for the prior of Mentola, and captain Guyot, they would have had no place wherein to abide, throughout the valley." They persevered, however, energetic in resolution, unscrupulous in means: how unscrupulous, may be estimated by the following extracts from a memoir, addressed by the jesuits to the propaganda, and still preserved among the royal archives at Turin (No. 425). "It is essential to obtain a *pariatis** to arrest three ministers of Pragela, whom the parliament of Grenoble has condemned to imprisonment (for having presided over their religious meetings) and who have taken refuge in the valley of Luzerna with two other criminals. The marquis de Pianeza must command the governors of Luzerna and St. Martin to seize them, wherever they are found. The people of Luzerna must be forbidden to lodge the merchants of Pragela, who trade in these parts. There are three heretics gone to trade at Turin, and who are lodging at the Red Horse: it is expedient to seize their merchandize, for as they cannot exist without it, the probabilities are, that they will be converted, if you promise they shall have their goods back. The governor of Suza, Meano, and Jalasso, must prevent the heretics of Pragela from living within his jurisdiction, for they preach their errors there in secret. You must expel from the valley of Luzerna, a person named Martino, a native of Balboutel in Pragela.

*An order to imprison *at sight*.

This young minister has succeeded the pastor Leger, whose house has been demolished; he is quite as seditious as Leger, and capable of doing still more harm than he. . . . The king of France must have notice sent him that the secretary to the governor, and a captain in the citadel of Pignerol, celebrate the protestant religion in their rooms, where they collect together for that purpose a number of Huguenot soldiers; a proceeding that may pervert the catholics. . . . The Waldenses of Pragela must be forbidden to trade with or to sojourn in Piedmont." Another means of conversion, bribery, was also had large recourse to, and had some effect upon the more impoverished among the Waldenses. "By the distribution of not more than two thousand crowns," writes Pelisson Fontanier, one of the proselyters, "we have converted from seven to eight hundred persons to the Romish faith. . . . I have sent word that no occasion is to be lost of converting families, and I have authorized their going as high as one hundred francs!" It is well known that a great proportion of these "converts" were foreign vagabonds, who passed themselves off as protestants in order to secure these wages of proselytism. Another influence to aid the catholic faith, was that of the dragoons, who were billeted, with full license of every kind, upon the peasantry who professed the evangelical faith, and not withdrawn until a *conversion* was operated. The governorship of the valley of the Clusone becoming vacant, the prince de Conti purchased the office, for a sum of eight thousand three hundred livres, and conferred it upon a zealous supporter of the missionaries, M. Bertrand, who applied himself fervently to his work. In order to augment the number of the propagandists, Alexander VII. granted (27th July, 1661) plenary indulgence to all brethren and sisters who should join the sacred congregation;

while, on the other hand, the prohibition to the Waldensian pastors to preach or teach beyond the strict limits of their assigned residence was rigorously renewed.

This was not enough; the members of the Waldensian church had established daily prayer meetings, even in the smallest hamlets, the elder, or the chief elder of the locality acting as pastor. There were sixty of these chapels, and each morning and evening the village bell summoned thither the faithful to prayer and thanksgiving. The ringing of these bells was prohibited: the people then made use of the horns with which they collected their herds together; upon this, severe penalties were denounced against all persons who should preside over these meetings; the Christians assembled none the less; each, in his turn, read passages of the Bible, in under tones, and offered up a prayer; no one of them, in special, had the direction of these pious and modest exercises; the Spirit of God alone presided over them.

"This race is incorrigible," cried the missionaries; "we cannot bend it; we must look to the rising generation." And to this effect, they began by forbidding protestants to keep schools; next, they forbade them to bring up their own children. "We have gained a great victory in the valley of Perosa," wrote one of the Jesuits, in October, 1677; "we have obtained a decree that all the children hereafter born of Huguenot mothers and catholic fathers, shall be baptized and brought up catholics."

In 1678, six new popish cures were established in the valley of Pragela, under the direction and superintendence of the prior of Mentola. In all these new parishes, the deputy-bailiff read the royal proclamation which placed the cures under the especial protection of his most Christian majesty, and prohibited any one from insulting them, in any way, under severe penalties; and the popish narrative of the proceedings sets forth, with great unction, a list of sacred banners, sacramental plate, chandeliers, copes, crucifixes, pictures, money, &c., the result of public and private subscriptions throughout France, which were bestowed, with infinite formalities, on the installed clergy.

The population of the valleys stood far more in need of subscriptions, for their poverty was greater than ever: "so great," writes one of the missionaries, "that we should be sure to convert a large number of them, in their distress, if we had only money enough." The unhappy Waldenses aided each other to the utmost of their power, establishing, for awhile, a sort of community of goods, and distributing supplies of food and other necessaries at the doors of the churches; but all their efforts, with such limited means, were inadequate to the purpose of preventing distress of the most overpowering degree. All this while, the greatest favours were lavished on the catholics, and, especially, on the recent converts; they were exempted from various taxes, they were received into the hospitals when ill, they had distributions of money, clothes, and food, regularly administered to them, they were relieved from penalties that they might have incurred, their daughters were promised dowries. Yet, despite all these disadvantages, the evangelical faith not merely remained unsubdued, but actually effected fresh triumphs over popery. This is manifest from a decree of the 11th of July, 1680, forbidding catholics, under rigorous penalties, to embrace protestantism, and protestants to receive catholics in their churches. In July, 1682, there was sent forth an edict prohibiting the Waldensian ministers from holding religious meetings anywhere except at the place of their own actual residence, under penalty of a fine of three thousand livres, and dismissal from their office. In the following August, a decree forbade laymen to assemble together, *under pretext of prayer, reading the Bible, or singing of psalms, seeing that such assemblies might become tumultuous.* The very means of temporal existence were taken away from the Waldenses, as an effectual mode of striking at their spiritual existence: in this same year, 1682, the Waldenses, by a succession of prohibitions, were forbidden to exercise any profession or trade, from that of lawyer or physician down to that of shoemaker or washerwoman.

The Waldensian church of Pragela, which had preceded the reformed church of France in the path of evangelical worship, was destined also to precede it to the Calvary of persecution and death. Five months before the revocation of the edict of Nantes, by an act of extreme and exceptional severity, the exercise of the protestant religion was expressly forbidden throughout Pragela, and all its churches were ordered to be demolished. Special edicts applied these revoltingly arbitrary orders to the valleys of Sezana, Oulx, and Exili. The churches of Fenile, Chaumont, and Salabertrans, in the valley of the Dora, were hereupon demolished, as were those of La Rua, Suchiere, Fenestrelle, and Usseaux, in the valley of the Clusone. Others were left standing, in order to be converted into catholic churches, and were used as such for four years, when they also were demolished to make way for new edifices. Among these were the churches of Villaret and Traversa, the house and garden of which became the glebe of the curé. The materials of the demolished edifices were applied to the construction of popish chapels; a portion of the con sistorial lands, lately enjoyed by the Waldensian pastors, was applied to the endowment of the popish livings, and the remainder to the establishment of two hospitals, one at Sestrieres, and the other at Fenestrelle.

It is easy to conceive the desolation which now overwhelmed these ancient churches of Pragela, which had so long enjoyed the privilege of evangelical worship. The Waldenses were plunged in inexpressible depression and anguish. The Bible, which had been transmitted from father to son among them, for so many ages, was about to be taken from them; the pastors whom they had cherished were already proscribed, and no man could give them refuge under the severest penalties. These worthy descendants of the Barbas, quitted, in bitter sorrow, their despairing flocks; their eyes, filled with tears, still turned on the path of exile, towards the summits, more and more remote, of their native hills, where they had preached the word of God. A great portion of their people soon followed them, and even many who had been deemed converts to the Romish church. On reaching Switzerland, these exiles sent deputies to the elector of Bradenberg, to request an asylum in his states: "There are already," they said, "six hundred of us, and in the spring of next year (1686), as many more of our countrymen will expatriate themselves."

The account of the Waldensian colonies in Germany has already been given. We will now inquire into the condition of the protestants who remained in the valleys.

Le Tellier, who had been intendant in Piedmont in 1640, recalled the Waldenses to mind, half a century afterwards, when, on his death-bed, he included them in the monstrous provisions of the decree revoking the edict of Nantes, which, with his dying hand, he signed, on the 22d October, 1685. By that revocation, the protestant worship was prohibited throughout the dominions of Louis

XIV.; its churches were ordered to be demolished, its schools to be closed. Its ministers, who refused to embrace catholicism, were to quit the kingdom within fifteen days, while those who consented to abjure, were to receive pensions one-third larger in amount than the salaries which had been paid them as pastors, half of which pension was to revert to their widows. Every child, thereafter born within the states of his most christian majesty, of whatever parents, was to be baptized a catholic. All protestant emigrants were to return under the paternal and most christian dominion of the French monarch, within four months, under penalty of the entire confiscation of their goods; and all protestants who should hereafter attempt to emigrate were to be condemned, the men to the galleys, and confiscation of goods, the women to imprisonment and confiscation of goods; confiscation being, in all cases, a leading feature in the proceedings. The "religionists," as the reformers were designated, were, by the last clause of the edict, permitted to remain in the royal dominions, *without practising any exercise of religion*, until it should please God to enlighten them.

But what, to the Christian, is physical existence deprived of all the action of spiritual life? The protestants, as Christians, prefered exile to the absence of religious life, and multitudes of them expatriated themselves at this epoch, only the very poorest remaining behind. Two thousand inhabitants of Pragela preceded or followed the expulsion of their brethren from the Piedmontese valleys; in 1686 and 1687, most of these also returned to their country, and were installed there, pursuant to the decree of Victor Amadeus in 1692. What, meantime, had become of those who remained on the banks of the Clusone?

Deprived not only of pastors, but of the right to hold

any religious meeting among themselves, they did not hesitate regularly to cross the lofty mountains and deep valleys which separated them from their co-religionists in Piedmont, in order to share with these the service of the Sabbath. From Upper Pragela they repaired to Macel by the Col de Pis, and from the lower part of the valley of Clusone to Pomaret, at the entrance of the valley of St. Martin. In order to accomplish these pious pilgrimages of edification and brotherhood, they had to depart on the Saturday evening, returning early on the Monday morning, happy, amid all the difficulties and privations of the journey, that it afforded them at least one opportunity in the week, of meeting together in common supplication and thanksgiving to God.

Even prayers and exhortations offered up beside the bed of the sick and the dying, became matter of denunciation against the protestants. "The other day,' wrote a popish missionary of the time, "the vicar-general of the provostry of Oulx gave information against John Challier, of Pourrieres, who was surprised, praying, after the manner of the protestants, at the bed-side of one Petre Pastré, labouring under a dangerous malady. This is an offence calling for severe punishment."

But even the arduous privilege of traversing the mountains to join in prayer with their less restricted brethren, was soon taken from the Waldenses of Pragela. The tyrant of Versailles wrote to his ambassador at the court of Turin: "The presence of the Waldenses of Piedmont on the frontiers of my dominions, occasions desertion on the part of my subjects, and you must represent to their prince that I am resolved no longer to endure this." The result of this haughty assumption has been already narrated. The Waldenses of Piedmont, were driven, *en masse*, from their native land; and these valleys, the last sanctuary wherein, amid the Alps, the word of God was heard, became silent as the tomb. Under such terrible and reiterated blows, felling, with each stroke, a branch of the ancient tree, utter destruction seemed inevitable. And such, indeed, befell the valley of Pragela, whose church subsided and became extinct, as a lamp without oil. This poor persecuted church, this spouse of Christ, had been deprived of her temples and her ministers, of her prayers, of her prayer-men; by-and-by, the Romish church claimed the secular possessions, also, of the fugitive Waldenses, and Louis XIV. readily granted the demand. The glebe-lands remained; these, too, in 1688, were seized by the spoiler-monarch, and transferred to various catholic establishments.

In 1684, and 1686, two new catholic curés were established in Pragela; in 1687, five doctors of the Sorbonne were sent thither from Pragela, to aid the missionaries in effacing, as closely as possible, the still vivid traces of the Reformed church. In 1688, several new popish chapels were built; and, in the words of a contemporary publication, "the catholic religion was making manifest progress, when, in 1690, war having been declared between France and Savoy, a great diminution of piety was observed."

The fact of the matter was, that the Waldenses of Piedmont had returned to their valleys, and during the terrible winter of 1689, which they passed at Balsille, their brethren of Pragela frequently supplied them with provisions, themselves indulging the hope that, by the chances of war, the valley of Clusone would remain in the possession of Victor Amadeus, and be incorporated with the other Waldensian valleys.

This prince invaded Dauphiny in 1692. As the result

of an incursion of his troops into Pragela, all that portion of the valley which lies between Fenestrelle and Perosa was given up to the flames, on the 25th of July, 1693, and four parishes were thus rendered uninhabitable. Their population withdrew, some to Savoy, others to the Brianconnais, but most into the Waldensian valleys of Luzerna and St. Martin. The latter there resumed the exercise of the reformed religion, and despite every impediment, continued its exercises, favoured by the war, which endured till 1696.

By-and-by, in virtue of the treaty of Turin, (18th August, 1696,) Louis XIV. required that Victor Amadeus should cease to give asylum and protection to protestants of French origin. The duke, in consequence, issued, 1st July, 1698, the decree by which all such protestants were ordered to quit the states of Savoy within two months. The Waldensian pastors were, in like manner, forbidden to enter the territories of France, under pain of ten years labour in the galleys. We have seen what vast misery, and what vast migrations, were the result of these severities.

In the countries rendered desolate by those migrations, the number of catholic churches multiplied in proportion to the decrease of the population. Towards the close of 1698, Louis XIV. had two new Romish chapels built in Pragela, and established eight new curés, in addition to those which he had already endowed there. Next, the ardent and unscrupulous zeal of the promoters of apostacy was applied to the work of furnishing these new parishes with parishioners; and, for several years, popish missionaries, clerical and secular, high and low, male and female, spread themselves over the district, seeking to gain proselytes by promises and menaces of every description and degree. In 1703, however, war once more broke out between Piedmont and France, and Victor Amadeus II. forthwith issued a proclamation in which he proffered protection and privilege to the Waldenses of the valleys, if they would take up arms against Louis XIV., and to the Waldenses of Pragela, if they would join their co-religionists in the struggle. The people, whom he had so persecuted, still came forward to defend him, and, ere long, to give him an asylum. They wrested Upper Pragela from the dominion of France and from the oppression of the Romish church. They raised up their prostrated altars, and, beneath the protection of their victorious arms, the protestant worship was once more re-established.

In 1708, Victor Amadeus having got possession of Fenestrelle, acquired dominion over the whole valley of Pragela, of which, theretofore, he had only possessed the upper portion. This valley was hereupon subjected to the same administration which already governed the other portions of the Waldensian territory, and the same governor was assigned to them. The courts of England and Holland at once applied themselves to the procuring for the protestants of Pragela the same privileges that were enjoyed by their brethren in the other Waldensian valleys. Queen Anne wrote, with her own hand, a letter on the subject to Victor Amadeus. This prince's reply, dated 3d of March, 1709, was of the most favourable character; but he represented that, for various political reasons, it was expedient to delay any public proceeding to the desired effect, until peace should be concluded. Meanwhile, in proof of the sincerity of his good-will towards the protestants, he enjoined the popish ecclesiastics of Pragela not to disturb the Waldenses in any way or degree, by reason of their doctrines, and even to permit those who had abjured protestantism to resume it if they so desired.

Four months afterwards, the archbishop of Turin directed his subordinates never to put forward the name or the authority of Victor Amadeus, when they had to do with the heretics.

There seemed, then, no obstacle now to the re-establishment of the Waldensian church at Pragela. The pastors of the adjacent valleys repaired thither for the celebration of divine service. Schools were re-opened, religious meetings resumed, family worship once more rendered happy the domestic hearth, and many of the emigrants returned to their homes.

At the Waldensian synod, held at Angrogna, 11th November, 1709, the deputies of Pragela presented themselves, furnished with a commission, signed by the consuls, councillors, and more than a hundred heads of families, in the name of all the protestants of the valley. They demanded admission within the body of the Waldensian churches, which was at once and gladly accorded; unity of body was with them only a visible manifestation of that unity of faith, which had never ceased to exist, and it was a joyful thing for the various representatives of the Waldensian church thus to render testimony to the spiritual union which had been maintained among all the members of that church, despite political divisions, despite all the cruel vicissitudes which had agitated their country.

Though separated, for more than a century, by the sword and the sceptre of two dynasties, they now met together such as they had been in ages long past, for the descent of the evangelical christians dates further back than the descent of kings.

Without possessing organized parishes, the inhabitants of Pragela had now the privilege of meeting together for the celebration of their worship; and, as a strong plant, whose branches are permitted to grow for awhile without being cut, their church made rapid progress. "We see with sensible grief," said the popish curés of Pragela in an urgent memorial to the duke, "inhabitants of this valley, who had been converted, reverting furiously to heresy, and we pray your lordship to put an end to such abominations." The royal council which had been established at Pignerol, and which had recently assumed the title of senate, applied itself to the restriction of a liberty so fatal to popery. To this purpose, it proceeded to impede the paternal relations which were being effected among the various Waldensian valleys ; the ministers of the valley of Luzerna were requested not to visit the valley of Pragela, and the Pragelans and other French refugees, who had settled in the valley of Luzerna, were ordered to quit that valley. The pastors, however, who had nothing to do with the political considerations which regulated the conduct of Victor Amadeus, and who rightly considered the evangelical Christians of Pragela as one of the most interesting portions of their flock, continued to visit them whenever they were required so to do, and the duties of their own special charge permitted. "On the 27th February, 1709," wrote the Romish missionaries, "there came to Pragela a heretic minister who perverted all the people. . . . On the 23d March, M. Bastia (pastor of La Torre), came here and baptized three children ; almost all the population were present."

The senate of Pignerol, though not vested with authority to take any repressive measure against the exercise of a liberty sanctioned by the sovereign, renewed, by way of manifesting its displeasure, the interdiction of the reformed worship in the valleys of Perosa and Pragela. The protestants, strong in their right, in their convictions, and in the necessity to protest against the tyranny from which they had so long and so severely suffered, replied to the manifesto of the senate by the most solemn act of their worship, and on the 7th April, 1710, for the first time in the past twenty-six years, they proclaimed at Usseaux the union of their beloved churches, the communion of all Waldensian hearts, by the celebration of the Lord's Supper, in which participated the inhabitants of all the valleys, fused in one sole family, with those of the Dora and the Clusone.

The catholic clergy of the latter valleys addressed to the senate of Pignerol (28th May, 1710) a manifesto concerning the disobedience of the Waldenses to the interdiction which had been directed against them, accompanied with an opinion, drawn up by some lawyers of the party, that the Waldenses of Pragela were not legally entitled to liberty of conscience. "His royal highness," said the lawyers, "promised, in the treaty of 21st January, 1704, and by the preceding convention of Utrecht, that the protestants who had emigrated from Pragela, might return thither and exercise their religion as freely as they had done before they quitted the valley; the same privilege being granted to all other persons of the religion who might settle there, on the condition that none of them should attempt, in any manner to divert the catholics from their religion, or to do them any harm. "Now these protestants of Pragela quitted that valley, precisely because their worship was interdicted there. They had not, then, liberty of conscience before they quitted it; in the terms of the treaty, liberty of conscience should therefore be withdrawn from them." In consequence of these proceedings, the duke of Savoy, by way of arriving at an estimate of the importance the protestants of Pragela, required from them a statement, in detail, of their numbers, and of the amount of their property. The return made to this requisition showing that their numbers and property were not such as to make them formidable, the vexations recommenced. The Dutch ambassador complaining of this, the marquis di San Tommaso, minister of foreign affairs, replied that the Waldenses were turbulent rebels, who were treated with far more consideration than they deserved. Soon after this, they were commanded to observe the catholic festivals, and in every way the propagandists resumed their work of oppression. All assemblages of more than twelve persons were prohibited, and next, the public exercise of the protestant religion was interdicted throughout Pragela. The English ministry, who had been favourable to the Waldenses, had meanwhile gone out of office, and, amidst more absorbing political events, the interests of the Waldenses were set aside by the protestant powers. By an arrangement with Louis XIV., Victor Amadeus, at the same time, succeeded in acquiring the valley of Pragela, on condition of extirpating protestantism from the district, while by the further exchange of the valley of Barcelonnette for the county of Nice, he deprived England of the sole ground upon which she should claim a right to intervene on the frontiers of Italy.

Thus was the religious future of a whole people sacrificed, by political machinations, to the ambition of popery. The treaty of Utrecht was signed on the 11th April, 1713. Towards the close of the preceding month, Victor Amadeus had manifested towards the Waldenses the most favourable disposition; but, the treaty concluded, the monarch assumed towards the unhappy protestants an altogether changed aspect, and repairing, for the purpose of being crowned, to Sicily, where he remained till the middle of 1714, he left the enemies of the Waldenses full time and opportunity to destroy the church of Pragela. First, the intendant Pavia ordered that, for the future, no Waldensian schoolmaster should be instituted without the consent and approbation of the catholic clergy; next, several schoolmasters, already instituted, were summarily expelled; then, the protestant councils, syndics, and other magistrates of the Valley, were replaced by catholic magistrates; and by-and-by, in May, 1714, the commandant of Perosa entered Pragela at the head of a body of troops, forced open, in the middle of the night, the houses of the leading Waldenses, and seizing the heads of these families in their beds, loaded them with chains, and carried them off as prisoners to Fenestrelle. The English ambassador at the court of Turin made hereupon strong representations, in the name of his own sovereign, and in that of Frederick William of Prussia, and these representations had, for awhile, the effect of modifying the tyranny practised upon the unfortunate Pragelans; but it was only for awhile; in all directions the pastors, the elders of the Waldensian communes, were seized, imprisoned, fined, compelled to pay the expenses of the arbitrary persecutions conducted against them, or, in default of payment, stripped of all their little possessions. The schools were closed; all private meetings for prayer, of more than ten persons, interdicted, under a penalty of ten gold crowns for each offence; they were forbidden to work on catholic festivals; and finally, on the 6th of February, 1719, came a decree prohibiting the celebration of the reformed worship in any shape whatever, and commanding that all future children, born of Waldensian parents, should within six hours after their birth, be baptized as catholics. To avoid this intolerable injustice, recourse was had to emigration, a fresh band departing after each fresh act of depression, until the Waldenses of Pragela disappeared from their valley, as snow from the mountain.

The great blow of all was the edict of the 20th of June, 1730, promulgated under the designation of *Instructions with respect to the Waldenses.* Under this edict, all persons born in the Romish church, or who had abjured protestantism, for whatever motive, and who had since returned to the reformed church, were condemned to death, unless they again reverted to catholicism, within six months, or quitted the country. The inhabitants of Pragela, Salabertrans, Bardoneche, and Chateau Dauphin, were all to be taken as being catholics, without reference to their own opinions, and no other religion than the Romish was to be permitted in any shape or degree, in these valleys. All French protestants who, since 1698, had settled in the Waldensian valleys, were to quit them within six months, never again to re-enter them, under pain of a public whipping for the first offence, and of five years' labour in the galleys for the second. After the promulgation of this edict, the number of the Waldenses who expatriated themselves became so great, that the government grew alarmed, and endeavoured to take measures for retaining the population; but it was to no purpose; before the end of the year, more than eight hundred protestants had quitted the Waldensian valleys for Holland, Switzerland, and Germany; the few who remained in Piedmont were compelled to accept the public profession of catholicism.

Chapter Thirty-first.

MODERN HISTORY OF THE WALDENSES.

FROM 1730 to the end of the eighteenth century, the Waldenses experienced various changes of fortune, which our limits do not allow us to dwell upon. Near the close of the century, they are found mixed up in the general conflict of the European powers, consequent upon the French revolution. One of the incidents connected with this part of their history is worthy of notice, for the atrocious conspiracy that was plotted against them, and the memorable deliverance which they experienced.

In 1793, Victor Amadeus III., now king of Sardinia, having joined Austria in the war against France, armed the Waldenses, and entrusted to them the guardianship of their own frontier, under general Gaudin. Papal fanaticism conceived the idea of a second St. Bartholomew against the protestant families thus deprived of their natural protectors, who were occupied, at a distance from home, in the defence of their country. The plan contemplated no less than the massacre of the entire protestant population. The execution of this plot was fixed for the night of the 14th May, 1793. The list of conspirators contained more than seven hundred names. A column of assassins, assembled at Luzerna, was, at a preconcerted signal, to spread themselves over the communes of San

Giovanni and La Torre, and put all to fire and sword. The house of the cure of La Torre, his church, the convent of the Recollets, and some other catholic houses in the place, were filled with cut-throats, alike ready for pillage and murder. But there were also generous catholics, who had refused to join this odious conspiracy.

Signor Odetti was a captain of the Piedmontese militia, then embodied, and acting against the French invaders, and a little before the fatal blow was to have been struck, he had been invited to join the conspirators in the massacre of the Waldenses. Signor Odetti was a rigid Romanist, and it was expected that the well-known severity of his principles would induce him to sanction any measure for the destruction of heresy. The curé of Luzerna, M. Brianza, was also admitted into the secret; but these two worthy men had too much of the real spirit of Christianity even to conceal, and much less to join in the plot. Brianza sent a private messenger to La Torre, to apprise the inhabitants of their danger, but did not succeed in putting them sufficiently upon their guard. Odetti, knowing that the hour of action was so near that nothing but very prompt measures could frustrate the sanguinary design, set out from Cavour himself, which is on the other side of the Pelice, and at some distance from La Torre, and hastened to his friend, to give him the alarming information. "I am afraid," said he, "that I am too late to prevent bloodshed. There is a conspiracy against you. The assassins are even now on foot; but if I cannot save you, I will perish with you. The honour of my religion is at stake; I must justify it by sharing your danger."

The consternation in La Torre was beyond all description at the horrible intelligence, which was now spread from house to house, and every habitation soon assumed the appearance of hopeless terror. The windows were closed and barred, and piles of stones were collected to hurl down upon the heads of the assailants; but aged men, and women, and children, were the only persons left to use them. The strength and flower of the population were eight or nine miles off, and occupied in defending the mountain passes against the French. Scarcely a man who could bear arms was away from this loyal duty; and yet this was the moment at which no less than seven hundred bigoted monsters had sworn to exterminate all the protestants of the valley of Luzerna, and to spread murder and devastation from San Giovanni to Bobbi.

Not an instant was to be lost; the day was already arrived when captain Odetti gave the information, and at sunset the murderers were to begin to assemble.

The only chance of safety consisted in sending notice of the plot to General Gaudin, a Swiss Officer, who commanded the Piedmontese troops on the nearest frontier. That brave man turned a deaf ear to the messenger, because he could not believe in the existence of so base a conspiracy. Another and another messenger arrived, but with no better success. At length several fugitives made their appearance from La Torre; the dreadful news reached the Waldensian soldiers themselves, and, in a state of the utmost apprehension for the lives of their families, they insisted upon being despatched to their succour. The general became sensible of his error, but not in time to give him hopes of being able to preserve the innocent victims. The day was wearing away, the fatal hour was named in which the work of blood was to commence, and nothing but extraordinary speed could possibly enable a detachment to reach the spot before it began. To repair his unfortunate error, the general commanded the brigade of Waldenses to march instantly, and followed himself with another division.

The wretched husbands and fathers pursued their way in almost frantic desperation. The imminent danger of their wives and children rendered any regularity of march out of the question; they precipitated themselves down steeps which they would have shuddered to encounter upon any other occasion, urged each other on with wild shouts, and prayed aloud to Heaven to give them additional speed. As they advanced on the road, they were repeatedly met by parties of distracted women and frightened children, sent forward from La Torre to hasten their pace. Many of these, in their terror and despair assured them, that they were too late: that the business of death was even then proceeding.

With breathless haste, and in a state of excruciating suspense, they hurried on. The shades of evening fell with increasing darkness, and with them a storm of rain that brought the torrents down the mountains, and threatened to impede their further advance. They began to accuse Providence of being leagued against them. The waters poured down from the heights in such accumulated violence, that it was almost madness to prosecute their march; nothing but desperation could have prompted them to go on. The last torrent that they had to pass was rushing with unusual impetuosity, but they dashed through it in safety, and in a few minutes after arrived within sight of La Torre. At the same moment they heard the tolling of the vesper bell of the convent of the Recollets; this, they had been told, was to be the fatal signal for the assassins to sally forth.

The unhappy men felt that they were too late. "We will revenge," they cried, "if we cannot prevent!"—and their speed was not abated. They rushed into the street of the village; the tramp of their feet, and the clangour of their arms, were heard within the houses; and, to the unutterable joy of these gallant deliverers, hundreds of voices were raised to welcome and bless their appearance.

The arm of God had done that which man's could not do. The time was not enough to allow of the arrival of the Waldenses, before the signal was to have been given for the conspirators to put themselves in action; but the rain-storm, and the violence of the torrents, which had no terrors for men advancing in a good cause, had alarmed and stopped the murderers. Many of those who should have arrived at the rendezvous had not reached it, and those who were there dared not move forward upon this sanguinary enterprise until their numbers were increased.

Considering the violent state of excitement to which the passions of the Waldensian soldiery were raised, it is natural to suppose that, surrendering themselves up to the feelings of the moment, they wreaked their vengeance upon the most criminal, at least, of their enemies. But no; not a drop of blood was spilt. Satisfied with the preservation of their friends, they were guilty of no violence upon the persons or property of any of the papists who were accomplices in the plot. The assassins escaped in the darkness of the night, and the Waldenses took no other steps towards their chastisement, than to forward a list of the conspirators to the government, who made no inquiry into the matter, and suffered them to go unpunished.

In 1799, Suwarrow invaded Piedmont at the head of a Russian army. In a threatening proclamation, addressed to the Waldenses, he reproached them with fostering the French, the enemies of public tranquillity. "The old attachment of your ancestors to Christian tenets," he said, "has procured for you the protection of England. The French declare themselves hostile to that power; and that power, your benefactress, is it not now our ally?" Already the Russian troops had arrived at Pignerol. "On the 3d of June, 1799," says Appia, in his memoirs, "foreseeing that the enemy would appear in great numbers towards Luzerna, I rose at the break of day; but before I was dressed, the Cossacks were already dashing about the streets of La Torre, uttering fearful hurrahs.

"My colleagues were absent; the invaders had already begun to pillage the houses; Pierre Volé defended his against them. I shuddered at the idea of presenting myself to three or four hundred furious men, who, perhaps, could not comprehend what I had to say. 'M. Appia, take care,' said a catholic who met me; 'you have your tricoloured cockade still on.' I thanked him for his suggestion, and substituted a piece of white paper for the dangerous cockade; I then, praying God to aid me, and hoping to be useful to my country, directed my steps towards the Cossacks. They had just massacred eight of Zimmerman's hussars. My heart trembled, as if it were hanging by a thread; I advanced towards the officer who seemed to be the chief in rank. 'What do you want, and who are you?' said he to me, in German.

"'I am a magistrate here,' replied I, 'and my name is Appia. What do you require of the inhabitants of La Torre?'

"'That they lay down their arms, and surrender all the French they have in their hands.'

"'No one is armed The French are gone.'

"'Do you answer for the truth of your words?'

"'Yes, sir.'

"'In that case, I will sound a retreat.'

"He did so, and I then began to search for my colleagues. The first two I saw had been afraid to come out, because they had heard that they were going to put the town to fire and sword. I re-assured them, and we set out together for San Giovanni. Arrived there, we met three patrols of troops, whom we could not make to understand us. At this moment an officer appeared on the bridge. We waved a white handkerchief to him; he answered in the same manner, and we advanced towards him. He told us to join him at Luzerna, at the house of colonel Worsach. We went there; he received us very courteously. After I had put some requests, which he immediately granted, he said to us:—'Gentlemen, return to your houses, tell the inhabitants to be tranquil, and to resume their labours without fear.'

"I begged him to give me this order in writing.

"'Go and write it, and I will affix my signature.'

"We entered the house of the curé, where we wrote the order; but the colonel was already on horseback; we hastened to carry it to him, and he signed it on the pommel of his saddle. I asked him for authority to establish patrols, to protect us from pillage.

"'Go,' replied he, 'all that you will do will be done well.' And he added this authorization to the note he had signed.

"He had spoken to us partly in Latin, and partly in German.

"We set out, very much gratified with the results of our mission, and immediately established a special guard in each Waldensian commune."

On the arrival of prince Bagration at Pignerol, a deputation of the Waldenses waited upon him, with the sub mission of their valleys. They were most kindly received by him, and, the next day, presented to Suwarrow.

"At the appointed hour," writes Appia, one of the deputation, "we were introduced in the dining-room; we saw a little old man enter in a white jacket, *à la Neyserlitz*, white breeches, a little leathern cap on his head, and with short, soft boots that fell down over his heels; . . . it was the marshal. The count took me by the hand, and presented me. I was about to repeat the act of submission, but he said to me, 'That is not necessary; I know it all:' he then embraced me, pronouncing these words—*Pace, amicizia, e fratellanza.*

"A servant then brought him a large glass full of raw brandy, which he drank off at once. The same servant then brought in a dish, on which were a dozen great radishes, with salt and oil. He crunched half a dozen of these between his hard gums, as though he had young teeth, and then coming up to me, put three into my hand, and had a glass of brandy brought for me. When we had eaten our radishes, he asked us—'Gentlemen, of what religion are you? Do you say *thou* or *you* to God?' We gave him an outline of our faith, and he then turned to an old Danish general, and said, 'Pray for these gentlemen.' The general clasped his hands, and began a prayer with infinite unction; but he did not please the marshal, who stopped him, and himself recited one, which the Danish general repeated after him, word for word. This singular scene at an end, we all went to breakfast, and after it the marshal sent count Zuccati with us to the president of the council, and by this intervention we procured the guarantee for the safety of our valley which we had sought."

When Napoleon, in 1805, went to Milan, to place on

his brow the iron crown, he received at Turin a deputation from the Waldensian Table.

Buonaparte noticed M. Peyrani, the head of the deputation, immediately, and accosted him in a style of unusual condescension, and even respect.

N. You are one of the protestant clergy?

P. Yes, sire, and the moderator of the Waldensian church.

N. You are schismatics from the Roman church?

P. Not schismatics, I hope, but separatists from scruples of conscience, on grounds that we consider to be scriptural.

N. You have had some brave men among you. But your mountains are the best ramparts you can have. Cæsar found some trouble in passing your defiles with five legions. Is Arnaud's "La Rentrée Glorieuse" correct?

P. Yes, sire, believing our people to have been assisted by Providence.

N. How long have you formed an independent church?

P. Since the time of Claude, bishop of Turin, about the year 820.

N. What stipends have your clergy?

P. We cannot be said to have any fixed stipends at present.

N. You used to have a pension from England?

P. Yes, sire, the kings of Great Britain were always our benefactors and protectors till lately. The royal pension is now withheld, because we are your majesty's subjects.

N. Are you organized?

P. No, sire.

N. Draw out a memorial, and send it to Paris. You shall be organized immediately.

The memorial was sent, but it was only after long delays, on Napoleon's return to Paris, that without waiting for the inquiry into the national property with which the Waldenses had been endowed by the executive commission, he confirmed for the Waldensian pastors the dotation they had received, without prejudice to the salary allowed them by the state. At the same time he signed the imperial decree of the sixth of Thermidor, year XIII. (25th July, 1805), by which their churches were formed into three consistories: one at La Torre, another at Parustin, and a third at Villa Secca.

There is nothing further to call for comment in the history of the Waldenses under the sway of Napoleen. The regular march of the government and the impartial observance of the laws pursued their course, without any remarkable incident.

In April, 1814, Victor Emanuel IV. regained the sceptre of Piedmont; he had been king since 1802, but had not yet reigned. An English fleet had gone to Sardinia to convey him from exile to the throne of his ancestors. The Waldenses thought it expedient to send a deputation to Genoa to receive him on his landing. Accordingly, the pastors and mayors of all the communes assembled at Roccapiatta on the 4th May, 1814.

The deputies, Messrs. Appia and Peyrani, went to Genoa, and sought to obtain an interview with general Bentinck, commander of the British forces; but, not being successful, they referred their request to his banker and to the reverend Mr. Wennock, chaplain of the British forces, who took a warm interest in their case. The request was simply that the king would treat the Walden ses as favourably as his other subjects; but Victor Emanuel, so far from complying with a request recommended by the representative of the great and generous nation which had just restored him to his throne, on his return to Turin issued an edict which revived all the ancient intolerant and exclusive measures against the Waldenses. By this edict, the injunction to lay aside all work on catholic festival days; the prohibition to acquire property beyond the valleys; the interdiction of all civil public employments; the obligation to have in their communal councils a catholic majority; and many other vexatious measures, were renewed.

The Waldenses sent a deputation to Turin, to endeavour to procure the revocation of the decree. The deputation was received on the 28th May, 1814. "I will grant the Waldenses all I can," replied the king. His intentions were very good, but the catholic clergy prevailed. The lands granted to the Waldensian pastors by Napoleon were resumed by the masters of its sovereign and foes of the Waldenses. The church which the Waldenses had built at San Giovanni was closed, and they were obliged to celebrate their religious services in the ruined church of Chiabasso, built on the confines of Angrogna.

The sole result of this second deputation was a *royal patent*, which confirmed the indulgences they had enjoyed before 1794. The deprivation of the resources on which the salary of their pastors depended, and the new impediments in the way of their worship, obliged them to have recourse once more to their sovereign.

The principal object of this third deputation was to claim the use of the church of San Giovanni. The king declined giving an immediate answer, but manifested favourable intentions.

The deputation then obtained an interview with the British ambassador, who promised to interest himself in their behalf. Meantime, the congress of Vienna had commenced its sittings. The Waldensian Board drew up a memorial, but, fearing to annoy a monarch whom they believed to be generous, forbore to issue it. This monarch had less consideration for them. A manifesto was published on the 4th January, 1815, to put in force all the ancient laws against them. It was in vain that the Waldenses renewed their representations: they were more severely oppressed.

The ancient edicts, however, which were now again in force, were still more rigid; and it was considered an indulgence on the part of the government to limit itself to the edicts it had issued.

Napoleon, returned from Elba to Paris, with the daring resolve to regain the throne by his sole presence, had, in two months, levied more than four hundred thousand men.

It was thought that the Waldenses, considering the liberties they had acquired from the emperor, and the oppressions they had suffered from Victor Emanuel IV. would take part with Napoleon.

The moderator of the valleys sent a despatch to them, advising them how to act: he prayed them to show that they were descended from those ancient Waldenses who, though sometimes ill-treated, did not allow the faults of their superiors to make them forget to rush to their succour in time of need; and expressed the hope, that the king, in consideration of the wisdom of their conduct and of their attachment to his royal person, would give the Waldenses unequivocal proofs of his attachment and paternal care. This hope was far from being realized; but the fidelity of the Waldenses was not shaken, and their good conduct was a permanent protest against the perfidious insinuations that were made against them. The government had announced their intention to take from the Waldenses all the property which they had held under the French administration, in order to restore it to the catholic parishes, which were now once more established. But the curés wanted them, besides, to make the Waldenses pay a sum equivalent to the revenues of this property, during the whole time they had enjoyed it.

Shortly afterwards, they sent a memorial to their sovereign, in which they set forth the *sufferings and misery of their pastors.* They reminded him that they used to receive two supplies from England, one of them termed *royal*, the other *national*, which, together, raised the income of each pastor to about four hundred livres Piedmontese. The British ambassador supported the prayer of the Waldenses; and in February, 1816, Victor Emanuel issued an edict, to this purport:—

First. That the pastors shall receive a fixed salary, the amount to be hereafter fixed.

Secondly. That the property acquired by the Waldenses without their ancient limits may be retained by the proprietors.

Thirdly. That the protestants shall be allowed to exercise civil occupations, such as those of engineer, architect, surgeon, &c.

Soon afterwards, the king consented to allow the Waldenses to resume their religious services in the church of San Giovanni. At this time a census was made of the Waldensian population, and there were found to be—

Protestants	16,975
Catholics	4,075
Total . .	21,050

The Waldenses took no part in the political events of 1821, which led to the abdication of Victor Emanuel IV., in favour of his brother, Charles Felix; but they suffered the displeasure and opposition of the new government, which seemed disposed to revive many of the former restrictive and oppressive edicts against them.

Chapter Thirty-second.

PRESENT CONDITION OF THE WALDENSES.

The Waldensian churches shared in the decline of vital piety which prevailed so generally in the protestant churches in the latter part of the last century. But there has been a blessed resuscitation of true piety and zeal, both among ministers and people, and there is now everywhere active among them the same undaunted, self-denying, Christian spirit that characterized them through so many long centuries of oppression. The first impulse of this awakened life has been traced to one remarkable individual.

A young officer of the artillery had exclaimed, in a moment of sorrow: "O God, give me to know the truth, and deign to manifest thyself to my heart." He then recommenced his studies, and devoted himself to the evangelical ministry.

That young man was Felix Neff, led by Providence to that part of the French Alps where the Waldensian church had been established. He triumphed over all obstacles; he taught the inhabitants to irrigate their meadows, to improve their lands; but he more particularly lent himself to the task of vivifying their souls.

The next year he went to the Waldensian valleys of Piedmont, and was forcibly struck with the richness of the vegetation, so strongly contrasting with the aridity of the

French valleys. But he was still more struck with the spiritual degeneracy of the Waldenses.

Prayer meetings were formed by him without the official circle of the church. These were denounced to the intendant of Pignerol, and by him to the moderator; but the latter pronounced them within evangelical legitimacy, and refused to allow any interference. Thus was religious zeal revived in the valleys, and with it came enlarged solicitude for the temporal wants of the church.

The idea of building a hospital in the valleys occurred to a few generous persons; the king authorized its foundation, and the representatives of the protestant powers, at Turin, gave, in every direction, facilities for the attainment of this important object. Count de Waldburg Truchsess the representative of Frederick William III. of Prussia, was especially prominent in promoting the undertaking. On learning that they were authorized to purchase a site for the purpose, he remitted to them the sum necessary for the purchase. This sum was part of a gift of twelve thousand francs, which had been made to the Waldenses by the emperor Alexander of Russia, at the instance of the count.

It was next determined to appoint a delegate, to collect the contributions which had been promised in foreign countries. The delegate departed in May, 1824; and after visiting Switzerland, Berlin, Paris, and England, returned in 1826. The protestant colonies in Genoa, Turin, and Rome, likewise contributed their charity and their sympathies. In Geneva, and other towns of Switzerland, as well as in other countries, committees were formed in aid of the funds, and considerable sums were collected. M. Paul Appia, pastor of the French protestant church at Frankfort on the Maine, visited the Netherlands, and afterwards Paris, and raised important contributions, by his eloquent sermons; the kings of Great Britain, Prussia, and the Netherlands, added their names to the list of subscribers, and at length a sufficient capital was raised, not merely to build the hospital, but, by the aid of subsequent collections, to endow it with a revenue of fourteen thousand francs.

This first establishment was erected in the valley of Luzerna; a few years afterwards, a branch institution was erected in the valley of St. Martin. At the same period, the reverend Dr. Gilly, having drawn the attention of the English public to the Waldensian valleys, by the narrative of his journey thither in 1823, became, so to speak, the founder of the college of the Holy Trinity, which was established at La Torre.

A branch of this institution was soon afterwards, by the exertions of Major Beckwith and others, formed in the valley of St. Martin. It is to Major Beckwith that is owing especially the erection or enlargement of a hundred schools in the valleys, with adequate endowments; but it is to Dr. Gilly that the valleys are indebted for the interest aroused by his works, in favour of the Waldenses, not only in Major Beckwith, but in the committee which, formed in London in 1825, has so materially promoted the ameliorations which have since taken place.

The more complete organization of the public services and of spiritual instruction, became next a leading object with the ecclesiastical staff of the valleys. The articles of discipline were scattered through a hundred synodical acts. M. George Muston, pastor of Bobbi, and assistant moderator, undertook to collect and classify them; he consecrated two years to the task, and the result of his labours was then submitted, first to the members of the Waldensian Board separately, and next to the aggregate synod, which, on the 5th December, 1833, adopted and enacted it. It is divided into seven chapters, and comprehends two hundred and sixty-nine articles. The number of parishes was about the same time augmented in the valleys. There had been but thirteen of these from 1686 to 1829, but in the latter year Macel was detached from the parish of Manilia, and Rodoret from that of Prali, thus forming two additional curés.

The introduction of lay members into the administration of the Waldensian church was made in 1823, and from that period the union has been closer between the pastors and their flocks, and the management of affairs far more satisfactory to all parties. Brotherly conferences are held, twice a year, by all the assembled pastors, and frequently by the pastors of each valley among themselves. A special school for the training of young men destined to the ministry was established in 1828; and, since 1848, all these candidates for the pastorship are instructed in Italian, with the view to the gradual restoration, in the valleys, of this their true national tongue, which became superseded by the French language, owing to the introduction, after the plague of 1630, of fifteen pastors from Geneva.

The library of the college of La Trinité has of late years greatly increased, and therein are now deposited all the attainable archives of the Waldenses.

The Waldenses were visited by the Rev. Dr. Baird, of the United States, first in 1837, and again in 1843. Dr. Baird has done much, by his printed publications, and by lectures, to make known in this country the present condition of this interesting people. In the spring of 1853, the Rev. Mr. Revel, the Moderator of the Waldensian Synod, visited the United States, and was present at the meeting of the General Assembly of the Presbyterian church, and of several other important ecclesiastical bodies, whom he addressed in reference to the present wants and condition of his people. The special object of his mission was to obtain the means of endowing their theological Seminary.

It is not surprising, after the great political movements of 1848, that tottering thrones should have extended to more than one people the tardy fruits of their liberties; and, thus considered, the civil and political emancipation of the Waldenses would be no extraordinary event: but the king of Sardinia had of his own free will engaged in a liberal course of policy, long before the revolutionary explosion of 1848. He had emancipated the Waldenses, and given a constitution to his people, without any pressure from without, and simply from the impulse of his own noble heart and lofty intelligence. It may have been seen that the rigour of the ancient edicts had been weakened by the individual act of the sovereign. These edicts, although still existing in form, had fallen into desuetude.

The Roman clergy had also changed its system of attack on the Waldensian church. Violence and oppression being no longer in vogue, they had recourse to a weapon already employed in former ages—discussion; which, however, now assumed the milder form of pastoral letters. Bigex, bishop of Pignerol, commenced this task; and on the appearance of the first of his pastorals, the Waldensian public was very much excited, whether from the novelty of the thing, or from the fear of possible consequences. Several pastors thought themselves bound to reply, and they did so by manuscript refutations, which, reproduced in many copies, circulated from family to family. This paper warfare soon ceased, producing no result to those who opened it. It was resumed by several of the successors of M. Bigex, but the only effect was, that public opinion inclined more than ever towards the Waldenses.

Charles Albert himself felt the influence. In his quality of grand master of the order of St. Maurice and St. Lazarus, he consented, in 1844, to be present at the dedication of the temple of the new church of St. Maurice and St. Lazarus, established at La Torre. Previous to the ceremony, orders had been given at La Torre to prepare lodgings for the troops of the line who were to come as his majesty's guard, and dark recollections clouded the thoughts of most of the people; when suddenly they heard that the king had dismissed the guard, saying, "I need no guard among the Waldenses."

Before quitting the valleys, the king placed in the hands of the syndic of La Torre, large alms for the poor of both communions; and when he resumed the road to Turin, he could see, like a sparkling diadem, a girdle of bonfires, which testified the joy and gratitude he had left behind him. Shortly afterwards, in memory of the good and loyal reception he had received from the Waldenses, he caused a small monumental fountain to be erected at the gates of La Torre, with this inscription:—

IL RE CARLO ALBERTO AL POPOLO CHE
L'ACCOGLIEVA CON TANTO AFFETTO.*
MDCCCXLV.

The decoration of the order of St. Maurice and St. Lazarus was afterwards given to General Beckwith, as to the benefactor of the Waldenses.

* "The king, Charles Albert, to the people who received him with so much affection."

Towards the close of 1847, the social and political reforms, long meditated by the Piedmontese government, began to be developed, in the amendment of legal procedure, the introduction of trial by jury, &c. On the 22d November, 1847, was promulgated the organic law of the communal and provincial councils, whereby all restrictions were removed from the election of Waldenses. This measure was soon followed by the institution of the national guard.

A petition to the sovereign, at the head of which appeared the name of the marquis d'Azeglio, was next drawn up, seeking the civil emancipation of the Waldenses and the Jews. The generous marquis himself presented this address to the sovereign, which was supported a few days afterwards by another petition from the Waldenses. Public opinion sustained the movement; and on the 17th of February, 1848, there appeared an edict, granting to the Waldenses a full participation in all the civil and political rights enjoyed by the other subjects of the king, including the privilege of frequenting the public schools, and of obtaining degrees at the university. No sooner was this decree known in the valleys than it excited an enthusiasm there, in which catholics alike with protestants took part. It was amidst the rejoicings occasioned by this edict, and by the constitution which had been granted to the Sardinian states by their beloved sovereign, that the revolution broke out in France, which, among its other effects, induced the abdication of that monarch in favour of his eldest son, Charles Emanuel V.

The Waldenses were, in especial, mourners at the abdication and subsequent death of him to whom they owed so much, by whom their political existence was changed, and under whom a new era commenced for them.

They are at this time enjoying a degree of civil and religious liberty to which for long centuries they had been strangers. The Sardinian government is now almost the only government, even professing to be liberal, that remains on the continent of Europe, and it continues to manifest every disposition to accord to the Waldenses the uninterrupted enjoyment of that freedom in which they are so abundantly prospering.

Appendix.

I. *Doctrines and Ecclesiastical Polity of the Waldenses.*

THE Waldenses disclaim the name of "*Protestant.*" They say they never came out *from* Rome, inasmuch as they were never *in* Rome. They are simply an Evangelical Church, and their proper title is "*The Evangelical Church of the Valleys.*" In the present work, they are sometimes called "Protestants," and their opponents "Catholics," for convenience, though the latter are more commonly designated "*Roman* Catholics," and "Papists."

In the matter of church order, the Waldenses are more closely allied to the Presbyterian Church than to any other. They are, in truth, in all essential particulars, Presbyterians. They have in each congregation a consistory, equivalent to the Church session. The consistory is composed of the pastor, the elders, and the deacons. The deacons have the care of the poor. The elders are first nominated by the congregation, and then elected by the consistory. They are regularly installed, after sermon, in the church, and have a charge to watch over the spiritual interests of the flock, to aid the pastor, to reprove the erring, to exhort to the performance of duty; and two of them are appointed to represent the congregation in the higher ecclesiastical tribunal. The Waldenses believe in the parity of the ministry, their pastors or "*barbas*" being all equal. They have ecclesiastical supervision by a court of review and control. They have but one superior ecclesiastical court, viz: the synod, which includes the functions of both presbytery and synod. The Waldensian synod anciently met every year, in the month of September. In times of persecution its meetings were, of course, liable to frequent interruptions. Later in their history, it met once in three years. It now meets once in five years. The synod is composed of all the ministers, who are actual pastors or professors in their college, and of two elders from each parish. The two elders from each parish have, however, but one vote. The synod elect one of their own ministers as mod erator, whose office continues till the time of the next meeting. His office, however, gives him no power beyond that of any presiding officer, and it expires with the appointment of his successor. He has no inherent right of ordination. When that rite takes place, the ordainers are the ministers as such, the presiding officer simply taking the lead. The ceremony of ordination is precisely similar to the corresponding rite as it is practised in the Presbyterian Church of the United States.

As there is considerable expense in getting from government the necessary permit to hold a synod, and sometimes this permit is withheld entirely for a time, the Waldenses have delegated the executive powers of the synod to a sort of committee ad interim, called the Board or Table. This committee consists of the moderator, the assistant-moderator, the secretary, and two elders elected by the synod. They carry into effect the decisions of the synod in the intervals of its meetings; superintend the churches and schools, including the conduct of both pastors and teachers; carry on the foreign and domestic correspondence; choose the deputations to foreign countries; suspend unworthy pastors and school-masters; examine and ordain candidates for the ministry; superintend the young men who are studying for the ministry; settle difficulties between ministers and their congregations, &c. They are in fact the executive of the synod, whenever the latter is not in session.

Among the ancient documents of the Waldenses, is one dating as far back as A. D. 1120, called "The Ancient Discipline of the Evangelical Churches in the Valleys of Piedmont." In this document, are two articles relating to the ministry. The education of ministers is described as consisting mainly in committing to memory a large part of the scriptures. They "get by heart all the chapters of St. Matthew and St. John, with all the Epistles called canonical, and a good part of the writings of Solomon, David, and the Prophets." They are represented as asking a call from the people, and being ordained by the imposition of hands. They are under the inspection of one another, and are provided with food and clothing by the persons whom they teach. Ministers committing gross sins are to be deposed. The church has the right to choose its own leaders. The pastors are to assemble statedly in general council or synod. But not a word is said of prelatical bishops, nor of superior and infe nor orders in the ministry. They had no such distinctions among them, at the time when they first became known to the Reformers, nor have they had any such since; and they have uniformly maintained, as they maintain now, that from time immemorial they have had but the one order of ministers, the barbas, or pastors of individual congregations, with elders and deacons in each congregation.

In doctrine, the Waldensian formularies are thoroughly Calvinistic. They hold the doctrine of sovereign unconditional election to eternal life; the doctrine that Christ died in a special sense for his elect people; the doctrine of justification by the imputed righteousness of Christ alone; of sanctification by the special power of the Holy Spirit, and of the final perseverance of the saints in holiness. They reject at the same time the doctrine of the mass, of purgatory, the worship of the Virgin, and, generally, they "account, as an unspeakable abomination before God, all these inventions of men, namely, the feasts, and the vigils of saints, the water which they call holy, as lifewise to abstain from flesh upon certain days, and the like."

II. *Extracts from the "Ancient Discipline of the Evangelical Churches, of the valleys of Piedmont," dated A. D.* 1120.

ART. II. CONCERNING PASTORS.

"All those who are to be received as pastors among us, while they remain with their relations, entreat us to receive them into the ministry, as likewise that they would be pleased to pray God that they may be made worthy of so great a charge; but the said petitioners present such supplications to give a proof of their humility.

"*We also appoint them their lessons and set them to get by heart all the chapters of St. Matthew and St. John, with all the Epistles called canonical, and a good part of the writings of Solomon, David, and the prophets.*

"And afterwards having good testimonials, they are by the imposition of hands admitted to the office of preaching.

"He that is last received ought to do nothing without the license of him that was received before him; and in like manner the former ought to do nothing without the license of his associate, to the end that all things among us may be done in good order.

"Our food and clothing are administered unto us, and given gratuitously, and by way of alms by the good people whom we instruct.

"Among the other powers which God hath given to his servants, he hath given them authority to elect the leaders who govern the people, and to constitute the elders in their charges, according to the diversity of the work in the unity of Christ, which is proved by the saying of the Apostle in the epistle to Titus, in chap. i. "For this cause left I thee in Crete, that thou shouldst set in order the things that are wanting, and ordain elders in every city, as I had appointed thee."

"When any of us, the aforesaid pastors, fall into any gross sin, he is both excommunicated and prohibited from preaching.

ART. IV. CONCERNING ELDERS, THE COLLECTIONS, AND COUNCILS.

"Rulers and elders are chosen out of the people, according to the diversity of the work, in the unity of Christ. And the Apostle proveth it to Titus, chap. i. "For this cause left I thee in Crete, that thou shouldst set in order the things that are wanting, and ordain elders in every city, as I had appointed thee."

"The money which is given us by the people, is by us carried to the aforesaid general council, and there delivered publicly in the presence of all; and afterwards the same is taken and distributed by our stewards; part of the money being given to such as are sent upon journeys for the occasion, and part of it given to the poor.

"We that are pastors assemble once a-year to treat of our affairs in a general council."

III. *A Confession of Faith of the Waldenses, bearing date A. D. 1120, taken from the Cambridge MSS.*

"Article I.—We believe and firmly hold all that which is contained in the twelve articles of the symbol, which is called the Apostle's Creed, accounting for heresy whatsoever is disagreeing, and not consonant to the said twelve articles.

"Article II.—We do believe that there is one God, Father, Son, and Holy Spirit.

"Article III.—We acknowledge for the holy canonical Scriptures, the books of the Holy Bible, viz:—

"The Books of Moses, called Genesis, Exodus, Leviticus, Numbers, Deuteronomy; Joshua, Judges, Ruth, 1 Samuel, 2 Samuel, 1 Kings, 2 Kings, 1 Chronicles, 2 Chronicles, Ezra, Nehemiah, Esther, Job, Psalms, the Proverbs of Solomon, Ecclesiastes, or the Preacher, the

Song of Solomon, the Prophecies of Isaiah and Jeremiah, the Lamentations of Jeremiah, Ezekiel, Daniel, Hosea, Joel, Amos, Obadiah, Jonas, Micah, Nahum, Habbakuk, Zephaniah, Haggai, Zachariah, Malachi.

"Here follow the books Apocryphal, which are not received of the Hebrews. But we read them (as saith St. Jerome in his Prologue to the Proverbs) for the instruction of the people, not to confirm the authority of the doctrine of the church, viz:—

"Esdras, Tobit, Judith, Wisdom, Ecclesiasticus, Baruch with the Epistle of Jeremiah, Esther from the tenth chapter to the end, the Song of the Three Children in the Furnace, the History of Susanna, the History of the Dragon, 1 Maccabees, 2 Maccabees.

"Here follow the books of the New Testament:—

"The Gospel according to Sts. Mathew, Mark, Luke, John, the Acts of the Apostles, the Epistle of St. Paul to the Romans, 1 Corinthians, 2 Corinthians, Galatians, Ephesians, Philippians, Colossians, 1 Thessalonians, 2 Thessalonians, 1 Timothy, 2 Timothy, Titus, Philemon, the Epistle to the Hebrews, the Epistle of St. James, the first Epistle of St. Peter, the second Epistle of St. Peter, the first Epistle of St. John, the second Epistle of St. John, the third Epistle of St. John, The Epistle of St. Jude, the Revelation of St. John.

"Article IV.—The books above said teach this, that there is one God, Almighty, all-wise, and all-good, who has made all things by his goodness; for he formed Adam in his own image and likeness, but that by the envy of the devil, and the disobedience of the said Adam, sin has entered into the world, and that we are sinners in Adam and by Adam.

"Article V.—That Christ was promised to our fathers who received the law, that so knowing by the law their sin, unrighteousness and insufficiency, they might desire the coming of Christ, to satisfy for their sins, and accomplish the law by himself.

"Article VI.—That Christ was born in the time appointed by God the Father. That is to say, in the time when all iniquity abounded, and not for the cause of good works, for all were sinners; but that he might show us grace and mercy, as being faithful.

"Article VII.—That Christ is our life, truth, peace, and righteousness, also our pastor, advocate, sacrifice, and priest, who died for the salvation of all those that believe, and is risen for our justification.

"Article VIII.—In like manner, we firmly hold, that there is no other mediator and advocate with God the Father, save only Jesus Christ. And as for the Virgin Mary, that she was holy, humble, and full of grace; and in like manner do we believe concerning all the other saints, viz: that being in heaven, they wait for the resurrection of their bodies at the day of judgment.

"Article IX.—*Item*, we believe that after this life, there are only two places, the one for the saved, and the other for the damned, the which two places we call paradise and hell, absolutely denying that purgatory invented by antichrist, and forged contrary to the truth.

"Article X.—*Item*, we have always accounted as an unspeakable abomination before God, all those inventions of men, namely, the feasts and the vigils of saints, the water which they call holy. As likewise to abstain from flesh upon certain days, and the like; but especially their masses.

"Article XI.—We esteem for an abomination and as antichristian, all those human inventions which are a trouble or prejudice to the liberty of the spirit.

"Article XII.—We do believe that the sacraments are signs of the holy thing, or visible forms of the invisible grace, accounting it good that the faithful sometimes use the said signs or visible forms, if it may be done. However, we believe and hold, that the above said faithful may be saved without receiving the signs aforesaid, in case they have no place nor any means to use them.

"Article XIII.—We acknowledge no other sacrament but Baptism and the Lord's Supper.

"Article XIV.—We ought to honour the secular powers by submission, ready obedience, and paying of tributes."

IV. *Catechism of the Ancient Waldenses for the instruction of their Youth, composed in the* 13*th century.*

Minister. If one should demand of you, who are you, what would you answer?

Child. A creature of God, reasonable and mortal.

Min. Why has God created you?

Ans. To the end that I might know him and serve him, and be saved by his grace.

Min. Wherein consists your salvation?

Ans. In three substantial virtues, which necessarily belong to salvation.

Min. Which are they?

Ans. Faith, hope, and charity.

Min. How can you prove that?

Ans. The apostle writes, 1 Cor. xiii., "Now abideth faith, hope and charity, these three."

Min. What is faith?

Ans According to the apostle, Heb. xi., "It is the substance of things hoped for, and the evidence of things not seen."

Min. How many sorts of faith are there?

Ans. There are two sorts, viz., a living and a dead faith.

Min. What is a living faith?

Ans. It is that which works by charity.

Min. What is a dead faith?

Ans. According to St. James, it is that which without works is dead. Again, faith is null without works; or a dead faith is to believe that there is a God, and not to believe in him.

Min. What is your faith?

Ans. The true catholic and apostolic faith.

Min. What is that?

Ans. It is that which in the result (or symbol) of the apostles, is divided into twelve articles.

Min. What is that?

Ans. I believe in God the Father Almighty, &c.

Min. By what way can you know that you believe in God?

Ans. By this, that I know and I observe the commandments of God.

Min. How many commandments of God are there?

Ans. Ten, as is manifest in Exodus and Deuteronomy.

Min. Which be they?

Ans. "Hear, O Israel, I am the Lord thy God, thou shalt have none other gods before me. Thou shalt not make any graven image, or any likeness of any thing that is in heaven," &c.

Min. What is the sum or drift of these commandments?

Ans. It consists in these two great commandments, viz., Thou shalt love God above all things, and thy neighbour as thyself.

Min. What is that foundation of these commandments, by the which every one may enter into life, and without the which foundation none can do anything worthily, or fulfil the commandments?

Ans. The Lord Jesus Christ, of whom the apostle speaks in the 1 Cor., "Other foundation can no man lay, than that is laid, which is Jesus Christ."

Min. By what means may a man come to this foundation?

Ans. By faith, as saith St. Peter, 1 Pet. ii. 6, "Behold, I lay in Sion a chief-corner stone, elect, precious, and he that believeth on him shall not be confounded." And the Lord saith, "He that believeth hath eternal life."

Min. Whereby canst thou know that thou believest?

Ans. By this, that I know him to be true God, and true man, who was born, and who hath suffered, &c., for my redemption, justification, and that I love him, and desire to fulfil his commandments.

Min. By what means may one attain to those essential virtues, faith, hope, and charity?

Ans. By the gifts of the Holy Spirit.

Min. Dost thou believe in the Holy Spirit?

Ans. Yes, I do believe. For the Holy Spirit proceeds from the Father and the Son; and is one person of the Trinity; and according to the Divinity, is equal to the Father and the Son.

Min. Thou believest God the Father, God the Son, and God the Holy Spirit; thou hast therefore three Gods.

Ans. I have not three.

Min. Yea, but thou hast named three.

Ans. That is by reason of the difference of the persons, not by reason of the essence of the divinity. For although there are three persons, yet notwithstanding there is but one essence.

Min. In what manner dost thou adore and worship that God on whom thou believest?

Ans. I adore him with the adoration of an inward and an outward worship. Outwardly, by the bending of the knee, and lifting up the hands, by bowing the body, by hymns and spiritual songs, by fasting and prayer; but inwardly, by an holy affection: by a will conformable unto all things that are well pleasing unto him. And I serve him by faith, hope and charity, according to his commandments.

Min. Dost thou adore and worship any other thing as God?

Ans. No.

Min. Why?

Ans. Because of his commandment, whereby it is strictly commanded, saying, "Thou shalt worship the Lord thy God, and him only shalt thou serve." And again, "I will not give my glory to another." Again, "As I live saith the Lord, every knee shall bow before me." And Jesus Christ saith, "There shall come the true worshippers, which shall worship the Father in spirit and in truth." And the angel would not be worshipped by St. John, nor St. Peter, by Cornelius.

Min. After what manner prayest thou?

Ans. I pray, rehearsing the prayer given me by the Son of God, saying, "Our Father which art in heaven," &c.

Min. What is the other substantial virtue appertaining to salvation?

Ans. It is charity.

Min. What is charity?

Ans. It is the gift of the Holy Spirit by which the soul is reformed in the will, being enlightened by faith, whereby I believe all that ought to be believed, and hope all that ought to be hoped.

Min. Dost thou believe in the holy church?

Ans. No, for it is a creature; but I believe that there is one.

Min. What is that which thou believest concerning the holy church?

Ans. I say, that the church is considered two manner of ways, the one substantially, and the other ministerially. As it is considered substantially, by the holy catholic church is meant all the elect of God, from the beginning of the world to the end, by the grace of God through the merit of Christ, gathered together by the Holy Spirit, and fore-ordained to eternal life; the number and names of whom are known to him alone who has elected them, and in this church remains none who is reprobate; but the church, as it is considered according to the truth of the ministry, is the company of the ministers of Christ, together with the people committed to their charge, using the ministry by faith, hope, and charity.

Min. Whereby dost thou know the church of Christ?

Ans. By the ministers lawfully called, and by the people participating in truth of the ministry.

Min. But by what marks knowest thou the ministers?

Ans. By the true sense of faith; by sound doctrine; by a life of good example; by the preaching of the gospel, and a due administration of the sacraments.

Min. By what mark knowest thou the false ministers?

Ans. By their fruits; by their blindness; by their evil works; by their perverse doctrine, and by their undue administration of the sacraments.

Min. Whereby knowest thou their blindness?

Ans. When not knowing the truth, which necessarily appertains to salvation, they observe human inventions as ordinances of God. Of whom is verified what Isaiah says, and which is alleged by our Lord Jesus Christ, Matt. xv., "This people honour me with their lips, but their heart is far from me. But in vain they do worship me, teaching for doctrines the commandments of men."

Min. By what marks knowest thou evil works?

Ans. By those manifest sins of which the apostle speaks, Gal. v., saying, "That they which do such things, shall not inherit the kingdom of God."

Min. By what mark knowest thou perverse doctrine?

Ans. When it teacheth contrary to faith and hope; such is idolatry of several sorts, viz., towards a reasonable, sensible, visible or invisible creature. For it is the Father alone, with his Son and the Holy Spirit, who ought to be worshipped, and not any creature whatsoever, when they attribute to man and to the work of his hands, or to his words, or to his authority, in such a manner, that men ignorantly believe that they have satisfied God by a false religion, and by satisfying the covetous simony of the priests.

Min. By what marks is the undue administration of the sacrament known?

Ans. When the priests, not knowing the intention of Christ in the sacraments, say, that the grace and the truth are included in the external ceremonies, and persuade men to the participation of the sacrament without the truth, and without faith. But the Lord chargeth those that are his to take heed of such false prophets, saying, "beware of the pharisees," that is to say, "of the leaven of their doctrine." Again, "Believe them not, neither go after them." And David hates the church or the congregation of such persons, saying, "I hate the church of evil men." And the Lord commands to come out from the midst of such people, Num xvi., "Depart from the tents of these wicked men, and touch nothing of theirs, lest ye be consumed in their sins." And the apostle, 2 Cor. vi. 14, "Be ye not unequally yoked with unbelievers. For what fellowship hath righteousness with unrighteousness, and what communion hath light with darkness, and what concord hath Christ with Belial, or what part hath he that believeth with an infidel? And what agreement hath the temple of God with idols? Wherefore come out from among them, and be ye separate, saith the Lord, and touch not the unclean thing, and I will receive you." Again, 2 Thess. "Now we command you, brethren, that you withdraw yourselves from every brother that walketh disorderly." Again, Rev. xviii., "Come out of her, my people, that ye be not partakers of her sins, and that ye receive not of her plagues."

Min. By what marks are those people known who are not in truth within the church?

Ans. By public sins, and erroneous faith. For we ought to fly from such persons, lest we should be defiled by them.

Min. By what ways oughtest thou to communicate with the holy church?

Ans. I ought to communicate with the church in regard of its substance, by faith and charity, as also by observing the commandments, and by a final perseverance in well-doing.

Min. How many things are there which are ministerial?

Ans. Two. The word and the sacraments.

Min. How many sacraments are there?

Ans. Two; namely, Baptism and the Lord's Supper.

Min. What is the third virtue necessary to salvation?

Ans. Hope.

Min. What is hope?

Ans. It is a waiting for grace and glory to come.

Min. How does a man wait (or hope) for grace?

Ans. By the mediator Jesus Christ, of whom St. John saith, "Grace comes by Jesus Christ." Again, "We have seen his glory, who is full of grace and truth, and we all have received of his fulness."

Min. What is that grace?

Ans. It is redemption, remission of sins, justification, adoption and sanctification.

Min. Upon what account is this grace hoped for in Christ?

Ans. By a living faith, and true repentance, saying, "Repent ye and believe the gospel."

Min. Whence proceedeth this hope?

Ans. From the gift of God, and the promises of which the apostle mentioneth, "He is powerful to perform whatsoever he promiseth.' For he hath promised himself, that whosoever shall know him, and repent, and shall hope in him, he will have mercy upon pardon, and justify, &c.

Min. What are the things that put us beside this hope?

Ans. A dead faith, the seduction of antichrist to believe in other things besides Christ, that is to say, in saints, in the power of that antichrist, in his authority, words, and benedictions, in sacraments, reliques of the dead, in purgatory, which is but forged and contrived, in teaching that faith is obtained by those ways which oppose themselves to the truth, and are against the commandments of God. As is idolatry in divers respects. As also by wickedness and simony, &c. Forsaking the fountain of living water given by grace, and running to broken cisterns, worshipping, honouring, and serving the creature by prayers, by fastings, by sacrifices, by donations, by offerings, by pilgrimages, by invocations, &c. Relying upon themselves for the acquiring of grace, which none can give save only God in Christ. In vain do they labour, and lose their money and their lives, and the truth is, they do not only lose their present life, but also that which is to come; wherefore it is said, that "the hope of fools shall perish."

Min. And what dost thou say of the blessed Virgin Mary? For she is full of grace, as the angel testifies—"I salute thee full of grace."

Ans. The blessed Virgin was and is full of grace, as much as is necessary for her own particular salvation, but not to communicate to others, for her Son alone is full of grace, and can communicate the same as he pleaseth, and "we have all received of his fulness. grace for grace."

Min. Believest thou not the communion of saints?

Ans. I believe that there are two sorts of things wherein the saints communicate—the first substantial, the other ministerial. As to the substantials, they communicate by the Holy Spirit, in God, through the merit of Jesus Christ; as to the ministerials or ecclesiastics, they communicate by the ministry duly performed, namely, by the word, by the sacraments, and by prayer; I believe both the one and the other of these communions of saints. The first only in God, and in Jesus Christ, and in the Holy Ghost by the Holy Spirit. The other in the church of Christ.

Min. Wherein consists eternal life?

Ans. In a living and operating faith, and in perseverance in the same. Our Saviour says, John xvii., "This is life eternal, to know thee the only true God, and Jesus Christ whom thou hast sent." And "he that endures to the end shall be saved."

V. *A Confession of Faith published by the Evangelical Churches of Piedmont, in* 1669.

"Having understood that our adversaries, not contented to have most cruelly persecuted us, and robbed us of all our goods and estates, have yet an intention to render us odious to the world, by spreading abroad many false reports, and so not only to defame our persons, but likewise to asperse with most shameful calumnies that holy and wholesome doctrine which we profess, we look upon ourselves as obliged, for the better information of those whose minds may perhaps be preoccupied by sinister opinions, to make a short declaration of our faith, such as we have heretofore professed and held, and do at this day profess and hold as conformable to the word of God; and so every one may see the falsity of those their calumnies, and also how unjustly we are hated and persecuted upon the account of our profession.

"*We believe,*

"1. First, that there is one only God, who is a spiritual essence, eternal, infinite, all-wise, merciful, just, and, in sum, all-perfect; and that there are three persons in that one only and simple essence, viz: the Father, Son, and Holy Spirit.

"2. That the same God has manifested himself unto us by the works of Creation and Providence, as also in his word revealed unto us, first by oracles in several manners, and afterwards by those written books which are called the Holy Scriptures.

"3. That we ought to receive those Holy Scriptures (as we do) for sacred and canonical, that is to say, for the constant rule of our faith and life: as also to believe that the same is fully contained in the Old and New Testament; and that by the Old Testament we must understand only such books as God did intrust the Judaical church with, and which that church always approved and acknowledged to be from God: namely, the five books of Moses, Joshua, the Judges, Ruth, 1 and 2 of Samuel, 1 and 2 of the Kings, 1 and 2 of the Chronicles, the 1 of Ezra, Nehemiah, Esther, Job, the Psalms, the Proverbs of Solomon, Ecclesiastes, the Song of Songs, the four great, and the twelve minor Prophets: the New Testament contains only the four Evangelists, the Acts of the Apostles, the Epistles of St. Paul—1 to the Romans, 2 to the Corinthians, 1 to the Galatians, 1 to the Ephesians, 1 to the Philippians, 1 to the Colossians, 2 to the Thessalonians, 2 to Timothy, 1 to Titus, 1 to Philemon, and his Epistle to the Hebrews; 1 of St. James, 2 of St. Peter, 3 of St. John, 1 of St. Jude; and lastly, the Revelation.

"4. We acknowledge the divinity of these books, not only from the testimony of the church, but more especially because of the eternal and undoubted truth of the doctrine therein contained, and of that most divine excellency, sublimity, and majesty, which appears therein; besides the testimony of the Holy Spirit, who gives us to receive with reverence the testimony of the church in that point, and opens the eyes of our understanding to discover the beams of that celestial light, which shines in the Scripture, and prepares our taste to discern the divine favour of that spiritual food.

"5. That God made all things of nothing by his own free will, and by the infinite power of his word.

"6. That he governs and rules all by his providence, ordaining and appointing whatsoever happens in this world, without being author or cause of any evil committed by the creatures, so that the defect thereof neither can nor ought to be any ways imputed unto him.

"7. That the angels were all in the beginning created pure and holy, but that some of them are fallen into irreparable corruption and perdition; and that the rest have persevered in their first purity by an effect of divine goodness, which has upheld and confirmed them.

"8. That man was created clean and holy, after the image of God, and that through his own fault he deprived himself of that happy condition, by giving credit to the deceitful words of the devil.

"9. That man by his transgression lost that righteousness and holiness which he received, and is thereby obnoxious to the wrath of God, death, and captivity, under the jurisdiction of him who has the power of death, that is, the devil; insomuch that our free will has become a servant and a slave to sin; and thus all men, both Jews and Gentiles, are by nature the children of wrath, being all dead in their trespasses and sins, and consequently incapable of the least good motion, or inclination to any thing which concerns their salvation: yea, incapable to think one good thought without God's special grace, all their imaginations being wholly evil, and that continually.

"10. That all the posterity of Adam is guilty of his disobedience, and infected by his corruption, and fallen into the same calamity with him, even the very infants from their mothers' womb, whence is derived the word of original sin.

"11. That God saves from that corruption and condemnation those whom he has chosen from the foundation of the world, not for any disposition, faith, or holiness that he foresaw in them, but of his mere mercy in Jesus Christ his Son; passing by all the rest, according to the irreprehensible reason of his free will and justice.

"12. That Jesus Christ having been ordained by the eternal decree of God to be the only Saviour, and head of that body which is the church, he redeemed it with his own blood in the fulness of time, and communicates unto the same all his benefits, together with the gospel.

"13. That there are two natures in Jesus Christ, viz., divine and human, truly united in one and the same person, without either confusion, separation, division, or alteration; each nature keeping its own distinct proprieties; and that Jesus Christ is both true God and true man.

"14. That God so loved the world, that is to say, those whom he has chosen out of the world, that he gave his own Son to save us by his most perfect obedience (especially that obedience which he expressed in his suffering the cursed death of the cross), and also by his victory over the devil, sin, and death.

"15. That Jesus Christ having fully expiated our sins by his most perfect sacrifice once offered on the cross, it neither can nor ought to be reiterated upon any account whatsoever, as they pretend to do in the mass.

"16 That the Lord having fully and absolutely reconciled us

unto God, through the blood of his cross, by virtue of his merit only, and not of our works, we are thereby absolved and justified in his sight, neither is there any other purgatory besides his blood, which cleanses us from all sin.

"17. That we are united with Christ, and made partakers of all his benefits by faith, trusting and confiding wholly to those promises of life which are given us in the gospel.

"18. That that faith is the gracious and efficacious work of the Holy Spirit, which enlightens our souls, and persuades them to lean and rest upon the mercy of God, and so thereby to apply unto themselves the merits of Jesus Christ.

"19. That Jesus Christ is our true and only mediator, not only redeeming us, but also interceding for us, and that by virtue of his merits and intercession we have access unto the Father, for to make our supplications unto him, with a holy confidence and assurance that he will grant us our requests, it being needless to have recourse to any other intercessor besides himself.

"20. That as God has promised us that we shall be regenerated in Christ, so those that are united unto him by a true faith ought to apply, and do really apply themselves unto good works.

"21. That good works are so necessary to the faithful, that they cannot attain the kingdom of heaven without the same, seeing that God hath prepared them that we should walk therein; and therefore we ought to avoid vice, and to apply ourselves to Christian virtues, making use of fasting, and all other means which may conduce to so holy a thing.

"22. That although our good works cannot merit anything, yet the Lord will reward or recompense them with eternal life, through the merciful continuation of his grace, and by virtue of the unchangeable constancy of his promises made unto us.

"23. That those who are already in the possession of eternal life by their faith and good works ought to be considered as saints, and as glorified persons, and to be praised for their virtue, and imitated in all good actions of their life, but neither worshipped nor prayed unto, for God only is to be prayed unto, and that through Jesus Christ.

"24. That God has chosen unto himself one church in the world for the salvation of mankind, and that same church to have one only head and foundation, which is Christ.

"25. That that church is the company of the faithful, who having been elected before the foundation of the world, and called with an holy calling, come to unite themselves to follow the word of God, believing whatsoever he teaches them, and living in his fear.

"26. That that church cannot err, nor be annihilated, but must endure for ever, and that all the elect are upheld and preserved by the power of God in such sort, that they all persevere in the faith unto the end, and remain united in the holy church, as so many living members thereof.

"27. That all men ought to join with that church, and to continue in the communion thereof.

"28. That God does not only instruct and teach us by his word, but has also ordained certain sacraments to be joined with it, as a means to unite us unto Christ, and to make us partakers of his benefits; and that there are only two of them belonging in common to all the members of the church under the New Testament—to wit, Baptism and the Lord's Supper.

"29. That God has ordained the sacrament of Baptism to be a testimony of our adoption, and of our being cleansed from our sins, by the blood of Jesus Christ, and renewed in holiness of life.

"30. That the Holy Supper was instituted for the nourishment of our souls, to the end that eating effectually the flesh of Christ, and drinking effectually his blood, by the incomprehensible virtue and power of the Holy Spirit, and through a true and living faith, and so uniting ourselves most closely and inseparably to Christ, we come to enjoy in him and by him spiritual and eternal life. Now to the end that every one may clearly see what our belief is as to this point, we have here inserted the very expressions of that prayer which we make use of before the Communion, as they are written in our Liturgy or form of celebrating the Holy Supper, and likewise in our public Catechism, which are to be seen at the end of our Psalms; these are the words of the prayer,—

"Seeing our Lord has not only once offered his body and blood for the remission of our sins, but is willing also to communicate the same unto us as the food of eternal life, we humbly beseech him so to give us of his grace, that in true sincerity of heart and with an ardent zeal we may receive of him so great a benefit; that is, that we may be made partakers of his body and blood, or rather of his whole self, by a sure and certain faith.

"The words of the Liturgy are these—Let us then believe first the promises which Christ (who is the infallible truth), has pronounced with his own mouth, viz., that he will make us truly partakers of his body and blood, that so we may possess him entirely, and in such sort that he may live in us, and we in him. The words of our Catechism are the same, *Nella Dominica* 53.

"31. That it is necessary the church should have ministers known by those who are employed for that purpose, to be learned, and of a good life, as well to preach the word of God as to administer the sacraments, and wait upon the flock of Christ (according to the rules of a good and holy discipline), together with the elders and deacons, after the manner of the primitive church.

"32. That God hath established kings and magistrates to govern the people, and that the people ought to be obedient and subject unto them, by virtue of that ordination, not only for fear, but also for conscience-sake, in all things that are conformable to the word of God, who is the King of Kings, and the Lord of lords.

"33. Finally, that we ought to receive the symbol of the apostles, the Lord's Prayer, and the Decalogue, as fundamentals of our faith and of our devotion.

" And for a more ample declaration of our faith, we do here reiterate the same protestation which we caused to be printed in 1603, that is to say, that we do agree in sound doctrine with all the reformed churches of France, Great Britain, the Low Countries, Germany, Switzerland, Bohemia, Poland, Hungary, and others, as it is represented by them in their confessions; as also we receive the Confession of Augsburg, and as it was published by the authors. promising to persevere constantly therein with the help of God, both in life and death, and being ready to subscribe to that eternal truth of God, with our own blood, even as our ancestors have done from the days of the apostles, and especially in these latter ages.

"Therefore we humbly entreat all the evangelical and protestant churches to look upon us as true members of the mystical body of Christ, suffering for his name sake, notwithstanding our poverty and lowness; and to continue unto us the help of their prayers to God, and all other effects of their charity, as we have heretofore abundantly found and felt, for the which we return them our most humble thanks, entreating the Lord with all our heart to be their rewarder, and to pour upon them the most precious blessings of grace and glory, both in this life and that which is to come. *Amen.*"

VI. *Extract from the "Noble Lesson," dated A. D.*, 1100.

But in this is clearly manifested the malice of those men,
That they who will curse, lie, and swear,
He that will frequently put his money to usury, kill,
And avenge himself on those who hurt him;
This they say is a good man, and to be accounted faithful.
But let him take heed he be not deceived at the end;
When he has received the stroke of death, and when death seizes him, and he becomes almost speechless,
Then he desires the priest to confess him:
But according to the Scriptures he has delayed too long, for that commands us
To repent while we have time, and not to put it off till the last:
The priest asketh him if he hath any sin,
He answers two or three words and so hath done;
The priest tells him he cannot be forgiven,
If he do not restore, and examine well his faults:
When he hears this, he is very much troubled,
And thinks with himself, if he restore entirely,
What shall he leave his children, and what will the world say?
Then he commandeth his children to examine their faults,
And buyeth of the priest his absolution;
Though he hath a hundred livres of another and better penny yet
The priest acquits him for a hundred pence,
And sometimes for less when he can get no more,
Telling him a large story, and promising him pardon,
That he will say mass for him, and for his ancestors;
And thus he pardons them, be they righteous or wicked,
Laying his hands upon their heads,
(But when he leaves them he maketh the better cheer)
And telling him that he is very well absolved.
But, alas! they are but sadly confessed who are thus faulty,
And will certainly be deceived in such an absolution,
And he that maketh him believe it sinneth mortally.
For I dare say, and it is very true,
That all the popes which have been from Sylvester to this present,

And all Cardinals, Bishops, Abbots, and the like.
Have no power to absolve or pardon,
Any creature so much as one mortal sin,
It is God alone who pardons, and no other.
But this ought they to do who are pastors,
They ought to preach to the people, and pray with them,
And feed them often with divine doctrine;
And chastise the sinners with discipline,
Namely, by declaring that they ought to repent.
First that they confess their sins freely and fully,
And that they repent in this present life,
That they fast and give alms, and pray with a fervent heart
For by these things the soul finds salvation:
Wherefore we Christians which have sinned
And forsaken the law of Jesus Christ,
Having neither fear, faith, nor love,
We must confess our sins without any delay,
We must amend with weeping and repentance,
The offences which we have committed, and for those three mortal sins,
To wit, for the lust of the eye, the lust of the flesh, and the pride of life, through which we have done evil;
We must keep this way.
If we will love and follow Jesus Christ,
We must have spiritual poverty of heart,
And love chastity, and serve God humbly,
For so we may follow the way of Jesus Christ,
And thus we may overcome our enemies.

THE END.

www.ingramcontent.com/pod-product-compliance
Lightning Source LLC
LaVergne TN
LVHW020100110826
845151LV00001B/40

* 9 7 8 1 4 2 5 5 4 5 0 7 9 *